INVESTING
MADE SIMPLE

Anthony L. Loviscek, Ph.D.
Seton Hall University

Randy I. Anderson, Ph.D.
City University of New York, Baruch College

BOOKS

A Made Simple Book
Broadway Books
New York

Produced by The Philip Lief Group, Inc.

INVESTING MADE SIMPLE. Copyright © 1992, 2003 by
Broadway Books, a division of Random House, Inc.

A previous edition of this book was originally published in 1992 by
Doubleday, a division of Random House, Inc. It is here reprinted by
arrangement with Doubleday.

Printed in the United States of America.

Produced by The Philip Lief Group, Inc.
Managing Editors: Judy Linden, Lynne Kirk, Hope Gatto, Jill Korot.
Design: Annie Jeon.

MADE SIMPLE BOOKS and BROADWAY BOOKS are
trademarks of Broadway Books, a division of Random House, Inc.

Visit our web site at www.broadwaybooks.com.

Library of Congress Cataloging-in-Publication Data
Loviscek, Anthony L.
    Investing made simple / Anthony L. Loviscek, Randy I. Anderson
            p. cm.—(Made simple series)
Includes bibliographical references and index.
ISBN 0-7679-1540-2
    1. Investments—United States. 2. Finance, Personal—United States.
I. Anderson, Randy I. II. Title. III. Made simple (Broadway Books)

HG4910.L678 2004
332.6—dc22

                                            2003055912

10 9 8 7 6 5 4 3 2 1

We dedicate this book to our families and friends who have unfailingly supported our efforts, at all hours of the day and night.

Tony Loviscek dedicates this book to his sister, Kathleen, and to his mother, Sylvia, as well as friends and colleagues Frederick Crowley and Randy Anderson, from whom he has learned much about finance.

Randy Anderson dedicates this book to his wife, Jennifer, who during much of the writing was very pregnant with a beautiful daughter, Ava, and to his wonderful son, Jackson, for all the patience and understanding a 4-year-old can give to a busy Daddy.

ACKNOWLEDGMENTS

This book reflects the efforts of many people who have helped and inspired us. First, we thank the Philip Lief Group for the invitation, with special thanks to Hope Gatto and Jill Korot for their editorial assistance, patience, and guidance throughout the process. Special thanks also go to Judy Linden and Ruth Mills, both of whom provided not only editorial assistance, but also substantive suggestions on improving the tone, clarity, and content of the book. Without their suggestions and support, this project would never have made it past the first draft.

We extend our gratitude to Kathleen Loviscek, who read early drafts and provided valuable feedback in the important role as an outside reader. We are also grateful to Aleksandar Miletic and Joanne DeStefano, who read portions of the manuscript and pointed out where changes were needed. We are indebted to Sean Salter, who served the invaluable role of checking facts and suggesting improvements. Without his diligence and dedication, in time of special need, our effort might not have passed muster. The same applies to Norman Fowlkes, who generously provided timely help in the area of retirement benefits.

CONTENTS

INTRODUCTION

Welcome to *Investing Made Simple*, a significantly revised and updated version of *Wall Street Made Simple*, which was published more than a decade ago. *Investing Made Simple* reflects a new reality: the evolution toward an ever broader, richer, and more complex investment environment. Previously obscure phrases, words, and acronyms, such as selling short, exchange-traded funds, puts, REITs, and Roth IRAs, have now become commonplace. Moreover, the rapid emergence of the "information age," across all forms of communication, has given investors ready access to an almost-overwhelming amount of financial data and up-to-the-minute financial news.

As both professors of finance (at Seton Hall University and the City University of New York, Baruch College) and active practitioners in the field, we have designed *Investing Made Simple* for the individual investor. It is a guide to investing in stocks, bonds, options, futures, and mutual funds. Whether you are trying to gain a perspective on the behavior of financial markets and the opportunities they offer or are actively trading securities, we believe you will find valuable information in this book.

Knowledge is power, and it is the key factor to investment success. For instance, do you know that $1,000 invested in stocks between 1950 and early 2003 would now be worth more than $400,000, even when accounting for the major declines in stock prices between 2000 and 2002? Do you know that the same $1,000 invested in bonds would be worth only about $24,000, and that the impact of taxes and inflation over that same period

would reduce both of these gains considerably, rendering the gains in bond investments to be worth almost nothing?

The message is clear: returns from safe, supposedly guaranteed investments can be so small that almost their only guarantee is a *loss* after inflation and taxes. You are better off accepting some risk in order to earn appreciable gains on your investments. As you read, keep in mind the phrase "return to risk," as that is the theme of this book. Return to risk means that higher returns are generally accompanied by higher risks, and that you should try to earn the highest investment gains possible for the risk that you are willing to bear.

To help you with your investment decisions, *Investing Made Simple* is divided into two parts. Part 1, comprising seven chapters, acquaints you with a variety of stocks, bonds, mutual funds, and derivatives. Part 2, consisting of four chapters, explores some ideas on developing your investment strategy, including building your investment portfolio and tracking its performance. At the end of each chapter you'll find a section titled "Some Things to Avoid," which is intended to help you increase the "return to risk" on your investments.

Chapter 1 introduces the discipline of finance: the art and science of money and asset management. There is a short quiz to help you assess your risk tolerance, so you can better select which investments are right for you. Rates of return on investments, the magic of compounded returns, and the risks involved therewith are also discussed; and suggestions on saving, including investments that grow tax-deferred and tax-free, are offered.

Chapter 2 provides you with perspectives on how stocks are issued, the exchanges on which they are traded, the differences between common and preferred stocks, fluctuations in stock prices, variables that reflect stock values, and the advantages and disadvantages of owning stocks.

Chapter 3 is a discourse on bonds, classified into the broader category of fixed-income instruments. They include short investments, such as certificates of deposits (CDs) and U.S. Treasury bills, and long-term investments in U.S. Treasury, corporate, and municipal issues. Also discussed is the separation of bonds into investment grade and noninvestment grade groups, and their respective ratings. You'll also find a discussion of the advantages and disadvantages of investing in bonds.

Chapter 4 describes mutual funds—from the very risky aggressive growth funds to the least risky money market funds. Included is a discussion on the costs of investing in mutual funds, from management fees to load charges that you need to be aware of. Also covered is a description and examples of exchange-traded funds.

Chapter 5 delves into the complex world of financial derivatives, with special attention given to options. It not only breaks down the arcane language of these contracts, such as calls, puts, covered calls, naked calls, and LEAPS, but also explains how you can use these instruments to reduce the risk of your investments.

Chapter 6 gives an overview of commodities markets—from grains and meats to lumber and precious metals. It explains forward and futures contracts and distinguishes between the "hedger"—the person who wants to

reduce risk—and the "speculator"—the investor who looks to take on risk.

Chapter 7 discusses financial futures markets. You will learn about trading in less tangible items than commodities, such as stock indices, interest rates, and eurodollars.

The first seven chapters lay the foundation for your decision-making process. Part II begins with Chapter 8, which introduces you to the world of active investing, with emphasis on defining and describing technical and fundamental analysis. It also explains the theory of efficient markets.

Chapter 9 expands on Chapter 8. It points out, based on recent research, where both technical and fundamental analysis are least likely and most likely to help you select investments that generate solid, risk-adjusted gains.

Chapter 10 is about portfolio analysis, introducing you to how you can put your investments together to earn the highest return possible for your risk-tolerance level. It provides a deeper discussion of diversification than found in many books and shows you how to apply it.

Chapter 11 provides a summary while adding some closing points. It distinguishes between the steps for active and passive investing, mentions the need to monitor economic activity, explains dollar-cost averaging, and describes how you can keep track of your investments.

Knowing the right questions to ask and the range of answers to expect may be the biggest boost to your investment-building program. *Investing Made Simple* is designed to help you do just that: ask the right questions and know how to find the answers.

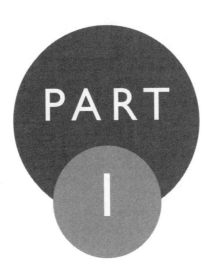

PART

I

INVESTORS MUST KNOW WHAT THEY WANT

—AND BE WILLING TO DO WHAT'S NECESSARY TO GET IT

KEY TERMS

finance, risk, rate of return, securities, compounding, rule of 70s, day trading, margin account, margin call, noise

In many ways, the title of this chapter is really about life, for it raises the question: Do you know what you want and how to achieve it? Whether your response involves a home, career, spouse, college degree, or early retirement, sooner or later, one way or another, reaching these goals involves the ubiquitous topic of money. In other words, how are you going to afford what you want?

The answer deals with a subject that we all are concerned with, regardless of race, gender, ethnicity, or income class: money management. This is truly what *finance* is all about. It really is quite simple: make sure your money is flowing *in* faster than it is flowing *out*. To state it even more simply, make sure you save some of this money.

Saving some of your money is, however, only the first step. The next step is equally important: what to do with your savings. Stashing it in the proverbial cookie jar, under the floorboards, or beneath the mattress have been replaced—fortunately—by making bank deposits and investing in bonds, stocks, mutual funds, and real estate; but simply putting your savings into one or more of these financial vehicles may not help you as much as you might wish. This brings us back to the opening question, but now it is being raised from a financial perspective: Do you really know what you want and how to get it?

Think of saving and investing along the lines of making bread. Assume your goal is to bake what you consider to be the perfect bread: a loaf with a thin, crispy crust and a moist, melt-in-your-mouth center. To that end, you use the highest-quality flour, eggs, sugar, salt, and yeast, and moisten only with filtered water. Yet you still face the most important step: putting the ingredients together. If you do not know which proportions to use and when to add them, your bread might end up looking like a soggy pancake—and tasting as bad!

The same is true for your investments. How much money will you need to set aside to reach your goal? Of equal importance, how will you reach your goal? Which "ingredients" will you use and in what proportions? In sum, what will you invest in and how much will you put into each investment? Like everyone, you want your investments to grow by large amounts because the higher the growth, the faster you will reach your financial goal; and the faster you reach that goal, the sooner you will reach your overall goal—that is, the home, the car, the college degree.

However, big investment growth rates carry a hefty price tag called *risk*. Risk is the chance that you will be disappointed, that the actual gain from your investments will be less than you had expected. Everyone likes big investment growth rates, or *rates of return* (on your investment), but very few of us are fond of risk. We classify stocks, bonds, and other financial assets into a broad category called *securities*, and although this is a reassuring name, it is difficult to earn consistently high returns without consistently taking high risks.

Do you know how much risk you can tolerate? If not, and if you have been investing your money, you might be setting yourself up for a major disappointment: you may find your returns are consistently too low to enable you to reach your goals; or you may find that your returns fluctuate, often unpredictably, beyond what you can tolerate; or you may find that your returns actually lose money.

You would be wise to remember these words: "It is all return to risk," which means that higher returns are generally accompanied by higher risks. For example, over the last hundred years (including 2000, 2001, and 2002—three bad years for stock investments), stock returns have been about three times higher, per year, than U.S. Treasury bills, which are considered to be the closest thing to a "risk-free" investment. At the same time, though, stocks would have exposed you to about six times more risk. While this is tolerable for some investors, it might not be so for others. Therein lies the next question: Do you

know how much risk you are willing to bear to get the returns you want? Let us try to gain some perspective on this vital question.

ASSESS YOUR RISK COMFORT LEVEL

Here's a quick overview of various risk levels:

- **Risk-free:** bank savings account insured up to $100,000

- **Low risk:** debt of the highest quality (e.g., U.S. savings bonds and U.S. Treasury bills)

- **Moderate risk:** investments in well-established industries (e.g., traditional manufacturing and services)

- **High risk:** investments in high-growth industries (e.g., high-tech companies and biotechnology)

- **Very high risk:** speculative deals (e.g., investments in companies suffering from severe financial distress and new firms in new industries)

To help you judge how much risk you can tolerate, take the quiz in Exhibit 1–1. There are no wrong answers. Be honest with yourself—as Shakespeare wisely recommended, "To thine own self be true." If you are not familiar enough with the investments listed in the quiz or are not yet comfortable with answering the questions, read the rest of the book first, especially the next two chapters, which deal with stocks and bonds, and take the quiz later. Keep in mind that the questions in this quiz are meant to serve only as a guide to help you assess your aversion to risk.

EXHIBIT 1–1.   DETERMINING YOUR RISK COMFORT LEVEL

1. **Which of the following appeals to you the most?**
   a. Investing in a risk-free security
   b. Investing in a low-risk, low-return security
   c. Investing in a moderately risky security
   d. Investing in a high-risk security
   e. Investing in a speculative security

2. **Which of the following makes you feel the most comfortable?**
   a. An investment in a safe, solid, low-growth company
   b. An investment in a well-diversified company
   c. An investment in a large technology company
   d. An investment in a small technology company

3. **Which of the following would be your first choice?**
   a. A portfolio of 20% moderately risky securities and 80% safe securities
   b. A portfolio of 60% moderately risky securities and 40% safe securities
   c. A portfolio of 100% moderately risky securities
   d. A portfolio of 80% moderately risky securities and 20% speculative securities
   e. A portfolio of 80% moderately risky securities and 20% speculative securities, with 40% of the portfolio financed with borrowed money

4. **You invest in a pharmaceutical company. One month later, the company announces it has developed a cure for breast cancer, and your investment gain is 30%. What will you do?**
   a. Sell off your investment and take your profits
   b. Hold your investment and hope for more gains
   c. Increase your investment and hope for more gains

5. **Which of the following one-year commitments would you prefer?**
   a. A bank account that gains 3% in six months
   b. A portfolio of moderately risky investments that shows no gain in six months
   c. A promising commercial land deal that loses 10% in six months

6. **Would you be happiest if:**
   a. You doubled your money in two years through prudent investing?
   b. You earned 10% on your investments when most other investments showed no gain?
   c. You earned 5% from your bank account when other investments dropped by 20%?

7. **Which of the following would give you the most satisfaction?**
   a. Winning a million-dollar lottery
   b. Tripling your money to $750,000 in two years on very risky investments
   c. Switching your $750,000 portfolio of high-risk investments to low-risk investments just before high-risk investments drop by 20%

8. **You have the opportunity to invest in a recently formed and very promising high-tech company. What would you do?**
   a. Nothing
   b. Invest 10% of your portfolio in the company
   c. Invest 20% of your portfolio in the company

9. **You are holding a portfolio of moderately risky securities. As inflation begins to rise, what would you be inclined to do?**
   a. Liquidate and invest the proceeds in a bank account
   b. Liquidate and invest the proceeds in land
   c. Liquidate and invest the proceeds in gold

10. **Assume interest rates are historically high and unemployment is up. What would you do?**

    a. Keep your money in a bank account until the economy improves

    b. Split your portfolio evenly between cash and moderately risky securities

    c. Buy a portfolio invested fully in moderately risky to very risky securities.

11. **You are on a televised game show. You have already earned $6,000, and you are in second place. There is one question left, and the only way you can win is to gamble all of it. The question deals with a category with which you are familiar but not an expert. What will you do?**

    a. Bet $1,000   b. Bet $3,000   c. Bet $6,000

Results: For each response, assign the following point values and add them together to get your score.

1. a = 1, b = 1.5, c = 2, d = 4, e = 6
2. a = 2, b = 2.5, c = 4, d = 5
3. a = 2, b = 3, c = 4, d = 5, e = 7
4. a = 2, b = 3, c = 5
5. a = 0.5, b = 2, c = 3
6. a = 3, b = 2, c = 1
7. a = 1, b = 3, c = 2
8. a = 1, b = 2, c = 4
9. a = 1, b = 2, c = 4
10. a = 1, b = 2.5, c = 5
11. a = 1, b = 2, c = 4

Score:

Less than 23: You tend to be very risk-averse.

23–34: You are a prudent risk-taker, willing to take on more risk for a higher return.

35–49: You tend to be an aggressive investor, willing to speculate or gamble.

To put the questions in Exhibit 1–1 in perspective (assuming you were holding a portfolio of stocks) how did you feel when the Dow Jones Industrial Average fell (during September 2001) from more than 10,000 to less than 8,000? If it made you physically ill, then you probably need to reduce your exposure to stocks. If you saw it as an opportunity to buy more stocks, then the opposite is true. Remember, be true to yourself: Do not take more risk than you can stomach, but, at the same time, don't be shy. After all, although fortunes have certainly been won and lost in the stock market, you won't get rich by investing exclusively in a bank savings account.

Although we will have much more to say about risk in forthcoming chapters, as a general guide, keep in mind the following risk levels, which are based on approximately 50 years of annual returns (to keep things simple, these numbers more or less represent fluctuations):

Risk of U.S. Treasury bills:	4%
Risk of U.S. corporate bonds:	8%
Risk of U.S. Treasury bonds:	9%
Risk of U.S. stocks:	20%

Think of risk in terms of driving. Suppose the speed limit is 65 mph; although that may be your average speed, to what extent does it fluctuate around 65? On some parts of the road, you might be driving at 50 mph; in other areas, your speed might be up to 70 mph. The more your speed fluctuates around 65, the more unpredictable your speed may be from one mile to the next. The same is true with the investment returns on securities. U.S. Treasury bill returns fluctuate the least; small company stock returns, the most. The greater the period-to-period fluctuation in the stock or bond returns, the less certain you are about the expected return, and the greater the chance that you will end up disappointed with your return.

As a final note about risk, consider that although stock investments have carried more than twice the risk of bond investments, the comparison is based on annual returns. If your investment horizon is longer than, say, ten years, then the risk of stock investments significantly drops, even to the point of being lower than bond investments.

DETERMINE THE KIND OF RETURNS YOU WANT

Risk is only one side of the financial coin. To be true to yourself, you should decide what kind of returns you want. Of course, everyone wants high returns, but as pointed out in the previous section, higher returns appear to go hand in hand with higher risk.

With that in mind, let's now see what insights finance can give us. To that end, we will use the phrase "doubling your money," which is often used in securities circles. For instance, if you have $10,000 to invest, wouldn't you like to know how long it will take to double this to $20,000? Going further, how long will it take you to double that to $40,000, and then to $80,000, and so on? By answering these questions, you will begin to understand the principle of *compounding*. Loosely defined, it means "return on return." With bank accounts, the interest earned from them is alternatively called "interest on interest."

Once you determine the size (i.e., the percentage) of your expected return, you can easily estimate, and with considerable accuracy, how long it will take you to double your money. To understand the next lesson, you need to

learn the *rule of 70s*, which involves numbers between 70 and 78, especially 72, 75, and 78. Each of these numbers will be used as a divisor. You choose which one to use by means of the chart shown in Exhibit 1–2, where the percent ranges represent the size of your rate of return.

EXHIBIT 1–2. DOUBLING YOUR MONEY

To determine how long it will take to double your investment dollars, divide the appropriate 70s number by the growth rate.

0%– 9%:	72
10%–18%:	75
19%–28%:	78
29%–38%:	81

Here are some examples of how to use the information in Exhibit 1–2:

- If you are consistently earning 8% per year on your investments, it will take you about nine years to double your money; that is, 72 (the 70s number from Exhibit 1–2) divided by 8, the percent you are earning.

- If you are earning 15%, it will take you approximately five years to double your money, or 75 divided by 15.

- If you are earning 26% per year (and if this is your normal return, you probably don't need to be reading this book), it will take you about three years to double your money, or 78 divided by 26.

Note that these are approximations. You will not get exactly a doubling. In some cases, you will get a little bit more, in other cases a bit less. For example:

- If you invested $10,000, and it earned 15%

per year for five years, you would have earned $20,113.57, or $113.57 over $20,000.

- If you invested $10,000, and it earned 18%, you would have doubled your money in about 4.167 years, or 75 divided by 18. That converts to $19,931.15, or $68.85 below $20,000.

When it comes to compounding, as you can see, the bigger the return, the faster you can reach your goal. This is why you should not only look for the highest return possible, given your risk tolerance, but also make sure that your investments are compounded as often as possible. Let the magic of compounding work its way through your investments!

By the way, as you read about investing, you might run across the acronym CAGR, which stands for "compound annual growth rate." It sounds sophisticated, but it is nothing more than compounding on an annual basis: "return on return" per year.

What should you do if your risk profile suggests that you are conservative? How can you make up for the lower returns that you expect compared with those earned by more risk-tolerant investors? The answer is simple: You will have to save more. How much more will depend on the rate of return you expect and how much you expect to accumulate, which takes us to the next topic: proper planning.

PROPER PLANNING CAN PREVENT POOR PERFORMANCE

Do you remember Aesop's fable about the grasshopper and the ant? Here's a summary: One summer day, a grasshopper was playing in a field. Chirping and singing, it asked a passing ant to join it. The ant, barely taking time to stop, declined, saying it had to store food away for the coming winter. Puzzled, the grasshopper wondered why the ant should be worrying about food when there was so much available. The ant, though, continued to work. When winter came, the grasshopper found the cold overwhelming and food scarce. Meanwhile, the ant was spending the winter deep in the warmth of its den, enjoying the protection of its community and an abundance of food. The moral is: hard work today ensures a better tomorrow.

Some people are like the grasshopper. They brush off recommendations to prepare for the future by saying, cavalierly, "We'll think of something," or "We'll cross that bridge when we come to it." Given the number of people who have large credit-card balances with little hope of paying them off in the near future, and others who are deeply debt-ridden by home, car, and other purchases, it is little wonder that the U.S. national savings rate is in the low single-digit range. Sure, this attitude may mean a lot of short-term pleasure, but it typically comes with high long-term costs. Yes, people generally find a way of getting by, but almost always at a lower standard of living, exacerbated by the stress of worrying about what they will do in the face of an unexpected crisis.

So how do you build a proverbial nest egg? Once again, the answer is simple: set some savings aside. Admittedly, that statement begs a few questions: How much should you set aside? Where do you put your savings? What kind of return can you expect? Let's assume that, regardless of your current age, you intend to be working at least ten more years. You undoubtedly have heard the finance cliché "time is money." Simply put, this means that the hands of time keep moving in one direction—forward—and that the longer you have to wait for your reward for saving, the less it will be worth to you. Fortunately, though, time can also be your friend. Exhibit 1–3 shows how time and compounding, together with just a small amount of savings, can work to your advantage. The savings rate is assumed to be 6%, close to the long-term U.S. average.

EXHIBIT 1–3. INCREASING YOUR INVESTMENT WITH COMPOUNDING, AT VARYING SALARY AND SAVINGS LEVELS

Given an investment return of 1% per month, over a 10-year period:

Annual salary:	$20,000, paid in monthly amounts of $1,666.67
Savings:	$100 per month, or 6% ($100 = 0.06 × $1,666.67)
Accumulation:	$23,001

Annual salary:	$30,000, paid in monthly amounts of $2,500
Savings:	$150 per month, or 6% ($150 = 0.06 × $2,500)
Accumulation:	$34,501.50

Annual salary:	$40,000, paid in monthly amounts of $3,333.33
Savings:	$200 per month, or 6% ($200 = 0.06 × $3,333.33)
Accumulation:	$46,002

Annual salary:	$50,000, paid in monthly amounts of $4,166.67
Savings:	$250 per month, or 6% ($250 = 0.06 × $4,166.67)
Accumulation:	$57,502.50

Annual salary:	$60,000, paid in monthly amounts of $5,000
Savings:	$300 per month, or 6% (0.06 × $5,000)
Accumulation:	$69,003

Annual Salary:	$70,000, paid in monthly amounts of $5,833.33
Savings:	$350 per month, or 6% ($350 = .06 × $5,833.33)
Accumulation:	$80,503.50

Annual salary:	$80,000 paid in monthly amounts of $6,666.67
Savings:	$400 per month, or 6% ($400 = 0.06 × $6,666.67)
Accumulation:	$92,004

Annual salary:	$90,000, paid in monthly amounts of $7,500
Savings:	$450 per month, or 6% ($450 = 0.06 × $7,500)
Accumulation:	$103,504.50

Annual salary:	$100,000, paid in monthly amounts of $8,333.33
Savings:	$500 per month, or 6% ($500 = 0.06 × $8,333.33)
Accumulation:	$115,005

There are a number of things to note from this exhibit:

- Compounded, 1% per month translates to about 12.6% per year. If you think this is too high, raise your savings rate.

- The accumulation far exceeds the amount invested. For example, at a salary of $50,000, the total amount invested for the ten years is $30,000, or $250 multiplied by 120 months. The accumulation, however, is $57,502.50. Once again, this is the power of compounding.

- You will get pay raises. The assumption in the examples is that you will be earning one salary for the entire ten-year period. More likely, over time you will receive raises that give you opportunities to enhance your accumulation.

- Begin early. If you were to increase the number of years from ten to twenty, then at $50,000, everything else remaining the same, the accumulation leaps to $247,314.89, more than a fourfold increase over $57,502.50.

- You can become a millionaire. To get to the magic mark of $1 million, you can combine a savings rate of 10% for twenty years with a salary of $130,000.

NEVER INVEST MORE THAN YOU CAN AFFORD TO LOSE

In the previous section, we assumed that you were saving 6% of your income. For some, 6% is too low—they can afford to save more—but for others, it may be too high. Although you need to be disciplined about your savings and investment habits, do not be foolish. Never invest more than you can afford to lose; and don't invest your food, clothing, housing, and medical money. As elementary as this may

sound, there are people who have done, and still do, make this mistake.

During the 1990s, a phenomenon called *day trading* became popular. Day trading is when investors buy and sell securities, such as stocks and bonds, on a daily basis. For example, say you buy and sell a security of a single company several times in one hour, trying to take advantage of near-constant fluctuations in the company's stock price. Although day trading, by itself, does not imply that you are investing more than you can afford to lose, it can become a problem for some people. For example, during the 1990s, a number of investors quit their jobs to devote more time to day trading—essentially making the practice their new job. People from all walks of life—from factory workers, desk clerks, and office supervisors to teachers, lawyers, and physicians—became very active participants in the stock and bond markets. In their desire to make a quick and easy buck, most failed to recognize that such a radical job switch placed their incomes in serious jeopardy. In many cases, these investors lost their cars, homes, and even their entire life savings, and they did not have their old jobs to fall back on.

You should also be careful about borrowing money to invest. When you do so, you are opening what's called a *margin account*. There are specific rules with which you have to comply when trading securities "on margin." The most important rule is that the amount you borrow cannot be above a certain percentage of the overall value of your portfolio. Say the percentage is 60% and you borrow $50,000 of a $100,000 portfolio. How far can your portfolio decline before you will be forced to come up with more cash, a situation known as a *margin call*, or a maintenance call? To get the answer, do the following calculation:

$$\$50,000 \div 0.60 = \$83,333.33$$

If you recieve a margin call notice, you must come up with more money—whether it is from your paycheck, your bank savings, or by making an outright sale of the stocks and bonds you own until the amount you owe is less than 60% of the total current value of the portfolio. Obviously, it might be difficult for you to come up with the necessary amount on short notice.

For example, say you borrowed $50,000 to build a portfolio of $100,000 If the market value of the portfolio falls below $83,333.33, say to $82,000, and if the margin call was issued, you would be required to make up the difference of $1,333.33.

Adding to the problem, if you are forced to sell some part of your portfolio, you will have to do so, in general, at a ratio of up to 3:1. In other words, for every dollar that your portfolio falls below the minimum, you will have to sell $3 in securities. If your broker determines that your portfolio value is short of the minimum requirement by, say, $5,000, you will have to sell $15,000 in securities. That can be a high price to pay, especially if all of the stocks and bonds in your portfolio have been incurring losses. The result will be a steep drop in your portfolio's value; and if it continues to drop, you will be asked for more money. And the only way you will be able to reduce your losses, for tax purposes, beyond the $3,000 level set by the Internal Revenue Service, is if you have gains to offset them—not likely to be the case in this situation. Once you are on this slippery slope, you may be forced into selling not only your investment portfolio but also all your personal assets, including cars and homes, and possibly forcing you into bankruptcy.

Fortunately, situations of this kind are unusual, if not rare. They do happen, but there is no reason for them to happen to you as long as you are prudent, and prudence begins with investing only what you can afford to lose.

IDENTIFY YOUR INVESTMENT GOALS

Be sure to keep your investment goals in mind. Depending on where you are in life, your mix of investments can, and should, vary. If you are saving for your child's education, for example, with at least ten years to invest (although it would be wise to begin before then), or if you are planning for retirement, you should think about taking some prudent risks, along the lines suggested in Exhibit 1–1. If you plan to buy a home in five years, a reasonable plan would be to follow the schedule for a very risk-averse investor. These guidelines are admittedly rough, because differences in risk-tolerance levels and investment goals could certainly move some investors to increase or decrease the proportion of their portfolio in stocks. (Chapter 10 provides more detailed guidelines for determining investment goals according to age.)

Always remember that investment returns are influenced by a subtle and significant factor: inflation. Inflation is a sustained increase in the overall price level. Its effect is to diminish the purchasing power of your income, much like termites eating away at the wood in your home. Over the past 75 years, the U.S. inflation rate has averaged over 3%. What are the implications of this?

A detailed article by Laurence Siegel and David Montgomery (see the References section at the end of this book) describes the impact of both inflation and taxes on investment returns. Although the article is somewhat technical, their main conclusion is that, after taxes and inflation, stocks have significantly higher returns than bonds or Treasury bills.

A simple illustration will drive the authors' point home. Assume you are earning 10% a year, which is close to the long-term return that stocks have provided, and that inflation is at 3.5%: your return, adjusted for inflation, drops to 6.5%. As a result, it will now take you longer to double your money. As disconcerting as this sounds, the impact on bonds and Treasury bills is worse. In fact, once taxes and inflation are subtracted, Siegel and Montgomery estimate that bonds yield less than 1% and Treasury bills yield a negative percentage. Thus, stocks, along with real estate, seem to hold their own against inflation better than bonds.

We suggest, then, that you keep a significant portion of your portfolio in stocks. And if you are under 50 years old, you should probably keep at least 70% of your portfolio in stocks.

BE TAX-SAVVY

Taxes can take a big bite out of your savings. Depending on your tax bracket, under current law, up to 38.6% of your investment income can be taxed. So, regardless of the amount that you can save, you should seriously consider taking certain financial actions to reduce the impact of taxes, especially if you are saving for retirement or your child's education.

Investment Vehicles for Retirement

Let's begin by discussing how you can both save for your retirement and reduce taxes. Consider the following three options:

Investment Retirement Accounts. Both the conventional Individual Retirement Account (conventionally, an *IRA*) and the *Roth IRA* are designed to shelter your savings from taxes. Even with the contribution limits ($3,000 for 2003–04, $4,000 for 2005–07, and $5,000 thereafter, with "catch-up" provisions for investors at least 50 years of age), this is a big deal. Of the two, the Roth IRA is preferred. Why? Although under certain conditions, the conventional IRA is tax-deductible while the Roth IRA is not, the Roth IRA offers an advantage that the conventional one does not: the ability to withdraw your money tax-free. Assuming you wait until your age is 59.5, when penalties for withdrawal are no longer imposed, the tax-free benefit will outweigh the tax-deduction benefit, unless you expect your tax rate to be much less than when you invested the savings. Note that if you are at least 50 years old, you may contribute to your IRA beyond the imposed limits, often called "catch-up contributions."

40l(k) and 403(b) Accounts. Available through employers [403(b) accounts are for not-for-profit employers], these plans offer the double incentive of allowing you to reduce your taxable income by investing in tax-deferred investment accounts, typically mutual funds. You do not have to pay taxes on the gains until you withdraw them, and you can begin doing so at age 59.5 without penalty. Often, employers will match the employee's (i.e., your) contribution, allowing for a double investment at the same risk, which is a good deal.

Other Plans. A Simplified Employee Pension (SEP) is an IRA-based plan designed for the self-employed and for employees of small-business owners. Annual employer contributions, as of 2003, are limited to the lesser of $40,000 or 25% of an employee's annual compensation. There is also the Savings Incentive Match Plan for Employees, or SIMPLE IRA, which has more flexible investment options than, for example, a 401(k). Its contribution limit, as of 2003, is $8,000 (to be raised to $10,000 by 2005).

To help you prepare for retirement, you might consider investing in a *defined benefit plan* or a *defined contribution plan*.With a defined benefit plan, you, as a business owner, receive a monthly check, depending on the amount you contributed and how long you were in business, for the rest of your life. This is more complicated than the defined contribution plan, but if you are raking in the money and retirement is not far off, you should consider talking with a financial advisor about it.

Alternatively, with a defined contribution plan, you have two choices: a money-purchase plan, in which the maximum contribution is the lesser of $40,000 or 20% of profits, or a profit-sharing plan with similar maximum contribution limits. The difference lies with the way the contributions are made. Once established, you must contribute to the money-purchase plan annually, regardless of your company's profits. With the profit-sharing plan, however, you have the choice whether or not to contribute.

Investment Vehicles to Assist with Education

When it comes to saving for your children's education, there are two important options to explore:

Coverdell Education Savings Account. If you understand the Roth IRA, you will understand this account. It allows you to make a nondeductible contribution to a special account for your child's education. The investment gains are tax-free, and so are the withdrawals, just as with a Roth IRA, as long as they are used to cover the child's education.

529 Account. Named after Section 529 of the Internal Revenue Code, this state-sponsored account is offered by all 50 states and the District of Columbia. Contributions must be in cash (as opposed to property), with large upper-limit maximums (e.g., in excess of $200,000). The 529 account operates in a manner similar to a 401(k), except the investment gains are also tax-free if used to pay for college-related expenses, such as tuition, room and board, and books. Currently, a single individual can contribute up to $55,000 (treated as an $11,000 payment, per year, for five years) with no adverse tax consequences; married couples can double this contribution.

SEEK GOOD ADVICE

It is common for investors of all stripes to seek the assistance of a financial advisor, one who knows not only about financial markets, but also about the various securities and laws that best suit the financial objectives of the investor. But do you need one? Even if you have reached your investment goals, it does not necessarily mean that you have finished running the financial race. In fact, in some ways, the race has begun anew. This is not to say that you need a financial advisor, but consider this: the more complex your situation—such as the need for long-term retirement planning, gifts, life insurance trusts, and the like—the more likely it is that you should seek advice.

But how do you select one? Start by talking to people you **trust**, for example:

- Referrals from relatives and friends
- Certified financial planners
- Registered investment advisors
- Accountants
- Lawyers

In addition, contact:

- Financial Planning Association
- American Institute of Certified Public Accountants

Note the emphasis on the word "trust" above. How do you know if an individual is trustworthy? The best way is to seek recommendations from satisfied customers; and you must ask them pertinent questions, such as where the advisor has met the referral's expectations and where the advisor has fallen short. In addition, pay attention to advisors who know how to listen, as opposed to doing all the talking. After all, to meet your individual needs, the advisor must understand not only something about your investment goals but also something about you. Remember, this is your money, so do not be shy about asking important questions, which should include, at a minimum:

- What are the advisor's qualifications?

- Is the advisor registered with the Securities Exchange Commission (SEC), the watchdog of financial markets?

- What is the advisor's experience and investment philosophy?

- What is the advisor's specialty (e.g., stocks, bonds, real estate, etc.)?

- What is the advisor's availability?

- Can you review a sample financial plan of an existing client?

If the advisor provides satisfactory responses to questions such as these, your next step should be to evaluate whether the advisor asks you the right questions, such as your investment horizon, your risk aversion, the kind of returns you are seeking, how much you can afford to lose, and your projected income.

Once you find an advisor, he or she might also be able to serve as your broker. There are two types: full-service and discount. Given the way financial markets are set up, you need to choose a broker to buy and sell securities. The basic difference between the two lies with one word: advice. The full-service broker can provide you with financial advice on what to buy and sell, and when to do so. The discount broker is not permitted to offer such advice; however, the discount broker, as the classification implies, offers services at a much lower price. In fact, Internet-based services can be as little as $7 per trade, unheard of before the 1990s. However, it is not clear that "you get what you pay for." Although full-service consultants no doubt offer a quality of service that discount brokers cannot, it does not necessarily follow that the extra cost carries additional benefits. Simply put, be careful. Just as with financial advisors, you need to shop around.

SOME THINGS TO AVOID

Given the discussion so far, there are a few things to avoid when getting started in investing:

- **Avoid being overly concerned with day-to-day movements in the prices of securities.** With few exceptions, investors should ignore these day-to-day movements, which statisticians call *noise*, or random fluctuations, that occur from buying and selling securities. There is no systematic way of profiting from these movements.

- **Avoid making too much of media information.** Interest in investing has led to popular television shows, such as CNBC's many finance-related programs, the *Nightly Business Report*, and *Wall Street Week*. They can be very informative in keeping investors up to date on the latest financial news, from broad market movements to individual stocks and bonds; however, it is far from clear that investors can profit from the information. Why? Because it is already known and has been priced into the securities.

- **Avoid buying on margin.** Unless you are an aggressive investor, avoid borrowing to buy securities. Although gains from borrowing can be high, so can losses, and the threat of margin calls might lead to many sleepless nights. In the end, it is all about return to risk, and the risks for most investors are not worth the returns.

SUMMARY

This chapter has explored some basic financial issues that all people face. It is human nature to live not only for today but also for tomorrow. Doing so implies building a nest egg. How you build that nest egg depends on your "taste" for returns and your "distaste" for risk. Remember the adage about "return to risk," and always be true to yourself. If it turns out that you are very risk-averse, then make sure you invest in securities that yield safe, predictable returns, such as low-risk stocks and U.S. government bonds. If you are more risk-tolerant, then look for high-risk securities that offer the potential for big gains. Regardless, based on what you know about compounding, the sooner you begin your financial journey the better. But as you set out on this important journey, keep these two important points in mind: never invest more than you can lose, and make informed choices.

INVESTING IN STOCKS

Probably the most-often-asked question in economics and finance is: What's the market doing? By "market" people usually mean the stock market, but they could just as easily be referring to the market for bonds, commodities, currency, futures, or options. But even if they do mean the stock market, what does that truly encompass? Does it include the Dow Jones Industrials, the S&P 500, the NASDAQ, the Russell 2000, and the Wilshire 5000, all of which you often hear about in the same breath as "stock market"? In this chapter, we will make the task of understanding all these entities simple.

In fact, the purpose behind the question about how the market is doing is itself simple: to figure out if you are gaining or losing on your investments. Let us begin where most of the action is: the stock market.

WHY A COMPANY SELLS STOCK

The stock market is like any other market where you buy food, clothes, or cars. Let's say you're thinking of buying a car, so you check the newspapers, television, and the Internet for ads on new and used models. Cars come in various styles (from sedans to minivans and SUVs) and sizes (small, compact, and large) with a variety of features (four-cylinder, six-cylinder, cloth or leather seats). Once you find one you like, you take a close look at it, whether by visiting the dealership or viewing "online" pictures and descriptions. Your goal is to find a reliable car at an attractive price.

The same applies to *stocks*, which represent ownership of a company. You begin by reading newspapers, visiting relevant Internet sites, and watching financial programs on television for information on stocks. Like cars, stocks come in various styles (from low-growth/low-risk to high-growth/high-risk) and sizes (from large companies to small companies) and they have different features (i.e., you can buy preferred or common stock). Once you find one of interest, you take a close look, usually by examining the company's financial strength, its market position, and its short- and long-term prospects.

But before we explore stocks in detail, you might be wondering, "Why do companies issue stock?" Concisely put, companies issue stock to raise funds. They do this by offering to sell shares of the company, called stocks, to the general public (you and me). This is called *going public*. The first time a company does this it is called an *initial public offering*, or *IPO* for short. The more shares of a company's stock you buy, the more of the company you own; and if you own more shares than anyone else, you can have a lot to say about how the company is run.

Raising money by selling stock is much the same as getting a loan for a car, a home, or an education. The bottom line is all about getting hold of more money. With stock, though (unlike with a loan), the company does not have to pay back anything. However, "going public" imposes a responsibility: the managers are now beholden to the stockholders, also called shareholders. In fact, the rules of finance state that the goal of the company is to satisfy its stockholders. How? By doing its job so well that the company keeps growing and the stock price keeps rising. As a result, management is always in the hot seat. Anytime the company does poorly and the stock price falls, management runs the risk of incurring the wrath of its shareholders. The outcome might be that management is ousted or that another company buys the company and replaces the management.

Primary and Secondary Markets for Stocks

Going public happens in two steps. The first step is the *primary market*, where investment bankers, such as Merrill Lynch, Morgan Stanley, or Salomon Smith Barney, buy large chunks of this primary stock issued directly from the company. This is where the company receives its money. In the second step, the investment bankers resell smaller pieces of the shares to their clients, who then trade those shares with other investors (again, the general public), which is the *secondary market*.

Keep this important point in mind: Unless a company issues new stock, the stock market activity that you hear and read about is from the secondary market. In the United States, almost all of the secondary market consists of three entities, or exchanges:

- The New York Stock Exchange (NYSE, or the Big Board)

- The American Stock Exchange (the AMEX)

- The National Association of Securities Dealers Automated Quotations (the NASDAQ)

Each of these exchanges has its own requirements for inclusion, but the bigger and more mature the company (such as General Electric or Coca-Cola), the more likely its stock is listed on the most prestigious of the exchanges: the Big Board. The smaller and newer the company, the more likely it is to be listed on the NASDAQ. If it's listed on the Big Board, the stock will have a ticker symbol of three letters or fewer (such as F for Ford, GE for General Electric, and AXP for American Express). Four-letter symbols are reserved for the NASDAQ (for example, MSFT for Microsoft and INTC for Intel). Mature companies, as intuition suggests, tend to be more predictable. Thus, their stock prices are less likely to show big swings than are growth companies. However, growth companies offer the promise of big gains in their stock prices.

There is one more place where stocks are listed: penny stocks, or stocks selling below $1 per share, are often relegated to an Over-the-Counter (OTC) exchange called the Pink Sheets (the name comes from the listings being printed on pink paper). It is not really an exchange in the sense of the NYSE or AMEX as much as it is a place where prices of thinly traded stocks are displayed.

Regardless of the exchange on which stocks are traded, stock markets are generally classified as either bullish or bearish. Although the origin of these words is not totally clear, a *bull market* refers to a period of sustained rising stock prices. A *bear market* is the direct opposite, namely, when stock prices display a downward trend. Bull markets have dominated bear markets. More than two-thirds of the last century included "up" years for the market. For example, since the end of World War II, the U.S. stock market registered rates of return of better than 10% in all decades except the 1970s. All told, bull markets tend to be long and bear markets short.

HOW A COMPANY SELLS STOCK: A CASE STUDY

"Taking stock" in a company means taking ownership in it, whether you buy one share or 10,000 (called a block). Owning one share in a business can be compared to owning one brick in a building. Whether you own just the one brick or a whole wall, you are still a part of the whole structure. When you purchase shares, you take claim to a piece of paper called a stock certificate, which shows the number of shares you own.

But why does a company issue stock? Again, simply put, the company wants to raise money. A business may be as small as one person, often called a proprietorship. Millions of small businesses dot the economic landscape, employing anywhere from one to a few hundred employees and taking in from a few hundred to millions of dollars in sales. Proprietorships, however, generally remain small because their access to money for expansion (or financial capital, as it is sometimes called) is limited to the resources of the owner.

Proprietorships are popular among professionals who offer services, including physicians, tax accountants, lawn care specialists, restaurant owners, house painters, or any

business that requires relatively little financial capital to get started. Proprietorships are simple to start. You simply proclaim your intent to do business. You may need to get a tax number or a license for certain kinds of services, but then you are qualified to "set up shop." As the need for capital expands beyond the resources of one person, two or more people may join in a partnership. Partnerships offer access to the one thing that proprietorships ordinarily do not: more financial capital. For example, many legal firms expand by increasing the number of partners in the business. However, while they provide the needed money, partnerships can also cause problems, in the form of, say, disagreements over location, expansion, even the day-to-day decisions about how to run the business.

Unlike your average proprietorship, big businesses and organizations require immense quantities of capital. Suppose you came up with a revolutionary way to build a very reliable and affordable car. Unless you happen to be fantastically rich, how will you come up with the money to build a large-scale factory, equip it with modern robotic technology, and pay the personnel who will work there? As a single person, you would encounter near-incomprehensible difficulty in rounding up enough money.

So, having ruled out a partnership because you don't know anyone with enough capital, your best bet is to create a corporation. You can then sell shares of the yet-to-be-built factory to acquire the capital needed to actually break ground. Each person who invests (i.e., buys stock) in your factory receives an ownership share in the business. With an almost unlimited number of people able and willing to buy stock, your new corporation can raise millions, even billions, of dollars.

Here is another illustration of corporation building. In our car scenario, suppose you develop a device for improving gas mileage to 100 miles per gallon for a fully equipped six-cylinder sedan. You test it in your own car, then in friends' vehicles. The device works flawlessly at all speeds. After producing a few dozen of them from a workshop in your basement and selling them below cost to neighbors (who rave about the results), you decide to devote your efforts full-time to the business.

Using your life savings, you buy a small manufacturing shop and begin production. You sell the device directly from the shop. Word begins to spread locally, then regionally, about your invention, requiring you to set up a retail sales store where people can buy the device without interrupting you at the shop. Unfortunately, you have already poured all of your funds into the manufacturing setup. Moreover, customers are beginning to order the device at a rate faster than you can produce, leading to back orders. You begin to sense that the shop—the whole operation, for that matter—is too small to satisfy demand. Complicating matters—and typical of new businesses—as promising as everything looks, you have yet to turn a decent profit (the money left over from sales after all expenses have been paid). So you have no new savings and you used your old savings to buy the shop. In short, you need more money. Without proof of a profit, however, bank financing will be hard to come by, or offered only at a high interest rate and on a short-term basis.

What should you do?

You expand by incorporating the business (forming a corporation), naming it, say, GSD, Inc., for Gas-Saving Device. You hire an attorney to prepare the paperwork and submit it to the secretary of state where you live. In effect, the state will treat the corporation as if it were a live person, allowing it to sell products, pay employees, sell shares to raise money (capital), and, generally, function the same as you.

Once you are officially incorporated, you can offer (i.e., sell) shares in GSD, Inc. to your friends, relatives, and business associates. But be aware, at this stage you are permitted to offer only a limited number of shares to these original investors—who are considered part of the corporation because they now own stock. These investors, of course, are looking to profit from the production and sale of your device. You set up a board of directors, an appointed group that oversees company operations (owning stock is not a prerequisite to being a member of the board). As the inventor, producer, and majority shareholder, you declare yourself the chief executive officer, or CEO, to be named to the board. Using the funds from the sale of shares, you expand GSD, Inc., setting up the retail outlet, buying more machinery, and hiring a small staff. Business is good, and you begin to generate profits, which you put back into the business to expand it further.

At this juncture, your device begins to catch on nationwide; orders are pouring in from all over the country. But soon you are right back where you started: demand is stronger than your capacity to produce. You have not yet generated enough funds from sales to keep paying current expenses and to finance additional expansion. So you go back to the original shareholders and ask if they would be willing to invest more money, that is, buy more shares. For various reasons, some agree, others do not. Regardless, you find that their additional contributions fall far short of what you need.

What should you do?

It is time to go public. But to sell shares to the general public, you first need to attract investors, and to do so you need to create a market for the company's shares. To that end, you hire financing specialists who develop a report on the objectives and history of GSD, Inc., called a prospectus, for submission to the Securities and Exchange Commission (SEC), the organization that oversees the operation of financial markets and financial reporting. Prior to the official offering date, when the new stock can be bought, the selling group, which is most often a collection of investment bankers, issues what is called a *red herring*, or a preliminary prospectus with all the details of the offering, excluding the share price, date, and disposal of the proceeds from the sale of the shares. The purpose of the red herring is to drum up interest among potential buyers of the stock. When the SEC approves the proposal, including the wording of the prospectus, the shares of stock become registered and available for sale to the general public.

Assume that GSD, Inc. originally authorized 2,000 shares of which 1,000 have been issued (750 to yourself and 250 to your friends), and 1,000 are held in reserve. In order to raise some money, you decide to sell 1,000 shares—200 of your own, plus 800 of the 1,000 in reserve. You hire a stock brokerage firm to buy the 1,000 shares (this buying process is usually called underwriting) and you set a price per share. This is the initial public offering. An underwriter buys the stock with a view to selling it to the public. It will likely contact a number of investment banks to create a selling group.

Before the stock is sold, you and the board of directors of GSD, Inc. vote to divide, or *split*, the stock 1,000 to l. This means that for every one of the original shares of stock, there will

now be 1,000 shares, and the total number of shares available for sale is now 1,000,000: the 200,000 shares that you own plus the 800,000 shares previously unissued. The shares of all the original owners are also split, 1,000 to 1. The IPO may be 1,000,000 shares, with 800,000 shares being sold by the company and 200,000 shares coming from your original ownership shares.

Assume the IPO is priced at $10 per share. You end up with $2 million in cash ($10 multiplied by 200,000 shares), and GSD, Inc. acquires $8 million of new capital. This is known as the primary market. The new shares are then marketed to investors, under the symbol, say, "GASD" in the NASDAQ market, who have their accounts with the underwriters. A market in the secondary area is now born for the shares.

Some of your friends and relatives may now decide to sell their shares. To do so, they must contact a stockbroker, who will be glad to sell them at the market price, which might now be greater or less than the original price of $10, in the secondary market. It all depends on how well the market receives the stock. If the company's future prospects are bright, and if business is brisk, the stock price could conceivably be higher than $10 per share, say, $15 or $20. If prospects are dim, then the opposite will occur.

This simple illustration describes what is referred to as *common stock*. Recall from the beginning of the chapter that corporations have a choice of issuing two kinds of stock, common and preferred. These will be defined and discussed in detail in the next two sections. For now, just keep in mind that the type of stock issued depends on the attributes of investors. As we will see, although common stock tends to carry more risk than preferred stock, it also promises higher returns. And it is the prospect of higher returns that attracts investors to buy stock to begin with. Why? Because stock investors tend to build their nest eggs quicker, accumulating greater sums than investors who concentrate in safer investments, such as bank savings accounts, certificates of deposit, bonds, or real estate.

The point is that a stock market benefits both issuers and buyers. To become a savvy investor, though, you need to recognize the differences between the various types of stocks and know how to evaluate the worth of the thousands of issues available, as well as know which to avoid. Understanding the basics is a must, even if you rely on others for investment advice. Keeping track of your investments calls for an understanding of how corporations distribute earnings to shareholders and the effects of a corporation's actions on the value of its shares as perceived by the market. With that in mind, next we'll take a close look at these basics, from common and preferred stocks to stock price movements.

COMMON STOCK: AN UNCOMMON INVESTMENT

Common stock represents ownership interest. Owners of common stock own the corporation. They may vote on numerous decisions affecting it, including a decision to sell or merge with another corporation. They elect a board of directors, whose members, in turn, hire managers to run the business. A majority shareholder is one who owns more than 50% of the outstanding shares in a corporation (i.e., the shares that have been "issued" or sold to the public) and, thus, can call the shots. All other shareholders are minority shareholders.

With ordinary common stock, the standard is one share, one vote. In large corporations, no single person or organization owns anywhere near a majority interest. In these corporations, a shareholder with as little as 10% of the shares may control the corporation in effect. If things go badly, a coalition of so-called dissident shareholders may gather enough shares/votes to replace the existing board. The new board may then fire the existing management and bring in its own management team.

Dividends, a distribution of the firm's earnings, may be paid on common stock at the option of the board of directors. Every dividend, whether paid in cash or additional shares of stock, must be declared, or passed in a resolution at an official meeting of the board, even if a dividend has been paid every quarter for the past fifty years. The dividend is usually stated as a specified amount per share. For example, your company might agree to pay $5 per share. This amount is fixed, regardless of what happens to the price of the stock. Five dollars per share on a current stock price of $50 is a dividend yield of 10% (i.e., $5 divided by $50). If the share price falls to $40, then the dividend yield becomes 12.5% (which is $5 divided by $40). However, many companies with stock outstanding pay no dividends. They may simply prefer to put the profit back into the company for further growth. Ordinarily, as a corporation grows and matures, it will pay dividends. This is one reason (although not necessarily the only reason or even the primary reason) that some investors buy stocks.

If dividends are important to you, be aware of the *ex-dividend date*, which begins two days before the holder-of-record date when buying shares. The ex-dividend date is the date when you, as a buyer, no longer have a right to the dividend. If you buy dividend-paying stock on or after the ex-dividend date, you will not be entitled to the dividend. It will end up in the hands of the seller of the stock, the holder of record. For example, if a stock is paying a dividend on July 15, 2003, you need to buy the stock well before this date to get the dividend. Otherwise, you will have to wait until the next quarter to receive it. Dividend payments actually consist of four dates: declaration date, holder-of-record date, ex-dividend date, and payment date. The last three dates have already been defined; the declaration date is the date on which the board of directors declares the amount of the dividend and the date whereby the company plans to pay it.

With the above example in mind, assume the board of directors of Coca-Cola met on April 16, 2003, and declared a dividend of $0.22, payable on July 15, 2003, to investors who held the stock as of June 15, 2003, the holder-of-record date. That means the ex-dividend date began on June 13. So you would have had to have bought the stock by June 12 to be eligible for the dividend on July 15, the payment date.

Speaking of dividends, you will find that some companies have *dividend reinvestment plans*, or DRIPs, as they are commonly called. DRIPs allow stockholders to use the dividends to automatically buy more of the company's stock. The plan can take one of two forms: either existing stock, in which a bank buys shares from the available pool, or newly issued stock to help the company raise more funds. Newly issued stock is usually offered at 3% to 5% off the existing market price.

Companies can issue more than one class of common stock. Each class carries a different set of privileges. The classes are usually noted as Class A, Class B, and Class C. Class A common stock may include voting privileges, whereas a

Class B stock is issued by the same company and permits dividend payments but not voting privileges. Investors need to make sure which class of stock they are buying and the characteristics of each. Class C stock is issued for specific purposes, such as financing a segment of the business or paying a special dividend, or is reserved for a special group of investors.

Although common stock usually carries voting privileges, it tends to be a risky investment. But with that added risk (compared to bank savings and bonds) comes higher expected return. In bull markets (when economic growth is strong and optimism high), the returns can be hefty—for some stocks, even more than 100% per year. In bear markets, though (when economic growth is not strong and optimism is low), the returns can be negative, and for some stocks, very much so.

PREFERRED STOCK: WHAT IS YOUR PREFERENCE?

Preferred stock differs from common stock in four ways:

- First (as the name suggests), preferred stockholders are first in line to receive dividends, and in greater amounts than their common-stock counterparts.

- Second, in the unfortunate event that the company goes out of business, preferred shareholders get earlier access to the company's assets.

- Third, preferred stockholders usually do not have voting rights. (The reason is that preferred stockholders receive dividends; therefore, the thinking is that they should have no voice in the management of the company.

Moreover, if the company goes bankrupt, preferred stockholders are paid before common stockholders.)

- Fourth, because of the large dividend payout, preferred stock prices tend to fluctuate less than common-stock prices, implying that the dividend yield is also unlikely to fluctuate much.

If the company should encounter hard times, there may be no cash available for the dividend. In cases like these, the board of directors will have to suspend payment until better times return. Some companies have provisions that the dividend is cumulative, meaning that the amount that has not been paid to date must be made up and paid to preferred stockholders before any dividends are paid to common stockholders. If the payment is noncumulative, whatever is not paid is lost forever.

Preferred stock is really a combination of a stock and bond (which, as we will see in Chapter 3, promises interest and principal payments). Its price can fluctuate like that of common stock, but not as much, and the dividend payment is fixed, just like the interest payment on a bond.

Preferred stock may be, under certain conditions, converted into common stock. Why would an investor want to do this? If the company has prospered, earnings on common stock can offer the investor higher returns, in some cases much higher, without having to incur a lot more risk. In other words, you can convert each $5 preferred share to a $75 common stock share. If the common stock price jumps to $125, you can convert the 100 shares of preferred stock to common stock at $75 per share (i.e., $7,500 total) and then sell the same shares at the $125 current market price (i.e., $12,500) for a nice profit of $5,000 (minus

transaction fees). This profit would be much greater than what the preferred shares would have earned you (100 shares at $5 per share, for a total of $500, minus transaction fees).

Speaking of profits, you should be aware that your profit is called a *capital gain*. It is the difference between the price you paid for an asset (e.g., stock, bond, home, etc.) and the price you sold it for. In the previous example, the profit of $5,000 is not considered "realized" until you sell the stock. If and when you do, the gain will be classified either as short-term or long-term. Any realized capital gain in excess of one year is considered long-term, with a current maximum tax rate of 20%.

Think about the tax implications of this for a moment. Let's assume your employer is paying you $60,000 per year. As a result, most of your income, everything above $27,950, will end up in the 27% tax bracket. If the $5,000 realized capital gain were short-term, then you would pay in taxes 27% of the gain (which would be $1,350, calculated by multiplying 0.27 by $5,000). However, if it were long-term, you would pay $1,000 in taxes (i.e., 0.20 × $5,000), a savings of $350. If at all possible, then, hold for the long term.

UPS AND DOWNS OF STOCK PRICES: HOW TO DECIDE WHEN TO BUY AND SELL

Stock prices are notorious for fluctuations. Why do they fluctuate? To put it simply, fluctuation is due entirely to attempts to determine the true worth of stocks. But what determines the true worth? Again, simply put, it depends on how much buyers are willing to pay for it. How much are they willing to pay? Much depends on how well a company is doing and is expected to do. The better it is performing and the brighter the prospects look, the more likely its stock price will rise. But what determines how well a company is doing, and for how long will these prospects remain bright? In general, it is all due to the demand for the stock and the supply of it. After all, all other things held constant, a high price leads to selling, and a low price brings buying, just like in any other market. Two things are for sure: when buying pressure exceeds selling pressure, stock prices rise. Like the cliché says, "a rising tide lifts all boats," as investors surely witnessed between 1995 and 1999. The opposite occurs when selling pressure dominates, as was seen from 2000 through 2002.

Overall market action may result from any of the following:

• Changes in national economic activity (such as in the case of recession or inflation)

• Changes in interest rates

• Changes in forecasts by respected economists

• Major political action in some part of the world (such as the invasion of Kuwait by Iraq in the summer of 1990, or the U.S. invasion of Iraq in the spring of 2003, or even a report that the president has had a heart attack)

• An anomaly such as the so-called January effect, a well-documented tendency for stock prices to rise in January

Despite the many explanations forthcoming from learned pundits and market watchers, no one really knows, at least day-to-day, why stock prices advance or retreat. To get a handle on market sentiment, market watchers will often refer to an advance-decline, which is the difference between the number of stocks that increased in price on a given day and the number that decreased. A day in which "gainers" significantly outnumbered "losers" would tend to be classified as bullish. When the opposite occurs, it would be thought of as bearish. A lot of fluctuation, though, is attributable to what statisticians call noise, or random movements, pushed by emotional buying and selling. Suffice it to say at this stage that the fluctuations in stock prices are the result of millions of individual buying and selling decisions being made throughout the day, which begins in the United States at 9:30 A.M. and ends at 4:00 P.M., EST.

Assessing the Value of a Stock

Although, on average, about 70% of an individual stock's price movement may be due to things other than general activity affecting the stock market, there are some variables you should know about when trying to value a stock's true worth.

Price-Earnings Ratio, or P/E Ratio. One of the most carefully watched variables, the P/E ratio is a common measure of a stock's value. A stock's P/E ratio is the price of the stock at closing on a specific day, divided by the stock's earnings (also called net income or profit) per share of stock for the previous 12 months.

For example, if the closing price for a stock is $40 per share, and the earnings per share for the past 12 months are reported to be $4, then the P/E ratio is 10 (i.e., $40 divided by $4). If the earnings per share were $2, then the P/E ratio would be 20 (i.e., $40 divided by $2).

A P/E ratio of 10 to 20 is fairly common. As a rule, the higher the earnings per share relative to the price per share, the lower the P/E ratio, and the less expensive the stock is considered to be. This makes sense: when a company is doing well, its earnings per share are rising. But if the stock price does not rise as well, its P/E ratio will be low. As a result, the stock might be a bargain, following the tradition of "buy low, sell high," or *going long* (as opposed to *selling short*, or "sell high, buy low" when the stock price appears expensive).

On the other hand, stocks with high P/E ratios are not necessarily expensive. Much depends on what investors expect of the stock, a topic we will explore in more detail in the chapters on selecting securities.

Price-Book Ratio. Similar to the P/E ratio, this is the price per share relative to the book value per share. The book value is the value that the company's accountants have placed in the company's financial records (i.e., its "books"). The lower its share price is compared to its book value, the less expensive the stock is considered to be. This also makes sense, because financially solid, well-performing companies should have relatively high book values per share. However, if its stock price is not much different from its book value price, the stock could well be a bargain. The same logic applies to the price-sales ratio, or the price per share of stock relative to the sales per share.

Dividend Yield. This is another variable worth looking at. Companies that pay high dividends but also have relatively low stock prices might well have attractive appreciation potential. In fact, for years there has been a stock value feature called "Dogs of the Dow" (see Exhibit 2–1 for a listing of eligible stocks in the Dow Jones Industrial Average), where investors are supposed to be able to find the lowest stock prices with the highest dividend yields.

Other Factors That Affect the Price of a Stock

The "rules" pertaining to the three variables just described are general. As always, you need to exercise caution across various industrial sectors because different investors place different values on various types of corporate performance. For example, the stock of an electric utility company may be evaluated as an income producer, much like a bond. (Bonds are covered in Chapter 3.) Utility companies typically pay out a substantial part of their earnings as dividends in order to attract new capital. As a result, income-oriented investors "buy an income stream" when they invest in utility or other high-dividend stocks. Thus, they tend to have low P/E and other valuation ratios. Growth stocks, on the other hand, offer investors the possibility that share prices will escalate to produce a sizeable capital gain, or the difference between the buying and selling prices.

At a more general level, actions by a company's board of directors can have a strong influence on the company's price, including those described in the following sections.

The Decision to Pay Dividends. Higher dividends, of course, appeal to income-oriented, risk-averse investors. When a board announces a higher dividend, the stock price may rise for any or all of three reasons:

- First, the higher dividend is worth more, and a pattern of increasing dividends attracts long-term investors who may be retired and living off this income stream.

- Second, rising dividends tend to counter some of the effects of inflation. For example, utility companies have been known to raise their dividends every year for 20, 25, 30, or more years, usually in the range of 3% to 6% each year.

• Third, and perhaps most important, a rising dividend is a signal from the company's board of directors that the future looks bright. The board is not going to commit funds that it feels will not likely be forthcoming.

Dividend actions can also have negative impacts on stock prices. For example, a board that has raised the dividend for years may choose, in order to preserve the company's financial health, not to increase the dividend. In stressful times, a board may cut a dividend or eliminate it entirely. Without some promise of imminent dividend restoration, disappointed investors will sell out, causing the stock price to decline. Other shareholders may bail out of the stock because cutting or eliminating the dividend is an indication that the business is doing poorly. Very few people may be interested in buying the shares of a company that is experiencing difficulties and is forced, by a lack of profits and/or cash flow, to forgo or reduce a dividend. However, if the stock price falls far enough, some bargain-searching investors may find the price attractive in the "buy low, sell high" tradition.

Stock Buybacks. In recent years, the boards of many cash-rich companies have chosen to buy back shares from its investors, called a *stock buyback*, instead of paying dividends. Buying back stock not only increases the demand for the stock, but also reduces the supply of it. The overall result tends to be a higher stock price, which keeps shareholders happy.

There are also reasons to believe that stock buybacks are superior to dividend payouts from the standpoint of corporate finance. For one, the company may elect a stock compensation program for its employees. Rather than issuing more stock and risk reducing earnings per share (and raising the P/E ratio), the com-

pany will buy back the shares. If soon after receiving the shares the employees sell them, the impact on the stock price is minimal because the number of shares has been kept relatively constant.

Corporate Mergers and Acquisitions. Whenever a board of directors approves its company's bid for another company, you can expect the target company's stock price to rise, sometimes very significantly. This is because the buyout bid, called the tender offer, is usually stated in terms of a share price that is currently above—sometimes well above—the target company's current share price. The market price generally rises, and very quickly, to just below the tender offer. The investors holding the target company's stock might elect to sell their shares rather than tender them, generally at an agreed-upon ratio, because they fear that the deal might fall apart, due to lack of financing, violation of law, or an uncooperative board of directors at the target company. In fact, there will be stock traders who actually will play the difference between the current market price and the tender price. These traders are called arbitrageurs.

Stock Splits and Stock Dividends. Occasionally, a company's stock price rises to a level that seems almost unmanageable for many investors interested in a *round lot* order, or an order consisting of 100 shares, as opposed to an *odd lot,* an order consisting of fewer than 100 shares. In such a situation, its board of directors may decide to divide the existing shares into more shares, called a *stock split.* Stock splits typically are issued in either two-for-one or three-for-two ratios.

For example, suppose you hold 100 shares in a stock priced at $100 per share. If the company's board issues a two-for-one split, then you would end up with 200 shares at $50 per share. If the split were three-for-two, you would have 150 shares at $66.67 per share.

In either case, the action does not affect the value of your investment, at least not initially. For one thing, the split does not occur immediately, but after a set date, sometime in the near future. In addition, if the company's fortunes continue to rise, the stock price will rise as well. The same logic applies to stock dividends. For example, a typical stock dividend is 10%, wherein the shareholder receives one share of stock for every ten shares owned.

Although rare, the opposite can occur, too: a reverse stock split. This is when the board attempts to raise the price of its stock. For example, a one-for-ten split at a price of $1.00 per share applied to 100 shares would raise the price to $10 per share and reduce the number of shares to ten. Once again, notice that this action does not initially change the value of the holdings.

MEASURING STOCK MARKET ACTIVITY

Now let's take a look at measures of stock market activity. That is what investors are referring to when they ask, "What is the market doing?" Recall that this was the question posed at the beginning of this chapter. Unfortunately, you will not find the answer by scanning the many small-print entries in newspapers, or on the Internet, or by watching ticker symbols glide by at the bottom of your television screen. You need some sort of summary, an average, like a batting average or grade-point average. And this takes us to our first and most recognized measure, the Dow Jones Industrial Average.

The Dow Jones Industrial Average

The Dow Jones Industrial Average (DJIA) is the granddaddy of stock market measures, and is the single most quoted indicator of market activity, as in "the market was up, with the Dow climbing 101.45 points." The report assumes the listener will recognize that "Dow" means the industrial average. But what does that mean?

The DJIA represents what happened to the stock prices of 30 particular companies over the course of a certain period—a minute, an hour, a day, a week, a month, a year, or whatever period is of interest. If the Dow has increased, it means that the stock prices of these companies, taken together, have risen. If the Dow decreases, it means the opposite.

Remember, however, that what is true for all the companies taken together may not be true for each of the companies taken individually. A positive number means that the "gainers" outpaced the "losers." It does not necessarily mean that the stock prices of all 30 companies rose. A little bit of history will help us understand more about the DJIA.

History of the Dow Jones Industrial Average. A precursor of the DJIA was started on July 3, 1884, when Charles Henry Dow issued his Dow Jones Average of eleven stocks, nine railroad companies, a steamship company, and Western Union. The closing prices of these eleven stocks were added and divided by eleven for a simple mean, or average, of the closing prices. For example, if the eleven prices added up to $165, dividing this by 11 gives an average price of $15.

The average was distributed as part of the *Customer's Afternoon Letter*, the forerunner of

The Wall Street Journal, the most well-known and widely circulated domestic financial newspaper. The DJIA first appeared in the initial edition of *The Wall Street Journal* on July 8, 1889. The composition of the average changed several times until 1896, when Dow added a twelfth industrial stock. The average was still computed as a simple mean of the closing prices each day. Companies continued to be deleted and added over time, and in 1916, the list was expanded to 20.

Due to stock price adjustments issued by the members of the industrials, such as stock splits, the average of stock prices was no longer comparable to what it had been in the past, and, beginning in 1916, the compilers changed the value of prices to reflect these adjustments. On October 1, 1928, 30 stocks were listed in the DJIA, which appeared for the first time in *The Wall Street Journal.* The average aimed to indicate market action among major big capitalization corporations. Over the years, the stocks included in the magic thirty have changed to reflect mergers and to improve the representation of the U.S. industrial base.

As of early 2003, the Dow Jones Industrials consisted of 28 stocks listed on the New York Stock Exchange (NYSE) and two on the NASDAQ, listed as shown in Exhibit 2–1 (their ticker symbols are shown in parentheses).

Because each of these companies has issued either a stock split or stock dividend over the years, the divisor is not 30, but a very, very small number, about 0.10. Once again, the Dow Jones Industrial Average is simply a sum of the stock prices of the 30 companies divided by the divisor—nothing more, nothing less.

You may ask, "What's so special about these companies, and why only thirty?" These are relevant questions, because the Dow is supposed to represent a broad base of stock market activity, and thirty stocks seems like a small number when you consider there are literally thousands of domestic stocks. Moreover, of the

EXHIBIT 2–1. THE DOW JONES INDUSTRIAL AVERAGE (AS OF EARLY 2003)

3M (MMM)	DuPont (DD)	International Paper (IP)
Alcoa Aluminum (AA)	Eastman Kodak (EK)	Johnson & Johnson (JNJ)
Altria Group (MO)	Exxon Mobil (XOM)	J. P. Morgan Chase (JPM)
American Express (AXP)	General Electric (GE)	McDonald's (MCD)
AT&T (T)	General Motors (GM)	Merck (MRK)
Boeing (BA)	Hewlett-Packard (HPQ)	Microsoft (MSFT)
Citigroup (C)	Home Depot (HD)	Procter & Gamble (PG)
Caterpillar (CAT)	Honeywell (HON)	SBC Communications (SBC)
Coca-Cola (KO)	Intel (INTC)	United Technologies (UTX)
Disney (DIS)	International Business Machines (IBM)	Wal-Mart (WMT)

current thirty, only General Electric is still around from the first groups in the 1890s. Unfortunately, as interesting as those questions are, they cannot be answered, because Dow Jones, the company that chooses the composition, does not reveal the selection criteria. So, because it does not reveal the selection criteria, and because there is no evidence that trying to determine which companies are the next candidates and which are likely to be dropped is a smart way to manage your investments, we will leave the speculation to other books. By the way, in one way or another, the same question and response holds for the other market measures, too, to which we now turn.

The Dow Composite

Broader than the 30 industrials (and thus more representative of overall stock market activity), the Dow Composite is made up of 65 stocks: the 30 industrials plus those of 20 transportation companies and 15 utility companies.

The 20 transportation stocks also form one of the offshoots of the Dow Industrials, and is called the Dow Jones Transportation Average. Nine of the original Dow companies were railroads because they were the dominant corporations of the day. A railroad average was begun in 1896, when the Dow was reconstituted to include only industrial concerns. In 1970, recognizing the growing importance of trucks and airlines in transportation, the transportation average was expanded to include the stocks of trucks and airlines.

The 15 utility companies (which make up another offshoot, the Dow Jones Utility Average) include electric power-generating companies and natural gas companies, but no telecommunications companies. Unlike the 30 industrial companies and the 20 transportation companies, utility companies tend

to be highly regulated. Thus, their stock prices tend to fluctuate less than those of their counterparts. Although this limits stock price appreciation, unlike their counterparts, utility companies are known to reward their shareholders with big dividends, which are a portion of the profits.

The Standard & Poor's 500

Because they include up to 500 stocks across the three market exchanges (NYSE, AMEX, and NASDAQ) and because of their superior construction, the Standard & Poor's indices are some of the most representative of all market indicators, according to many market watchers who recognize the limits of the Dow 30. The Standard & Poor's Corporation (usually referred to as "S&P," the trademark of the company) is a major stock and bond analysis firm that publishes detailed information for use by investors.

The Standard & Poor's 500 Composite Index (or simply the S&P 500) differs from the Dow Jones industrial, transportation, and utility averages in three important ways.

First, because it includes 500 stocks that are mostly industrial companies, with the remainder split among financial companies, transportation companies, and utilities, the S&P 500 more accurately reflects overall market activity than any of the Dow Jones averages. It reflects a broad sampling of the market, similar to the Dow Jones Composite Average but with a wider spread.

Second, it is an index, not an average, of stock prices. An index is expressed in terms of a number and a time period, often called a base number and base period. The base number could be almost any number. The point is that these bases make comparisons much easier and more realistic than when referring to the Dow Jones averages.

For the S&P 500, the base period is 1941–43 and the base value is 10 (which was the value of the S&P 500 during that period; that is, the value of the market in 1941–43 was averaged and given a value of 10). When the market doubled from that period, the S&P 500 reached 20.

Even during the three "down" years of 2000, 2001, and 2002, the S&P 500 has advanced significantly since 1941–43. As of early 2003, the S&P 500 was at approximately 850, which means that the capital gains of the S&P 500 had advanced about 85 times the initial value of 10 in 1941–43. By comparison, a similar inference from the Dow 30, or from any of the Dow averages, is not possible because none are an index.

Third, the index values are weighted. The price of each stock in the index is multiplied by the number of shares of each stock outstanding. This weighting means that major corporations have a greater influence on index values than smaller corporations. Thus, a stock that makes up 1% of the S&P 500's valuation exerts 10 times as much influence on the index as a stock with 0.10% of the S&P 500's valuation.

Unlike the Dow, the S&P 500 includes a great variety of companies, and across relatively new sectors, such as telecommunications, computing technology, and biotechnology. These high-tech companies, once they are established on a profitable operating basis, tend to grow faster than more mature corporations in established industries, as in the automotive, beverage, and pharmaceutical sectors.

The composition of the S&P 500 changes more frequently than that of the Dow Jones averages due to mergers, acquisitions, and declines in company fortunes. For example, when a corporation is merged into another corporation, or if it ceases to be a leader in its category, it is dropped from the S&P 500 listing. With 500 corporations, these changes occur more frequently in this index than in the 30 companies in the DJIA.

Compared to the DJA, investors should focus on the S&P 500. Not only is it a more accurate representation of overall stock market behavior, but it also is a good benchmark for investors who want to hold a broadly diversified set of stocks. These investors take the passive position of not choosing individual stocks, instead investing in a broad portfolio of stocks. As we will see in coming chapters, this is a sound investment strategy.

The New York Stock Exchange Composite Index

The New York Stock Exchange (NYSE) Composite Index includes all common stocks listed on the NYSE, a total of about 2,100. As an index, it has the same features as the S&P 500, but in terms of sheer numbers, the NYSE is a more broadly diversified index.

Although its history traces to about 57 years ago, the NYSE Composite Index has only been computed and reported since 1964, and the index is based on 50, with the base period being December 31, 1965. The NYSE Index is weighted and computed in a similar fashion to the S&P 500. Each common stock's price is multiplied by the number of shares outstanding to determine the stock's current aggregate value. These aggregate values are totaled and compared to the aggregate value of all NYSE stocks for the base period.

The American Exchange Index

The American Exchange Index measures activity from the American Stock Exchange, which consists of about 1,000 stocks. Like the S&P 500 and the NYSE Index, it is weighted, and it reflects the aggregate value of the stocks that comprise it.

Perhaps the most well-known and watched listings on the AMEX Index are not stocks, but portfolios of stocks known as exchange-traded funds, or ETFs. These portfolios comprise stocks that make up major stock market measures, and various groups of them. One is the S&P Depository Receipts, sometimes called "Spiders" for the acronym SPDR (with the symbol SPY). Another group is the Dow DIAMONDS, for Dow Jones Industrial Average Model New Deposit Shares (with the symbol DIA), which is made up of the Dow Jones Industrials. In other words, an ETF is a security made up of a group of stocks that trade just like a single stock.

The NASDAQ Index

The NASDAQ Index reports activity on the National Association of Securities Dealers Automated Quotations index. It began on February 5, 1971, with a base of 100. The stocks are weighted by capitalized value (price per share multiplied by the number of shares outstanding), similar to the S&P 500.

It's important to point out the impact of growth stocks (which include many technology stocks) on the NASDAQ. Over the last 30 years, the rate of return on the S&P 500 was about 11% per year. In contrast, the rate of return on the NAS-DAQ (which has many more high-risk stocks) was about 17%. In fact, by the end of March 2000, it had increased by about 25% per year. The decline to 17% reflects the decline in the

fortunes of NASDAQ firms during the early years of the twenty-first century, an indication, as outlined in Chapter 1, that higher risk generally accompanies higher return.

The Wilshire 5000

The biggest of all stock market measures, in terms of the number of stocks and their total value (which is the price of the stock multiplied by the number of shares) is the Wilshire 5000 Index. It began in 1974 and is maintained by Wilshire Associates of Santa Monica, California. It gets its total of more than 7,000 stocks by including all stocks on the New York Stock Exchange, all stocks on the American Exchange, and all frequently traded stocks on the NASDAQ exchange.

By including stocks from the NASDAQ, the Wilshire 5000 includes small-company stocks, ones not included in either the S&P 500 or the NYSE Index. Thus, not only is the Wilshire 5000 the biggest, it is also the most broadly diversified. As an index, the Wilshire 5000 is unique in that a one-point change in the index represents roughly $1 billion of assets, so that a 10-point drop in the index would represent a $10 billion decline in the aggregate value of the stocks within the Wilshire 5000.

The Value Line Index

The Value Line Index is published by Value Line, which is well known in investment circles for its ratings of stocks and mutual funds. The index is broad-based, including about 1,700 stocks from nearly 100 sectors, across all major industrial segments of manufacturing, mining, utilities, real estate, and services.

The company actually publishes two indices, one called the Arithmetic Index and the other the Geometric Index. The Arithmetic Index, which began in 1988, is based on computing an average of all price changes for a particular period. The Geometric Index is based on the growth rate in prices dating back to 1961.

The Russell 2000

The Russell 2000 is a stock index that attempts to capture the performance of small-company stocks. In particular, the index contains 2,000 of the smallest stocks—often called small-cap stocks, or just small caps—contained in the Russell 3000, which represents about 98% of the total value of all U.S. stocks. Historically, small-cap stocks have earned higher returns than large-cap stocks, but at the expense of greater risk.

TRACKING STOCKS

So, where do you go to see how your stocks are performing? Stock listings are reported each business day in *The Wall Street Journal*, *Investor's Business Daily* on CNBC, and on the Internet. In addition, the business sections of most metropolitan newspapers report listings of frequently traded stocks. As a guide, you can find the closing price from the previous day, as well as the high and low prices, and price changes for certain time intervals, such as the last fifty-two weeks. Many small-cap stocks are traded off Pink Sheets that can be viewed at www.pinksheets.com. You can also call your broker.

Regardless of where you find your information, as stated in Chapter 1, try not to get too caught up in day-to-day movements of stock prices. Most of the movement is unpredictable and attributable to "noise," and trading on noise is almost surely not going to be profitable.

ACTIVE VERSUS PASSIVE INVESTING

Do you find all this daunting? Do you feel you do not have the time or the inclination to try to pick winning stocks? Do you doubt your ability to do so? If your response to any or all of these questions is yes, then you might well be a passive investor. Despite the term, there is absolutely nothing negative in investment circles about *passive investing*. It is simply an acknowledgment that you do not feel that you can devote the time and effort required to pick good stocks, which is called, not surprisingly, *active investing*. As we will see in later chapters, there is a lot of evidence to support the view that many, perhaps most, investors should be passive and not try to pick "winners," but instead invest in broadly diversified mutual funds or exchange traded funds. It is interesting to note that the investment performance of passive investors often exceeds that of active investors.

ADVANTAGES AND DISADVANTAGES OF STOCKS

Advantages

There are many advantages to investing in stocks:

- As reported in Chapter 1, the long-term rate of return on stocks is among the highest of all investments. Since the end of World War II, they have earned double-digit gains per year, enabling investors to double their money in about six and a half years. This return is almost 50% more than what you could have earned on bonds.

- The high return has made stocks a better hedge against inflation than most alternative investments.

- Preferred stocks provide attractive dividend yields that sometimes compare favorably with bonds.

- The price gains on stock (called capital gains) are not taxed until you "realize" the gains; that is, until you sell your stock.

- Capital gains are taxed at favorable rates—that is, lower than those earned on ordinary income, such as wages and salaries—and there is pressure on Congress to lower them further.

Disadvantages

In a word, the main disadvantage is risk. Investing in the stock market is typically several times riskier than investing in bank accounts and similar low-risk investments. Most stocks are decidedly not for the highly risk-averse investor. Some stocks, in fact, suffer from wide swings in price, and thus big fluctuations in returns. This is especially true in the case of emerging sectors in technology and communications. Unfortunately, strong financial performance does not always mitigate these swings. Complicating matters, as seen in the early years of the twenty-first century, are financial accounting scandals that have sent stock prices of seemingly healthy companies plummeting.

These problems bring up a well-known problem with stocks, a feature that does not hamper investments in debt instruments (which we examine in Chapter 3): when to buy a stock and when to sell it. There are no hard rules. In fact, Brad Barber and Terrance Odean (2000) have found that active investors tend to do two things that are detrimental to their portfolios: they appear to hold their losing stocks too long and sell their winning stocks too soon. Moreover, frequent trading in stocks, as appealing as it may seem, does not appear to produce superior rates of returns. In fact, it tends to do the opposite.

SOME THINGS TO AVOID

Although we will go into more detail on this topic later in the book, at this point, there are two things that we think deserve attention: IPOs and so-called *penny stocks*.

- **Avoid Initial Public Offerings (IPOs).** Unless you really know something about the company, such as dealing with it directly, watching it grow from a small shop operation to large enterprise, or using the company's products and finding them to be superior to others on the market, you should avoid investing in IPOs. This is because there is no information on them. There are no P/E or other valuation ratios, revenue figures, or risk measurements to guide your purchase.

Of course, the investment bankers who underwrote the issue will tout the stock as a great "buy" (as their analysts are supposed to), and you will hear about the new offering in media reports, suggesting its bright prospects. Nevertheless, you would be wise to keep your hands away from it. It is just too risky. In addition, evidence of investors getting rich quick on new offerings is hard to find. You will find exceptions, of course, but counting on an exception is not a savvy way to invest.

- **Avoid penny stocks.** As mentioned, these are usually "small caps," listed on the Pink Sheets, that literally sell for pennies on the dollar, such as $0.18, $0.29, or $0.91. In terms of "buy low, sell high," these look great. Dreams of buying a block of one of these stocks, or 10,000 shares, and riding it up to, say, $20 per share in a few years, float attractively through investors' minds.

Who would not jump at the prospect of a $10,000 investment increasing to $200,000 in just a few years? The problem is that the likelihood of such an event, or any kind of sizeable gain, is remote. The reason the stocks are selling so cheap is because their prospects are so poor. If their prospects were good, the stocks would not be selling for pennies because investors would scoop them up now, "on the cheap," in the hope of cashing in big profits.

SUMMARY

Now you have an overview of stocks, common and preferred, and their markets. Stock is a form of ownership in a company. It is bought and sold in markets just like any other product. Corporations issue it to raise money, often referred to as financial capital. By selling stock to a variety of investors, large and small, private and public, a corporation can raise billions of dollars.

To become a good stock investor, you need to know about the attributes of a stock: its prospective returns, its risks, and ways used to evaluate its worth. These ways include an examination of price-earnings and similar ratios, dividend yields, stock buyback programs, and stock splits.

INVESTING IN BONDS, CDs, AND T-BILLS

(AND OTHER DEBT INSTRUMENTS)

Bonds are simple: they are debt instruments, essentially IOUs—someone or some organization owes money to someone else. Like stocks, they come in many different styles (such as high, medium, and low "grades," which indicate degrees of risk). They come in many sizes (such as $1,000, $5,000, and $10,000), and have various features (such as short-term, long-term, coupon, zero, tax, and no-tax). In addition to bonds, other debt instruments include certificates of deposit, Treasury bills, Treasury notes and commercial paper, all of which will be defined and explained in this chapter.

All debt instruments are set up along very familiar and simple lines: borrowing and lending. The key element common to all is that they pay interest to the lender. For example, when you purchase a bond, you are lending money to someone or an organization (public or private) with the promise of a reward. The reason is simple: the only way you will save some of your income (which is to postpone spending it) is if you are compensated for doing so. In this case, to get your money for a specified period, the borrower agrees to pay you (the lender) interest plus the amount originally loaned (called the *principal*)

on a timely basis. The period depends on the agreement. When the agreement runs out, the bond is said to have matured. The length of time this takes is referred to as the bond's *maturity*. A bond has the longest maturity of any debt instrument, lasting for more than ten years, typically at least twenty years. If the maturity is two to ten years, it is called a *note*. If the maturity is no longer than one year, it is called a *bill*.

Some features of a debt instrument—such as whether it is "callable," "rated," a "zero," or "convertible"—can make bond holding seem complex; to understand this type of investment, you really need to focus on two words: fixed income. This means that whatever kind of debt instrument you hold, the income earned from it (i.e., the interest payments) does not vary. Thus, bonds tend to be more predictable and stable investments than stocks, which make no promise of fixed income.

Keep these thoughts in mind as you read the rest of this chapter, which describes various types of fixed-income investments, beginning with certificates of deposit.

CERTIFICATES OF DEPOSIT

Among the most common debt instruments are *certificates of deposit* (CDs), issued by commercial banks, savings banks, and credit unions. (For convenience, we'll call all three of the depository institutions "banks.") A CD is a contract between you and a bank. The bank agrees to pay you a specific rate of interest in exchange for your agreement not to withdraw the money before a specified date. If you break the contract and withdraw your funds early, the institution imposes a penalty. CDs come in all shapes, sizes, and various maturities, and can be bought for as little as $500 and for over $1 million. At a broad level, there are advantages and disadvantages of investing in CDs, with reference to the discussion on stocks in Chapter 2.

Advantages of Investing in CDs

CDs are considered risk-free when insured by the Federal Deposit Insurance Corporation (FDIC) for up to $100,000. By risk-free, it means that the chance of your not receiving interest and principal is zero. So, when you invest up to $100,000 in an insured CD, you are assured by the Federal Deposit Insurance Corporation or National Credit Union Administration that you will receive your interest when due and the return of your principal at maturity.

In addition, CDs are readily available at your local bank, and they are a good place to "park" your money for a while in the event that the stock and bond markets seem uncertain. Along these lines, during a time of rising interest rates, CDs may well be the preferred investment. This is because rising interest rates, as we will see, reduce stock and bond values.

Alternatively, "rolling over" a series of short-term CDs (i.e., investing in three-to-six-month CDs successively during a time of rising interest rates) would earn for you increasingly higher interest returns while preserving the principal of your investment—something that isn't guaranteed with stocks.

Some investors also seem reassured when dealing with an organization in which they have built a relationship of trust. They like working with people they know, face to face, even to the point of sacrificing higher returns elsewhere.

Disadvantages of Investing in CDs

Since the passage of restrictive legislation in the late 1980s, deposit insurance is more limited. All accounts under one name at one bank (or a single depository institution) are now aggregated when applying the $100,000 limit rule.

For example, if you have a savings account balance of $5,000, a checking account balance of $5,000, and a CD worth $100,000, the two smaller accounts totaling $10,000 will not be covered, unless they are in an IRA, which would be separately insured up to $100,000. Therefore, if your balance is approaching the $100,000 limit, you should avoid allowing interest accretions to boost the balance beyond that limit. Although bank failures are very unusual, to be safe, you should transfer any excess over $100,000 to another depository institution.

In addition, you need to be aware of two other forces that can negatively affect your investment gains in CDs: inflation and taxes. After accounting for each one, it is not unusual for the returns to be very small, even negative. For example, during 2002 and 2003, many banks were paying rates on short-term CDs of around 2%. Unfortunately, inflation during this period exceeded this rate. Thus, investors in CDs were actually losing purchasing power: the ability to buy goods and services.

This problem became worse because the interest earned on CDs is fully taxable— another disadvantage. If the investor were paying an income tax rate of 33% (which includes federal, state, and local rates), then the after-tax return on a CD paying 2% is 1.34% (1 minus 0.33 multiplied by 2); adding the inflation impact leaves the investor decidedly worse off. As explained in Chapter 1, even in a no-tax, no-inflation world, it would take you 36 years to double your money (72 divided by 2). This is not reassuring. Neither is it reassuring to discover the interest penalty if you should have to withdraw your money before maturity; it can be substantial.

Pay Attention to How Often Interest Is Compounded on CDs

As an added caveat, make sure you understand how the interest is computed on your CDs. Here is where we can tackle the sometimes-tricky area of compounding, or "interest on interest," which we introduced in Chapter 1 with the "doubling rules." Simply stated, you want to earn as much money as possible as fast as possible. To do so, you want your money compounded as often as possible because the more often it is compounded the higher your rate of return.

To illustrate, assume you have a one-year CD at $1,000 at 10%. At the end of the year, you will have at least $1,100:

$$0.10 \times \$1,000 + \text{the original } \$1,000$$

Note that we said "at least." There could be more. Say that the interest is compounded monthly, as is often the case. As a result, the monthly rate of interest, sometimes called the periodic rate, is 0.00833 (0.10 divided by 12).

Now do the following:

$$\$1,000 \times (1 + 0.00833)^{12} = \$1,104.67$$

That is $4.67 more! We took the expression to the twelfth power because that is how often your investment was earning "interest on interest." At the end of the first month, you had earned:

$$\$1,000 + (\$1,000 \times 0.00833) = \$1,008.33$$

By the end of the second month, you earned:

$$\$1,008.33 + (\$1,008.33 \times 0.00833) = \$1,016.73$$

Note that your investment for the second month began at $1,008.33, not $1,000. That is what "interest on interest" is. The process continues up through the twelfth month. Once again, the point is to look for CDs whose returns are compounded as often as possible.

We'll close this discussion with two more tips:

- **First, you might want check into zero CDs.** The word "zero" means there is no interest paid directly on the CD. They are attractive for Individual Retirement Accounts, or IRAs, not only because the interest earned is tax-deferred, but also because the amount is easier to follow than that on a regular CD. Instead, you purchase them at a discount, or an amount below the face value, thus requiring less up-front outlay of cash.

- **Second, shop around for CDs, and not just locally, but nationally.** In fact, you can usually ask your financial advisor (or your broker) to find the best rates for you, and often without a brokerage charge. Or, you can search the Internet for the best rates. Make sure, though, that the offering institution is insured by the Federal Deposit Insurance Corporation. The difference in rates of return can be as high as one percentage point, even higher. Every dollar counts, so do not overlook opportunities to increase your returns.

U.S. TREASURY BILLS: INVESTING $1,000 OR MORE

The U.S. Department of the Treasury, the fiscal arm of the federal government, issues three basic types of debt securities: bills, notes, and bonds. These securities are widely available and are easily bought and sold. Moreover, they have "deep" markets, which means the markets are very active and can handle virtually any amount, from an individual $10,000 Treasury bill to billions of dollars worth of Treasury bonds.

The difference among the three is simply the maturity, as explained previously. U.S. Treasury bills, familiarly known as T-bills, are short-term debt instruments issued as discount securities; that is, they are sold for less than their face value. They are available in 1-, 3-, 6-, and 12-month maturities. T-bills for 3- and 6-month maturities are auctioned weekly by the Federal Reserve System, the nation's central bank, commonly known as the "Fed." (Note: The U.S. Department of Treasury is *not* related to the Federal Reserve System. In fact, each has a different role. The Treasury is concerned with federal government taxes and spending; the Fed is concerned with the amount of money available for spending and financing, and with interest rates.)

Auctions for 12-month T-bills are held monthly on a Thursday. T-bills are issued in denominations of $1,000, $10,000, $15,000, $50,000, $100,000, $500,000, and $1 million. Each amount is the maturity value, because the bills are sold at a discount and pay no interest directly. Buyers gain income from the difference between the original amount paid (i.e., the discounted amount) and the maturity value. For example, if you bought a 6-month $10,000 T-bill at auction for $9,800 and received $10,000 after holding the T-bill for six months, the $200 difference would be your investment gain. Incidentally, there are two reasons that the rate of return is higher than 2% (or $200 per every $10,000), even though 2% is the rate often seen in newspapers. First, in the preceding example, what you actually paid was $9,800, not $10,000. That alone implies that your return is at least 2.04% ($200 divided by $9,800). Second, the fact that you earned the interest in six months implies an even higher annual rate of return.

You buy T-bills at original issue one of several ways. Your bank or broker can buy your T-bills, and will charge you a fee, typically around $25 for the purchase of one T-bill. Brokers may also charge a percentage of the amount invested.

You can also buy T-bills directly from either the U.S. Treasury or from the Fed; it is a fairly simple process, and there is no service fee or commission. To do so, either search the Internet or if there is a Federal Reserve Bank or branch nearby, visit the bank to ask for instructions on how to buy directly. (Note: There are Federal Reserve Banks in Boston, New York, Philadelphia, Richmond, Atlanta, Cleveland, Chicago, St. Louis, Minneapolis, Kansas City, Dallas, and San Francisco.) If there is no Federal Reserve Bank or branch near you, write to the Fed in your area for instructions on buying T-bills by mail. Your banker can provide you with the address of the Federal Reserve Bank that services your area.

To place a competitive bid, you must file an application, or tender, before 1:00 P.M. eastern time, on the day of the auction. Your certified check or a bank cashier's check must accompany your application. The Fed will return the difference between the price you paid and the amount it will mature to, usually by a direct deposit to your checking account. At maturity, the Fed deposits electronically the face amount into your checking account, unless you elect to roll over the principal into a new T-bill. And be aware: You must notify the Fed before your existing T-bills mature if you elect to roll over the principal.

The maximum for a single noncompetitive bid per auction is $1 million. Only the highest bids are accepted by the U.S. Treasury. Small buyers agree to accept the average of the competitive bids as the price for their T-bills. All noncompetitive bids are totaled, and the total dollar amount is set aside first for small investors before any competitive bids are accepted.

An active secondary market permits you to sell T-bills before maturity for ready liquidity. This market is operated by dealers in Treasury securities. Rates vary daily according to the overall level of interest rates and supply and demand for T-bills among investors. Thus, if you buy a 6-month T-bill, then need cash after holding it for a month, you can sell it through your broker, who will charge a commission. There are specific steps to follow, with which your broker will help you.

As with certificates of deposit, there are advantages and disadvantages to investing in T-bills.

Advantages of Investing in T-Bills

Some advantages to investing in T-bills are:

- T-bills are very liquid, so they are easily bought and sold.

- They are considered to be risk-free, in that there is no question about the federal government's ability to make timely payment of the amounts owed.

- As with CDs, T-bills are good investments when capital markets (such as in stocks and bonds) are unsteady or when uncertainty abounds.

- For many investors, in good and bad times, U.S. Treasury bills are the investment of choice whenever they are liquidating their stock holdings.

- They are also worthy investments during periods of rising interest rates, times in which stocks and bonds will appear unattractive.

- Adding to their attractiveness is that the interest return is free of state income tax.

Disadvantages of Investing in T-bills

The biggest disadvantage of investing in T-bills is their small rate of return. Because they are considered virtually risk-free, and have short maturity schedules they carry a low interest rate, the lowest among all debt instruments. In fact, throughout much of 2002 and 2003, T-bill interest rates were less than 2%. As a result, they serve to protect your investment gains much more so than they advance them.

In addition, over long periods, when T-bill returns are adjusted for taxes and inflation, they tend to yield negative rates of returns. So they should not be held for long periods.

COMMERCIAL PAPER: CORPORATE IOUs FOR INVESTORS WITH $100,000 OR MORE

Essentially, commercial paper is a short-term IOU issued by a high-quality corporation. The only thing backing it up is investor confidence that the company will live up to its promise, its creditworthiness. Thus, unlike with U.S. Treasury bills, there is some risk, however small, that the company will fail to make its payments. This is what is called *default risk*. Although there is no case of the U.S. government failing to make interest and principal payments on time, the same cannot be said about corporations. History is replete with instances of corporations that have gone broke, some slowly, others quickly. In any event, the default risk typically leads to higher returns on commercial paper than on U.S. Treasury bills.

Commercial paper, like U.S. Treasury bills, is sold at a discount. The difference between the discount issue price and the face value at maturity represents the *yield*. Commercial paper maturities tend to be short, usually between 30 and 90 days. Few private investors buy commercial paper because of its high minimum investment, often at $100,000 or $250,000. However, you can buy it indirectly through money market accounts, which are covered in Chapter 4.

U.S. TREASURY NOTES AND BONDS

U.S. Treasury notes and bonds, or T-notes and T-bonds, are traditional instruments called coupon securities. The term originates from the former practice of issuing bonds with coupons attached, which were clipped and forwarded to the U.S. Treasury when interest was due.

T-bonds are now issued as registered certificates with the buyer's name and taxpayer identification number printed on the certificate. T-notes and T-bonds are also issued in data entry (or book entry) form in the name of the buyer, who receives a confirmation of ownership. Interest checks are mailed semiannually (i.e., twice yearly) to registered owners, or the interest is transferred electronically to the owner's bank account. Notes or bonds in data entry form may be converted to certificates for sale in the secondary market (that is, the time after original issue but before maturity).

T-notes and T-bonds are similar, differing only in maturity. T-notes are issued with maturities ranging from two to ten years, and T-bonds mature in excess of ten years. The U.S. Treasury sells T-notes and T-bonds regularly, to finance the federal deficit (when federal government expenditures exceed tax revenues) and to pay off maturing notes and bonds. So this market, as with the T-bill market, is very deep, and the securities are very liquid.

How and When to Buy T-notes and T-bonds

T-notes and T-bonds may be bought directly from Federal Reserve banks in a manner similar to T-bills. T-notes and T-bonds are issued in denominations of $1,000, $5,000, $10,000, $100,000, and $1,000,000. Most of these are sold at auction to dealers who bid for them at prices they expect will yield a profit during resale to individuals and/or various institutions, including foreign investors.

If you wish to buy T-notes or T-bonds at original issue from the Fed, contact the branch in your area or your bank for details on the procedure. The U.S. Treasury regularly updates Internet announcements that provide current information on how to buy T-notes and T-bonds online. The sale of notes and bonds follows a general schedule. Specific dates for sale are usually released in newspapers about two weeks in advance.

In terms of frequency of offerings, 2- and 5-year notes are offered monthly; 3-year notes are offered quarterly; and 10-year notes are offered 6 times per year. For a long time, the U.S. Treasury issued 30-year bonds, which investors viewed as the leader of bond investments because they carried the lowest interest rate among all bonds. However, by the end of the 1990s, the Treasury began to retire the bonds, and indicated that, until further notice, it would not issue more of them.

Like T-bills, most T-notes and T-bonds are sold at auction by competitive bidding. Unlike T-bills, T-notes and T-bonds can be bid at either a price or a yield. However, most individual investors submit noncompetitive bids without specifying a yield or a price. Instead, they agree to accept the average yield and equivalent price determined from the average of the competitive bids, similar to the procedure for T-bills.

If securities are to be sold at less than their maturity, or *par* (i.e., the value as a result of the auction), investors receive a discount, which is the difference between the selling price and the par value. If, however, the T-note or T-bond sells for more than the maturity value, the investor must pay a premium, which is the difference between the selling price and maturity value. Original-issue T-notes and bonds may also be purchased from commercial banks and brokers, both of which will probably add a fee.

Two Ways to Earn Money on T-notes and T-bonds

T-notes and T-bonds have two yields: current yield and the yield to maturity.

Current Yield. This is the annual interest on the bond divided by its current price. Although the par value is typically $1,000, fluctuations in interest rates can change the price of a note or bond, which in turn can change the current yield. For example, if you bought a new 10-year Treasury note at an interest rate of 5.2%, your current yield would be 5.2% (i.e., the $52 in interest you would receive, divided by the $1,000 price). If market interest rates then decline during the next year to 4.2%, your bond would be worth more than $1,000—around $1,075. The current yield drops to about 4.84% (which is the $52 in interest divided by the new price of $1,075) for any investor interested in buying your note—and there will indeed be many investors interested, especially if they expect interest rates to fall further.

Why did the price rise? Your 5.2% note promises to pay $52 a year for 9 more years, which is $10 more than the $42 promised on a newly issued 10-year note. In the eyes of prospective note investors, compared to 4.2% notes, your note looks more attractive, so the market bids up its price. In fact, if interest rates continue to fall, your 5.2% note will continue to rise in value. You benefit in two ways: a higher interest return and a higher value of your note.

The process works in reverse, too. If you initially buy a note that pays 4.2%, and interest rates rise to 5.2%, then your note will be worth less than $1,000 if you suddenly need to sell it. Who will want to receive $42 dollars per year from your note when $52 dollars is available from a newly issued one? No rational investor, and the market for your note will reflect this.

The previous illustrations reveal a critical relationship that cannot be underestimated: interest rates and note/bond prices move in opposite directions. If interest rates fall, note/bond prices rise, and when interest rates rise, note/bond prices fall. With this mind, you want to buy notes/bonds at high interest rates and hold cash at low interest rates. This way, if interest rates fall, you get the higher rate on your note/bond while also enjoying an increase in its value, a capital gain that is not taxable until you sell the note/bond, if you ever do.

The Yield to Maturity, or YTM. This is a bit more complicated than current yield, but simple to explain and approximate. YTM is the interest rate that bondholders can expect over the life of a bond (or note) if they hold it to maturity and collect the face value of the bond (or note).

For example, if you bought a $1,000 T-bond for $800 with a coupon rate of 8%, the $80 interest would be equal to a current yield of 10% ($80 divided by $800). If the bond were due to mature in 10 years, the YTM would be higher than 8% because you would receive $1,000 at maturity, a $200 gain over your purchase price of $800.

For a quick approximation of the YTM, divide the gain between price and maturity value ($200) by the number of years to maturity (10), and add to this number the annual interest payment of $80. Then divide this figure by the purchase price of

$800 to arrive at 0.125, or 12.5%. A word of caution: This is only an approximation, as YTM is linked to compound interest. The true YTM in this illustration affects the annual amount of gain. You will need a calculator capable of handling compound interest to figure a true YTM, or you can ask your broker to look it up in his or her yield tables. In this example, the true YTM is about 11.4%. In any event, note that the rate of return is not 8% ($80 divided by $1,000), the ordinary yield, nor is it 10% ($80 divided by $800), the current yield. It is higher than both of these numbers because it takes into consideration the number of years before the bond matures. Fortunately, the YTM for listed bonds is included in most media reports.

The advantages and disadvantages of investing in T-notes and T-bonds are covered at the end of the discussion on all notes and bonds backed by the U.S. Treasury and other government agencies.

U.S. SAVINGS BONDS: GOOD FOR SMALL INVESTMENTS

So far, we have discussed U.S. Treasury bills, notes, and bonds, but many investors are more familiar with U.S. Treasury securities known as *U.S. savings bonds*. These are not negotiable, and prices do not change. You can buy them at local banks, Federal Reserve Banks and branches, and through payroll deduction programs.

Savings bonds are issued in three series, EE, HH, and I. They are available in small face amounts of $50, $75, $100, $200, $500, $1,000, $5,000, and $10,000. Prices are half of the maturity values (i.e., a bond with a $50 face value and maturity value costs only $25 to buy), with a classification of zero-coupon bonds, also called *zeros*.

As of early 2003, interest rates on EE-bonds amounted to around 2.70%. The market interest rates are based on 90% of the rates being paid on 5-year T-notes. Owners of EE-bonds must hold them for a minimum of five years to earn the market rates. Otherwise, short-term rates are less and depend on how long the owner holds the bonds before redeeming them. Savings bonds issued in June 1959 and earlier no longer pay interest, nor do bonds issued from December 1965 through June 1969. It is estimated there are currently about $6 billion in savings no longer paying interest.

EE-bonds are sold at a discount, with a classification of zero-coupon bonds. These are bonds whose interest payments are reflected in an appreciation in the value of the bond. Think of them along the same lines as a U.S. Treasury bill. You pay $9,800, redeem it at $10,000, with the interest reflected in the difference between the price paid and the redemption, or maturity, value. Unlike coupon securities in which the interest payment is set when you buy the bond, with zeros the interest payment is not explicit. The interest may accumulate tax-deferred until the bonds are redeemed (i.e., when you cash them in), or they mature without extension.

Interest accrues on EE-bonds by increasing in value every six months. Because the redemption value remains constant for six months until it jumps again, you should plan redemptions for the first part of the month that the value increases. Thus, if you are buying EE-bonds, plan to buy them near the end of any month. Because they earn interest as if you had bought them earlier, you gain a full month's interest. You can check maturity values for the bonds by asking at your bank, by writing for a table of redemption values from the Bureau of the Public Debt, or by checking the Internet.

Advantages of Investing in U.S. Savings Bonds

EE-bonds offer four major advantages for small investors:

- There is no cost or commission to buy or redeem them.

- The interest on EE-bonds is free of all state and local taxes.

- Unlike other zero-coupon bonds, you have the choice of paying federal taxes on each year's redemption value increase or deferring payment until you redeem the bond. If you elect to pay the taxes annually, all of the final redemption value (except for the final year's interest) will be not be taxed.

- All interest earned from EE-bonds that is used to pay for a child's education are excluded from federal taxes. Restrictions, of course, apply.

Series HH savings bonds, or HH-bonds, are no longer available for sale. You can acquire them, though, by exchanging mature EE-bonds for them. The exchange defers the tax on the interest payments from the EE-bonds. The normal maturity of HH-bonds is 10 years, but it is routinely extended to 20 years. HH-bonds pay semiannual interest and are coupon bonds, unlike their EE counterparts. Interest is taxable at the federal level, but not at state and local levels. However, at the time of this writing, the Bureau of the

Public Debt is mulling over the discontinuance of HH-bonds by mid-2004.

Series I-bonds offer inflation protection. They increase in value on a monthly basis, and the increase is tied to the Consumer Price Index, a measure of inflation. They are offered in the same denominations as EE Series bonds and can be bought at any institution that sells EE Series Bonds. Like HH-bonds, though, I-bonds are sold on a coupon basis; they are not zeros. The yield has two components: a fixed rate of return and the inflation component.

AGENCY BONDS AND RELATED ISSUES: GINNIE MAES, FANNIE MAES, FREDDIE MACS, AND SALLY MAES

In addition to the U.S. Department of Treasury, other entities routinely issue bonds. These are best known by their nicknames, each of which is discussed in full in the following sections.

Ginnie Maes: Mortgage Bonds Backed by the U.S. Government

The most well-known of these other-agency bonds is the Government National Mortgage Association, commonly known as "Ginnie Mae." Ginnie Mae bonds, also called certificates, are backed by the "full faith and credit of the U.S. government." To clarify, the federal government guarantees the timely payment of both interest and principal. Ginnie Mae certificates are highly prized as income producers, because they yield a bit more than U.S. Treasury bonds, up to about 1.5 percentage point. Interest paid on Ginnie Maes is, however, exempt from state and local taxes.

These bonds are sold in a variety of allotments, with the minimum being $25,000, and are used to keep liquid what is otherwise a very illiquid mortgage market. The mortgages that apply are guaranteed by the Federal Home Administration and Veterans Administration. Interest paid on these mortgages is "passed through" to the bondholders in proportion to their holdings. This pass-through feature has led to these, and similar, mortgage-backed bonds to be called pass-through securities. This is because mortgage payments are passed through the lenders to the bond investors.

Although Ginnie Maes have a high minimum price on original issues, $25,000, with additional increments at $5,000, small savers can easily get around this problem by investing in mutual funds (covered in Chapter 4) that concentrate their holdings in Ginnie Maes. In addition, although they mature in 30 years, early payoff of mortgages by homeowners trims the term to about half of this, on average.

When traded on the secondary market through brokers, partially paid Ginnie Maes may be bought for $10,000 to $20,000, with the broker collecting a commission for making the trade. When the mortgage pool is paid off, whether partially or totally, the principal is distributed to the Ginnie Mae bondholders in proportion to their holdings. Having to reinvest the capital received irregularly and in odd amounts can, however, be a nuisance if you want to avoid spending capital and paying commissions. A popular solution to both problems is to buy Ginnie Mae securities through a mutual fund. In this way, when portions of the principal are returned, the fund manager reinvests the portions into other Ginnie Maes.

Fannie Maes and Freddie Macs: Bonds Backed by Mortgage Lenders

Similar to Ginnie Mae are the Federal National Mortgage Association, also known as "Fannie Mae," and the Federal Home Loan Mortgage Corporation, also known as "Freddie Mac." Both Fannie Mae and Freddie Mac also issue pass-through securities and use the funds to buy mortgages from mortgage lenders, including banks, mortgage finance companies, and state and local housing finance. Although neither group lends money directly, they do so indirectly by helping replenish mortgage lenders with the funds needed for additional mortgage loans. This process of financing the purchase of mortgages with bonds sold to investors is a form of securitization, the process of creating a security by combining other assets.

Although both organizations guarantee timely payment of interest and principal, they cannot guarantee to the same extent as the U.S. government, which protects Ginnie Maes. To compensate for this additional default risk, Fannie Mae and Freddie Mac bonds are issued at higher interest rates than Ginnie Mae's. Moreover, both Fannie Mae and Freddie Mac have stock that is actively traded on the New York Stock Exchange, under the symbols FNM and FRE, respectively. So if you want to tap this market, you have several choices:

- You can buy Ginnie Mae, Fannie Mae, or Freddie Mac bonds.

- You can invest in mutual funds that concentrate in this mortgage pass-through market.

- You can buy the stock of Fannie Mae and/or Freddie Mac.

- You can invest in a combination of two or more of these choices.

Sallie Maes: Bonds Backed by College Education Loan Programs

Another organization that helps to keep the loan markets liquid is the Student Loan Marketing Association, also known as "Sallie Mae." Sallie Mae holds college student loans backed by the Federal Family Education Loan Program, as overseen by the U.S. Department of Education. Sallie Mae actively trades on the New York Stock Exchange (symbol: SLM). The debt it issues, however, is not guaranteed by the U.S. government or by state and local governments.

Advantages and Disadvantages of Investing in Notes and Bonds

Consistent with previous discussions, let us now look at the advantages and disadvantages of U.S. Treasury and government agency notes and bonds. First, the advantages:

- They are practically free of default risk, and they are a safe haven in times of uncertainty.

- If bought when interest rates are relatively high, they can be a reliable source for capital gains income when interest rates fall, because falling interest rates mean higher note/bond prices.

- They are also easily sold in secondary markets and are an effective way to help diversify a stock portfolio. In fact, financial planners strongly recommend that a percentage of your portfolio be in Treasury notes/bonds.

Here are some disadvantages to investing in U.S. Treasury and government agency notes and bonds:

- Because of their default-free status, the interest earned on them is relatively low, in the single digits. Consequently, they are not a good means to increase portfolio value, especially after accounting for taxes and inflation.

- During times of rising interest rates, the value of the notes and bonds can drop significantly, not unlike drops in stock prices. Thus, these investments can, at times, display surprising volatility.

- Although price fluctuations do not affect EE-bonds, these securities are not negotiable (i.e., they cannot be subsequently sold once purchased).

CORPORATE BONDS: IN SEARCH OF HIGHER RETURNS

The corporate world of bonds is a bit more complicated than the government world of bonds. For one thing, corporate bonds are riskier because corporations do not have pockets as deep as those of the federal government. So even when the bonds are secured by claims on company assets, such as plant and equipment, these collateralized bonds do not guarantee that you, as a bondholder, will get your money back in the unfortunate event that the company goes bankrupt. As a result, to compensate for the added default risk, corporate bonds pay significantly more interest than Treasury or agency bonds; in the cases of cash-strapped corporations, a lot more. In addition to collateralized bonds, there are two categories of investment vehicles, *debentures* and *convertible bonds*, which are subdivided into groups known as *investment-grade* and *noninvestment-grade*.

The overall idea is simple, and the following sections describe these types of corporate bonds and explain how to invest in them.

Debentures

These are bonds that are not collateralized; that is, they are not secured by claims or liens on company assets. They are issued with only the backing of the good faith and credit of the corporation. In the hierarchy of debt repayments, debentures rank behind collateralized debt. As a result, they have more default risk and have higher interest rates to compensate for the added risk. (As we will see, the added risk makes itself felt through bond ratings.) Nonetheless, many large corporations issue debentures, and bond buyers accept them. This is not to say that you should avoid debentures; just be aware that they are different from bonds backed by a lien.

Debentures are often callable; that is, issued with the provision that they can be "called in" and reissued at a lower interest rate than at the original issue. (However, the company will have to pay for this in the form of, say, one year of interest payments plus the full face value of the bond; and generally at least five years have to pass before the bond can be called.)

Even lower on the hierarchy of debt repayments than regular debenture bonds are subordinated debenture bonds. As the name implies, subordinated debentures rank below regular debentures and, therefore, are more risky. When you consider bonds of any kind, equate risk with interest rate; for example, if there's high risk, there will be high interest. Check for a sinking fund, which is a means for a company to accumulate cash each year. The sinking fund usually requires that some percentage of the bond holdings be paid off each year, which reduces the debt buildup and helps reduce the risk of nonpayment should the company become strapped for cash in the future.

Convertible Bonds

As the name implies, these bonds can be converted into stocks. This provision is designed to make the bonds more attractive. They work just like convertible preferred stock (discussed in Chapter 2). If the company prospers and its common stock prices rise dramatically, bonds may be converted to stock for an immediate profit.

Convertible bonds are hybrid securities. They act like bonds to provide a floor of value as interest payments generate income, and they may act like stock when the price of a company's stock price approaches the point where conversion of the bonds would generate a profit. Investors may buy bonds with the idea of converting them at a profit when and if the company's stock rises. Unfortunately, convertible bonds may also pay lower interest rates than similar bonds and dawdle for years at a price below a profitable conversion price for the stock. You pay a premium of sorts when you buy a convertible bond; that is, either the interest payout is low or the price of the bond is high for value received.

Investment-Grade/ Noninvestment-Grade

Regardless of whether a bond is collateralized, a debenture, or a convertible, it can be graded into any of a number of classifications in the investment-grade/noninvestment-grade area. These grades are really bond ratings. Those with the highest rating, (i. e., those with the lowest default risk), are called *blue chips*. Three major rating agencies are Moody's Investor Services, the Standard & Poor's Corporation, and Fitch Investor Services. These organizations will, for a fee, rate a corporation's bonds in terms of default risk. The idea is to help the corporation broaden the market for its bonds by providing investors with an easy-to-follow classification system in terms of default risk. The smaller the default risk, the higher the rating. Exhibit 3–1 shows the rating systems of these three companies.

In regard to Exhibit 3–1, please note there are "degrees" of the listed ratings that are not included in the exhibit. For example, Moody's uses the numbers 1, 2, and 3 to indicate the strength of the rating (with 1 being the highest and 3 being lowest), while S&P uses plus (+) and minus (−) signs. Also, be aware that these organizations are slow to change ratings; and when they do, it is done gradually. As a result, speculating on when a bond might be upgraded or downgraded in order to take advantage of changes in bond prices is not a wise approach. You should also note that the ratings organizations are sometimes—though not often—wrong. For example, just prior to its collapse in 2001, due to a financial scandal, the Enron Corporation enjoyed an A rating of its debt.

Given our discussion so far, collateralized bonds, because they have a claim on assets, are likely to be given higher ratings than debentures and convertibles, which cannot make such claims. As a rule, risk-averse investors (which includes the vast majority of all investors) should stick to bonds rated among the first four classifications. (You can find ratings on the Internet and the publications produced by these rating companies housed in many libraries.)

Of these ratings, the noninvestment-grade ones have generated considerable interest since the mid-1980s. Bonds rated in these categories are referred to as high-yield, a description that has replaced their original term: *junk*. These bonds

			EXHIBIT 3–1. BOND RATING AGENCIES: MOODY'S, STANDARD & POOR'S, AND FITCH
Moody's	**S&P**	**Fitch**	**Description**
Aaa	AAA	AAA	Blue chip, lowest default risk
Aa	AA	AA	Blue chip, low default risk
A	A	A	Good "financials," some default risk
Baa	BBB	BBB	Lowest investment-grade, susceptible to default risk; lowest grade for most risk-averse investors
Ba	BB	BB	Speculative; significant default risk; noninvestment-grade
B	B	B	High-risk, noninvestment-grade; risk-averse investors look elsewhere
Caa	CCC	CCC	Close to default; for risk-tolerant investors only
Ca	CC	CC	Highly speculative; lowest grade prior to default
C	D	C	Lowest grade; in default; interest payments likely suspended; most speculative

have been issued by the billions to finance corporate takeovers and buyouts. They can pay up to double-digit interest returns, as compared to the single-digit returns offered on investment-grade bonds. The problem for the issuer, and in turn the bondholder, is coming up with the cash needed to make timely debt payments. This turned out to be the case for many corporations during the 1980s and 1990s. Their deep indebtedness at interest rates well exceeding 12%—the average rate of return on corporate investment projects—exceeded the cash they were able to generate to pay their debts. It was to overcome the stigma associated with the word "junk" that companies trying to sell the bonds to investors now refer to them as high-yield bonds, as mentioned above.

All that said, a debt rating one or two notches below Baa/BBB/BBB may not be as onerous as it seems. Few firms carrying debt with these ratings actually go bankrupt. As a result, some evidence indicates that risk-tolerant investors can do well by investing part of their portfolios in these bonds, especially if a company appears well poised for a recovery, which could easily lead to a bond rating upgrade and, in turn, a higher price for the bonds.

Municipal Bonds

Municipal bonds, or *muni-bonds*, are the last major class of long-term debt to be covered. They are issued by states, counties, cities, and local taxing authorities such as schools, water and sewer systems, port authorities, and toll bridge authorities. Muni-bonds are probably the most complex of all bond markets, for the following three reasons:

• The issuers come in many different sizes and structures.

- Reports on the financial condition of the issuers are not always easy to obtain, as the issuers are usually small and unknown.

- Muni-bonds are infrequently traded, so it is not easy to find out just how much a bond issue is selling for. In other words, the market for municipal bond issues tends to be "thin," unlike the market for U.S. Treasury bonds and even some corporate bonds.

These characteristics make the ratings of municipal bonds, which are rated just like corporate bonds, crucial for investors.

Municipal bonds have a feature unlike any other bond: the interest income is forever free of federal income taxation, and if you buy bonds issued within your home state, they are usually free of state income taxes as well. These are sometimes called "double tax-frees."

It is possible to further your tax-free cause by buying a muni-bond from the city in which you live. For example, if you live in New York City and buy a local muni-bond, it could be free of city, state, and federal income tax. Such bonds are called "triple tax-frees." In contrast, if you live in New York and buy the California muni-bond, you might be liable for New York's income tax on the California muni-bond's interest. Before you conclude that muni-bonds belong in your portfolio, however, you need to examine what the tax-free implications are for you personally, compared to the tax implications on alternative investments. More on this below.

You need to be aware of three classes of muni-bonds:

- The first class, called general obligation, comprises bonds issued to finance essential services, such as the construction of roads, bridges, and schools, and similar activities. The interest on these muni-bonds is exempt from federal income tax for everyone.

- The second class, called revenue bonds, is issued to finance projects that generate revenue (e.g., a parking garage). The interest on these bonds is also tax-exempt.

- The third class comprises muni-bonds issued to provide low-interest loans to a business as an inducement to locate in a community or to help first-time homeowners with lower mortgage loan rates. These so-called nonessential muni-bonds pay a slightly higher interest rate than muni-bonds issued for essential services. More important, these bonds generally do not carry the tax-exempt status that essential-service muni-bonds do. Thus, high-income taxpayers in particular should avoid this class of bonds.

All other things held constant, your tax bracket should dictate whether you invest in tax-free muni-bonds or taxable bonds, such as U.S. Treasury, agency, or corporate bonds. The key is after-tax income, and the rule is that the higher your tax bracket, the more favorable a muni-bond will be. So investment-grade muni-bonds tend to be good investments for risk-averse, high-income investors.

It is simple to figure out which is the better choice for you: a taxable corporate bond or a tax-free municipal bond. First, you need to determine your overall marginal tax rate, which is the total of your federal, state, and local taxes. After doing so, divide the tax-free rate by 1 minus your marginal tax rate.

EXHIBIT 3–2. TAX-EQUIVALENT RETURNS ON MUNICIPAL BONDS

Tax Bracket	Tax-free Rate of Return	Taxable-equivalent Rate of Return
31%	4.0%	5.80%
31%	4.5%	6.52%
31%	5.0%	7.25%
31%	5.5%	7.97%
31%	6.0%	8.70%
31%	6.5%	9.42%
31%	7.0%	10.14%
34%	4.0%	6.06%
34%	4.5%	6.82%
34%	5.0%	7.58%
34%	5.5%	8.33%
34%	6.0%	9.09%
34%	6.5%	9.85%
34%	7.0%	10.61%
39%	4.0%	6.56%
39%	4.5%	7.38%
39%	5.0%	8.20%
39%	5.5%	9.02%
39%	6.0%	9.84%
39%	6.5%	10.66%
39%	7.0%	11.48%

For example, say you have a choice between a Aaa-rated taxable bond yielding 7.3% and a tax-free, Aaa-rated bond yielding 5% in interest, with your federal marginal tax rate being 27% (0.27) and your state and local income tax rate 4% (0.04). First, add the two tax rates to get 0.31 (0.27 + 0.04). To find the taxable equivalent rate, subtract that 0.31 from 1, which gives you 0.69. Now divide 5% by 0.69 for a taxable-equivalent rate of 7.25%. That is,

a Aaa-rated taxable bond yielding 7.25% percent leaves you with the same after-tax, or spendable, income as a tax-free bond yielding 5%. Thus, the bond yielding 7.3% looks attractive. Exhibit 3–2 offers additional numbers for perspective, based on current federal tax rates plus 4% for the combined state and local income tax rate.

By looking carefully at the numbers in Exhibit 3–2, you can see that the higher your tax bracket, the higher the tax-equivalent rate of return for each tax-free rate of return. This is to say that, for example, a Aaa-rated muni-bond paying 5.5% is equivalent to a Aaa-rated corporate bond paying 7.97%, if your marginal tax rates add up to 31%; 8.33%, if they add up to 34%; and 9.02%, if they add up to 39%. So if the corporate rate of return, for example, is greater than each of these numbers, you would earn more income by investing in corporate bonds than in muni-bonds for all tax rates between 31% and 39%.

Given the way bond markets work, you will have to do your homework. As muni-bonds increasingly look like the bond of choice, their prices will be bid up. At the same time, corporate bond prices will be bid down. The result is that both types of bonds, for the same investment-grade, end up at equivalent after-tax yields.

Trading Bonds

You can trade corporate and municipal bonds through your broker. The maturity, normal, or par value for corporate bonds is $1,000; for muni-bonds, it is $5,000. A round lot, as with stocks, is 100; and investors in these quantities are generally institutions, but odd-lot dealers have expanded the bond markets to individuals who want to purchase fewer than 100.

Beware, though, that buying fewer than five bonds might not be very economical because of three costs: a buying commission, a selling commission, and the difference in market buying and selling prices (known as the *bid-ask spread*). Bonds typically trade according to their yield to maturity, or YTM. For maturities far into the future, the current yield is a good approximation, but the closer to maturity the bond gets, the more the YTM should be used. Bond prices listed in *The Wall Street Journal*, for example, or on the Internet, have one place dropped. Thus, a bond price listed as 98.5 is really $985.

Advantages of Investing in Bonds

Here are some of the advantages of investing in bonds issued by entities other than the federal government:

- The rates of return on highly rated corporate bonds, from A to Aaa/AAA/AAA, are significantly higher than on U.S. Treasury bonds, sometimes exceeding two percentage points. In a world of compounded returns, over long periods, this can lead to significant gains in income over Treasury bond returns, especially in tax-deferred investments, such as IRAs.

- The prices of these bonds tend to fluctuate about the same, if not a bit less, than the prices of U.S. Treasury bonds. For investors who would like to tap the stock market for high returns but are concerned about losing money on stocks, there are convertible bonds, which have both bond and stock-like features.

- For very risk-averse investors in high-income tax brackets, highly rated muni-bonds offer attractive and very reliable rates of return.

Disadvantages of Investing in Bonds

Here are some of the disadvantages:

- The risk of default, even on highly rated bonds, appears to be a cause of concern for many investors. History is replete with examples of corporations and municipal units that have failed to make timely payment of interest and principal.

- In addition, because these bonds have maturities of at least 20 years, changes in interest rates can produce wide swings in their values, by more than 20% in some cases. Thus, although the interest income is fixed, the capital gain/loss is not easily predicted in the event that the bond must be sold before it matures.

SOME THINGS TO AVOID

There are at least three things to avoid when investing in bonds:

- **Avoid junk/high-yield bonds.** Stick to investment-grade bonds. Although there is evidence that some junk bonds are not really junk, trying to separate the wheat from the chaff (especially where there is some question about accounting practices) is difficult. Moreover, as stated earlier, the rating organizations are slow to change ratings; they do not want to be accused of acting on whim, nor do they want to be accused of misinterpreting financial information. So unless you really know something about the company and its near-term and long-term prospects, you would be well advised to stick with bonds whose ratings are no lower than a strong Baa/BBB/BBB.

- **Avoid investing in bonds at low interest rates.** Admittedly, this is tricky. What is a low interest rate? What is a high one? Because long-term Treasury bonds have yielded, on average, about 5.5% over the past 75 years, you should be wary about investing in new bonds anytime the 20-year Treasury bond rate falls below 5.5%. Why? Recall that interest rates and bond prices have an inverse relationship; namely, as interest rates rise, bond prices fall, and vice versa.

For example, if you bought a $1,000 bond with a coupon rate of 6%, you would receive $60 per year until the bond matured. But if you had to sell the bond early, and interest rates had since risen to 7%, you would get less than $1,000 for it. In short, you would incur a capital loss on your bond. In addition, the lower the interest rate is on your bond, the smaller the after-tax, inflation-adjusted rate of return. After adjusting for taxes and inflation, it is not uncommon for bonds to yield less than 1% per year.

- **Avoid investing too much of your portfolio in Treasury bills and certificates of deposit.** Most investors are risk-averse, but don't be so risk-averse that you hold most of your investment portfolio in nearly risk-free assets (unless you have retired or are nearly retired and feel safe with the interest income from these investments). On the one hand, many investors would love risk-free, double-digit rates of return, especially rates that were available between the late 1970s through the early 1980s. On the other hand, this period was exceptional. Such returns do not exist at this time, and are not likely to reappear anytime soon, if ever. For example, by early 2003, interest rates on Treasury bills and comparable certificates of deposit were under 2%. After adjusting for taxes and inflation, these returns are negative. Moreover, given the doubling rules mentioned in Chapter 1, you will not build much of a nest egg by investing almost exclusively in short-term investments.

SUMMARY

Investors have many choices in the area of bills, notes, and bonds. These can be thought of as fixed-income securities. When the future is very uncertain, you will find it prudent to stick with short-term investments, as found in certificates of deposit, U.S. Treasury bills, and U.S. Treasury notes with maturities less than five years. These are also sound investments during times of rising interest rates. As the investments mature, you will be able to "roll over" the certificates and bills into new ones paying higher interest rates. These investments, however, typically yield low rates of return, so they are more effective in protecting investment gains, or as a means of holding cash when waiting for more favorable stock/bond market conditions, than as a means of building up a portfolio's value.

To enhance portfolio return with debt instruments, you should use bonds, such as Treasury, agency, corporate, and municipal. Of these four, Treasury bonds are the safest, being free of default risk, but they also offer the lowest returns. Corporate and municipal issues rated from A to Aaa/AAA/AAA by Moody's, Standard & Poor's, and Fitch are attractive alternatives. Municipal issues, given their tax-exempt status, are appealing, particularly if you are in a high-income tax bracket.

MUTUAL FUNDS AND EXCHANGE-TRADED FUNDS

When trading securities, individual investors are no match for institutions. For one thing, institutions execute the vast majority of trades on the New York Stock Exchange (NYSE). Institutions that buy and sell shares in large volumes can send prices up or down with breathtaking speed. These trades can generate price fluctuations that may be scary and costly for some investors. In addition, markets are global now and are so closely interlinked that a sneeze on Wall Street can send a chill over European and Asian markets. The "big boys" play hardball, sometimes with savage intensity, and can intimidate smaller, amateur investors who lack the expertise and savvy of the pros. Program trading engages big investors who buy or sell groups of stocks against contracts that involve hundreds of millions of dollars.

So what can the individual investor do? The answer is simple: If you do not want to trade individual stocks and bonds, invest in *mutual funds* and *exchange-traded funds*, the topics of this chapter.

INVESTING IN MUTUAL FUNDS

What are mutual funds? What are exchange-traded funds (ETFs)? First, let us explore mutual funds. A mutual fund is a portfolio of assets you can buy into—called shares— that is managed by a financial specialist. The shares you buy are just like the shares you buy in a corporation. The share price, though, is somewhat different from the typical stock price. It is called the *net asset value* (*NAV*) per share, which is the value of the fund's assets, minus the value of its liabilities, divided by the number of shares outstanding. Thus, the NAV is an approximation for the price per share.

For example, if the NAV of a stock mutual fund (i.e., one that invests exclusively in stocks) is $10, and you sent the company a check for $1,000, you would be buying 100 shares. The shares would represent the stocks that the manager believes will do the best job of meeting the fund's objectives. The objectives represent any of a number of what are called "styles," such as "aggressive growth," "growth," "growth and income," "balanced," "income," and "money market."Here are explanations for these mutual fund categories:

- **Aggressive growth.** Includes stocks of companies with strong growth potential, such as in the semiconductor, telecommunications, and biotechnology sectors. Many of the companies may be small and recent IPOs. This kind of fund is geared toward risk-tolerant investors.

- **Growth.** Includes stocks of companies with good growth potential. The stocks are risky but represent established companies, most of which pay little or no dividend. Some representative sectors include the pharmaceutical, computer, entertainment, and medical services sectors.

- **Growth and income.** Stocks of companies in the growth sector that are balanced with stocks that also pay a significant dividend. In addition to the sectors in the growth area, you would see, for example, stocks of dividend-paying conglomerates, beverages, and traditional manufacturers.

- **Balanced.** The holdings include a mix of about 60% high-quality, or nonspeculative, stocks and 40% high-quality bonds, such as U.S. Treasury bonds and investment-grade corporate bonds.

- **Income.** These funds are similar to the holdings in the balanced fund, only more conservative, with a substantial portion held in high-quality bonds.

- **Money market.** The safest of all funds (although certainly not risk-free), the holdings include U.S. Treasury bills, certificates of deposit, highly rated commercial paper, and other short-term and medium-term fixed-income securities.

Note these are broad classifications and that some funds will not follow these definitions. For example, you can find growth funds that specialize in small-company (called small-cap) stocks; there are income funds devoted exclusively to Ginnie Maes; there are international funds geared toward emerging markets of developing countries; and there are sector funds that focus on stocks of companies that make up one or a few industries. Each of these funds will have its own return and risk features.

Referring back to the example of the $10 NAV and 100 shares: the fluctuation in the NAV, or its swing around $10, depends on the performance of its stock holdings. In the case of an aggressive growth fund (which would hold high-risk stocks with a lot of growth potential), the wide swing in the prices accompanying the stocks could cause the fund's NAV to fluctuate a lot, say in one year, from as low as $7 to as high as $14. If, however, the fund is one of income (i.e., whose holdings would include well-established companies that pay big dividends), its NAV would likely fluctuate much less, say in a range of $10 to $12, because the prices of the stocks and bonds that would make up the fund would not fluctuate nearly as much as those of aggressive growth stocks.

Exhibit 4–1 shows examples of mutual funds in each of the categories, with the asterisk (*) representing a benchmark.

Compared to their respective benchmarks, the best-performing funds, based on the ten-year results as of the first quarter of 2003, were Liberty Acorn, Fidelity Low-Priced, Legg Mason Value, Dodge & Cox Balanced, and Alliance Americas Government. As expected, the biggest variation in returns is in the aggressive growth group while the smallest variation is in the income group. The difference in variation reflects the risks inherent in each group of funds.

ACTIVELY AND PASSIVELY MANAGED FUNDS: HARE VERSUS TORTOISE

As of early 2003, there were literally thousands of mutual funds for the investor to choose, of all sizes, shapes, and compositions. Many were *actively managed*; others, *passively managed*.

EXHIBIT 4–1.   SOME MUTUAL FUNDS AND THEIR CHARACTERISTICS

Name	Style	Annual Ten-Year Return
Invesco Technology	Aggressive Growth	6%
Janus Mercury	Aggressive Growth	11%
Liberty Acorn	Aggressive Growth	13%
White Oak Growth	Aggressive Growth	8%
*Vanguard Small Cap	Aggressive Growth	9%
Fidelity Contrafund	Growth	10%
Fidelity Low-Price	Growth	13%
Janus	Growth	6%
Strong Opportunity	Growth	9%
*Vanguard 500 Index	Growth	9%
Gabelli Equity Income	Growth & Income	10%
Legg Mason Value Trust	Growth & Income	14%
T. Rowe Price Equity-Inc	Growth & Income	10%
Van Kampen Exchange	Growth & Income	10%
*Vanguard Growth-Inc	Growth & Income	9%
Dodge & Cox Balanced	Balanced	11%
Elfun Diversified	Balanced	8%
Fidelity Puritan	Balanced	8%
Janus Balanced	Balanced	10%
*Vanguard Balanced	Balanced	8%
Alliance Americas Govt	Income	9%
Dodge & Cox Income	Income	8%
USAA Income	Income	7%
*Vanguard Total Bond	Income	7%

Actively managed funds require that the mutual fund managers try to pick winning stocks and bonds with the expectation that the fund's overall performance will exceed a designated benchmark. For example:

• For medium-sized to large company stocks (also called mid-caps and large-caps), the benchmark is the S&P 500.

• For small-company stocks (or small-caps), the benchmark is the Russell 2000.

• For bond funds, it is the Lehman Bond Index.

Outperforming the benchmark is a big deal, because the fund manager who does is often awarded a bonus. Outperformance, especially consistent outperformance, attracts investors and generates income for the fund. Conversely, the manager whose performance is consistently less than the respective benchmark will not likely hold the position for long.

Passively managed funds hold securities that are the same as, or very similar to, an index, which is considered a passive benchmark. One of the most well-known funds, and one of the largest in terms of assets, is Vanguard's 500 Index Trust fund. The fund tracks the holdings of the S&P 500. The objective is not to outperform the index but to mimic it. As we will see in coming chapters, there is considerable evidence to suggest that this strategy is compelling, especially for investors who choose not to select their own securities or have an investment advisor do so.

For a quick comparison, the Vanguard Funds in Exhibit 4–1 represent a passive investment approach. You can readily compare the performance of each Vanguard fund with respect to its group. In Exhibit 4–1, the five best-performing funds outperformed their respective Vanguard benchmarks.

THE FUND PROSPECTUS: READ THE FINE PRINT

You can find a description of a fund, including its objectives, in a fund's *prospectus*. The Securities Exchange Commission (the SEC, the watchdog of financial markets) requires every open-end mutual fund (discussed later in this chapter) to provide you with a prospectus before or at the time you purchase a fund's shares. Even when you buy shares from a broker, the broker must provide a prospectus to you. For your own protection and to avoid misunderstandings, insist on

receiving a prospectus before buying mutual fund shares, and read it carefully. Admittedly, a prospectus is dry reading, but it supplies you with valuable information. Although the SEC can require a mutual fund to send you a prospectus, it cannot, unfortunately, require you to read it. Remember the admonition *caveat emptor*, meaning "buyer beware."

Two parts of the prospectus are especially vital: the summary of fees and expenses and the summary of important information. Read these brief sections even if you choose not to read the entire document.

Summary of Fees and Expenses

This section of the prospectus notes all commissions, redemption fees, exchange fees, and any other transaction fees, plus annual operating expenses. Projections of these costs and expenses over one, three, five, and ten years, based on a 5% annual return and redemption at the end of each period, permit comparisons among funds.

Two categories of expenses are incurred by all mutual funds. Expenses are deducted from income earned by the securities held in a fund's portfolio. The first category of expenses includes the necessary operating expenses: transfer agent fees, legal fees, and custodian bank fees. The expense ratio relates operating expenses to the fund's assets. Small funds typically report higher expense ratios because they spread expenses over fewer shares. Specialty funds (such as gold and international funds) may also incur higher-than-average expenses because managers must travel more widely to examine whether an investment, for example, in an overseas company, is worthwhile. In short, information about foreign companies is not as readily available as information about companies in the United States. Probably the lowest expense ratio in the industry is the one posted by Vanguard's 500 Index Trust fund. It is typically in the range of 0.15% to 0.20%.

The second category of expenses includes, among other things, management fees for a fund's advisors. Management fees cover the salaries of clerks and telephone operators, printing costs, and the myriad costs of running a business.

Earning the management fee is the primary reason mutual funds exist. It is the fund's main source of income. Look for it in the prospectus. Fees are typically in the 0.5% to 1% range, and drop on a sliding scale as the fund's assets grow. A combined rate of expenses plus management fee of around 1.5% is fairly typical, but the range is wide. You want the sum of the expenses and fees to be as small as possible.

Summary of Important Information

The prospectus' summary of important information is usually on the cover or the first text page. Look for a statement of the fund's objectives in addtion to the managers' plans for achieving them. For example, a growth fund summary may include a statement like this:

> The [fund] is a no-load mutual fund with the primary objective of long-term growth of capital and with secondary objectives of regular income and preservation of capital. The [fund] invests primarily in common stocks.

An income stock fund prospectus may state something like this:

> The investment objective is current income with the prospect of increasing dividend income and the potential for capital appreciation. The [fund] invests primarily in higher than average dividend-paying common stocks of well-established large companies.

The prospectus for an aggressive mutual fund may include statements of policy such as:

> The [fund] may borrow money from banks to purchase or carry securities. This use of leverage must be considered a speculative investment activity.

Other important information contained in the prospectus includes initial purchase minimums, repurchase minimums, how to redeem shares, whether check writing is permitted, and restrictions (if any) on carrying out these transactions by telephone, in writing, and/or electronically.

Although a fund's holdings (such as the stocks, bonds, and cash that the manager holds at any time) will not be listed in a prospectus, a fund will send you an expanded version of the document that lists its holdings of securities as of a specific date. All you need to do is ask for one. More useful information on the makeup of a fund's portfolio can be found in a recent annual or quarterly report of the fund's activities. You can also find important information on a fund's profile and performance by going directly to two Internet sources:

- *www.yahoo.com*. Go to the finance section, where the company displays stock quotes. You can look up the ticker symbol for a mutual fund, type it in to get its quote, and then check its profile and historical performance.

- *www.morningstar.com*. This lists specific mutual funds, and you can find information by typing the ticker symbol of the fund.

OPEN-END AND CLOSED-END FUNDS

There are two kinds of mutual funds, *open-end* and *closed-end*, each of which can be broken down into two more groups, *load* and *no-load* funds.

Open-End Mutual Funds

Open-end funds are the most common. They get their name from the fact that the number of shares the fund can hold is open-ended, that is, has no limit. An open-end fund stands ready to sell more shares or redeem shares from current owners on any business day. New money flowing into the fund expands the number of shares. As money flows in and shares increase, total assets rise to keep the NAV, which is the total value of the fund's portfolio less liabilities, relatively constant. Market action and the adeptness of a fund's manager may cause the NAV to rise. Or, despite the best efforts of the manager, market action may cause the NAV to decline. Remember, the NAV is calculated at the end of every business day and seldom remains constant.

Shares in an open-end fund trade only at the fund's office, and only the fund manager can issue new shares or redeem shares owned by investors. Shares are tracked almost exclusively by computer entry with each new purchase or redemption being acknowledged by a computer-generated confirmation, rather than a certificate, which serves as evidence of ownership. Issuing certificates complicates trading and is discouraged.

When you buy shares in an open-end fund, the price is the NAV computed at the end of the day. If you send the minimum amount that is required to open an account (e.g., $500, $1,000, $5,000, or $10,000) and it arrives (by mail or wire transfer) on a Tuesday before 4:00 P.M. EST, your investment is then translated into shares at the price computed at the end of that Tuesday. Some mutual funds may set earlier deadlines for money to be invested at that day's closing NAV. For example, if the NAV at the end of Tuesday is $17.31 per share, and you sent the fund $1,000, you would end up with 57.77 shares, ($1,000 divided by $17.31), assuming the fund is no-load (does not charge a commission).

If you were to submit a request to redeem $1,000, the manager would reduce the fund's holdings and your account by 57.77 shares, then send you a check within ten days. Taking care of a variety of different requests to purchase and sell shares means that the total number of shares held by the fund will fluctuate daily. Thus, the number of open-end fund shares may be, and usually is, different every day. Mutual funds require that instructions to redeem shares arrive in good order at the manager's office.

Closed-End Mutual Funds

Closed-end funds operate differently from open-end funds. Closed-end funds derived their name from the fact that the number of shares the fund can hold is constant—that is, closed-end funds have a limit. When the fund opens for business, it offers a specific number of shares—say 10 million, for instance—through an underwriter (a firm that raises investment capital from a variety of investors on behalf of the firms that are issuing equity and/or debt). Once shares are sold under an initial offering, they are traded on one of the stock exchanges.

A second way that closed-end funds are different from open-end funds is that the price of shares depends on supply and demand. The NAV is computed daily (as with open-end funds), but the actual share trade price may be, and usually is, considerably different from the NAV on the trade date. Shares in a closed-end fund trade just like the shares of other corporations on an exchange. If the trade price is less than the NAV, the fund's shares sell at a discount. If the trade price of shares exceeds the NAV, the shares are said to be trading at a premium. Most closed-end funds typically trade at a discount from the NAV. Because these shares trade on an exchange, the price for each trade may be fixed at any time during the day. It does not depend on the value of the NAV at the time of the trade or at the end of the day.

A third way that closed-end funds are different is that shares in these funds trade through brokers; therefore, you should expect to pay a commission on each trade, whether you are buying or selling. (Unlike load and no-load funds, discussed in the next section of this chapter, there is no such thing as a no-load or load closed-end fund.) This brokerage fee has a big impact when a closed-end fund is first opened to investors; therefore, you should avoid buying shares of a closed-end fund at the initial offering.

Initial shares are sold without a commission; however, a concession to the broker directly from the fund managers reduces the value of the shares by up to 7% below the initial offering price. This means there may be shares and/or cash in a closed-end fund's portfolio worth only $0.93 for every dollar in share value initially offered. Wait for a few days, weeks, or even months before buying shares in a new closed-end fund. During the first week or two, the underwriters and broker network usually maintain a firm price while all shares are being placed (sold). After that, the issue is turned loose to find its own level of value. Typically, within a few months, closed-end shares drop about 20% from their offering price. There are exceptions, of course. As you are learning, nothing is fixed in the market.

LOAD AND NO-LOAD MUTUAL FUNDS: DO YOU GET WHAT YOU PAY FOR?

Load funds sell shares through brokers who earn a commission on each sale. In the jargon of Wall Street, the commission (or brokerage fee) is known as a load, from the definition of load as "a burden." The maximum commission allowed by the SEC is 8.5% of the money invested. A dwindling number of stock and specialty funds charge this maximum load due to growing competition from no-load mutual funds, which do not charge commissions. At the 8.5% rate, for every $1,000 you invest with a broker to buy shares in a load fund, $85 stays with the broker and the brokerage firm as a *front-end commission*, with $915 left to buy the shares in the load fund. The front-end commission is the full charge for a so-called round-trip, meaning you pay nothing more to redeem shares at a later date. Note that no part of the commission or load goes to the mutual fund itself. The load is an *incentive* for the broker to market the fund's shares. Load percentages typically vary from 0% for money market mutual funds, to around

4% for bond funds, to about 8% for specialty funds (such as international funds, emerging market funds, and precious metals funds).

In contrast, with no-load and low-load funds, shares are sold directly to individual investors. They spend part of their earnings or assets to advertise in newspapers, such as *The Wall Street Journal*; in magazines, such as *Forbes* or *Money*; and by direct mail to shareholders or lists of potential investors. You pay no broker-age expenses (i.e., commissions), unlike in the load fund example above, where only $915 of your $1,000 investment is left to buy shares. With no-load, your total investment buys 100% shares, enabling all of your money to work for you. (With low-load fund, the com-mission charge is generally from 1% to 3%, so most of your money goes to work for you.)

No-load fund families offer an exciting variety of funds from which to choose, across all major categories. Because their growth, or even their existence, depends on service to individuals, no-load funds offer ready advice by telephone or mail. Investing in a no-load fund is easy. Call or write the fund for an application and return it with your check in the envelope provided. A few of the large no-load fund families maintain sales offices in major cities for personal service.

In recent years, load funds have been feeling the pressure from no-load and low-load funds, not only because of the absence of load charges (or at least minimal ones), but also because load funds have not had as promising a track record as the loads might suggest. In addition, no-load and low-load funds offer enough variety to satisfy almost every invest-ment objective. Even more compelling, the evidence tilts in favor of no-load funds once mutual fund returns are adjusted for loads.

On average, you would be better off with a no-load fund than a load fund. But before you invest again, make it a point to get to know each fund that interests you. Read the mutual fund's prospectus and check the respective Web sites. And speaking of getting to know about a fund, it is wise to check for what are called 12b-1 fees, perhaps the most misunderstood of all mutual fund charges and fees, to which we now turn.

12B-1 FEES: A HIDDEN COST OF INVESTING IN MUTUAL FUNDS

The number 12b-1 refers to the section of regulations set by the SEC that permits open-end mutual funds to charge up to 0.75% of a fund's assets for marketing and distribution each year. Note that 12b-1 fees are not charged against a fund's earnings or new money being invested. The charge is against assets. For example, if a fund's assets total $100 million, and the fund's management decides to charge a 0.75% 12b-1 fee, the fund's asset base declines by $750,000, thus depleting the assets available for investing. If a fund's asset base declines, shareholders can expect earnings to decline because less money is being invested in the market.

Once started, 12b-1 fees continue year after year, but not all funds use them. For example, some mutual funds that charge front-end loads also levy 12b-1 fees, while others do not. Of the two kinds of funds, closed-end and open-end, the 12b-1 fees are more common with the latter, as managers tap the fund's assets to bolster marketing efforts in the hope of attracting more investors.

REDEMPTION CHARGES: ANOTHER HIDDEN COST

Another fee that you need to watch for is called a contingent redemption charge. It is a deferred sales charge that reduces the amount you receive when you cash out your shares. This redemption charge (also called a contingent deferred sales charge) will reduce the amount you receive if you elect to cash out of some funds. A few mutual funds market their shares through brokers on a no-load basis. When you buy shares in these funds from a broker, you pay no commission, as in the case of a true no-load fund. There is a hitch, however. The broker actually does receive a concession from the mutual fund manager equal to about 4% of your investment, unless your investment is relatively large, over $100,000, for example. So, when you decide to redeem shares, you will find that a deferred sales charge—a fee that depends on how long your investment stayed in the fund—reduces the amount you receive.

A typical redemption charge may be 6% if you redeem shares within the first 12 months, 5% during the second 12 months, and so on, with a one percentage point reduction for each additional year; after six years, you may redeem all shares with no redemption fee.

The rationale for the redemption charge is that the fund needs time for your cash to earn a return that recoups the concession paid to the broker. Another reason is to discourage frequent switching between mutual funds. The sooner and more often you switch between funds, the bigger the redemption fees will be. Some brokers may not explain the contingent redemption fee clearly, opting to emphasize the no-load feature instead. Do not be afraid

to ask questions and check the prospectus for details regarding a possible contingent redemption fee. After all, it is your money.

In particular, watch for noncontingent redemption charges. These can be more onerous than the contingent variety. A redemption fee may apply for a specific period, or indefinitely. A redemption fee fixed as a percentage of the NAV at redemption can be particularly burdensome after several years of an increasing NAV. As the fund's NAV grows, so does the size of the redemption fee. Some noncontingent redemption fees may be stated in dollars alone or in combination with a percentage fee.

All things considered, these fixed redemption fees act like large brokerage charges, and are designed to discourage frequent switching between funds. If you have to pay a redemption fee every time you move out of a stock or bond fund into the safety of a money market mutual fund, you probably will switch less frequently. To reiterate, do not be afraid to ask questions and check the prospectus for details.

MONEY MARKET MUTUAL FUNDS AND MONEY MARKET DEPOSIT ACCOUNTS

Money market mutual funds invest shareholders' cash in money market instruments, such as bank certificates of deposit, Treasury bills, commercial paper, and similar short-term IOUs. These funds were invented in 1972 to offer small investors a chance to earn the same high-interest rates of return as large depositors. They effectively circumvented regulated interest rates on savings deposits as set by the Federal Reserve System, the nation's central bank.

By the mid-1970s, large investment banks (such as Merrill Lynch and PaineWebber) began to offer interest rates on accounts that permitted limited check writing. The rates were much higher than investors could earn on checking accounts and bank savings accounts, so investors flocked to these funds. In fact, the difference was, at times, larger than ten percentage points, for example, 18% versus 5 1 w %, the highest rate that investors could earn on bank passbook savings accounts at the time. To stem the deposit outflow, which deeply hurt banks, Congress allowed the formation of the money market deposit account in the early 1980s, essentially an interest-bearing checking account with limited check-writing features. All told, the effects have been to revolutionize banking and money systems in the United States.

There is one basic difference, at least as far as investors are concerned, between money market mutual funds and money market deposit accounts. Unlike money market deposit accounts, which are insured up to $100,000 by the Federal Deposit Insurance Corporation, money market mutual funds are not federally insured. Even so, the SEC closely regulates them. The funds maintain a constant NAV, usually $1 per share, by keeping maturities short to avoid interest rate risk. Managers turn over their funds often, buying short-term securities that may mature in ten days, and reinvesting the cash in new short-term securities.

Although the capital value of shares remains constant, interest rates change daily. The SEC requires that interest rates be stated as a 7-day average. Average maturities may range from twenty days to seventy days. When interest rates appear to be heading higher, fund managers will shorten maturities; for example, they will buy CDs and other money market instruments due to be repaid in twenty-one rather than twenty-eight days. This tactic enables the manager to regain control of the money and reinvest it sooner at what he or she perceives will be a higher interest rate. If the manager believes interest rates are headed lower, he or she will invest in securities with longer maturities to lock in higher rates for longer periods. This behavior on the part of money fund managers can provide a useful clue to the possible direction of short-term interest rates, and in turn, perhaps long-term rates as well.

This can be found in the consensus view of money market fund managers. As mentioned in Chapter 3 on bonds, understanding something about the views on interest rate movements can help you make your choice between short-term versus long-term fixed-income investments.

Money market mutual funds and money market deposit accounts offer a near-term safe place to park savings while giving you quick access to your funds. Typically, money market mutual funds pay somewhat higher interest rates than money market deposit accounts. This is to compensate for the lack of deposit insurance (higher return for higher risk). Thus, you gain the liquidity of check writing along with more income from your money. Check writing can also offer instant access to money you have invested in other types of mutual funds within a family of funds. Suppose you own shares in a fund with the Vanguard Group and want to open another account. Rather than having to send a check to the company or liquidating a portion of the fund you are currently holding, the money market account allows you to transfer the funds simply by calling the company's 800-number and telling the manager what you want to do. Such services are now also available through the Internet.

DIVERSIFICATION CONSIDERATION: NOT TOO MANY EGGS IN THE BASKET, PLEASE

Although we will cover the topic of diversification in more detail in later chapters, at this point it is prudent to discuss the diversification benefit that mutual funds offer individual investors. Diversification means investing in securities whose returns are not closely related to each other. The idea is to protect your portfolio from being greatly impacted by the negative return of one or a few securities, following the proverb "don't keep all your eggs in one basket."

With a few exceptions, most mutual funds carry diversification benefits. For example, if you are interested in stocks but feel overwhelmed by the choices, you can invest in a broad-based stock mutual fund that by its sheer size alone guarantees diversification (e.g., the Vanguard 500 Index Trust invests in 500 stocks). That way, if the automotive sector has negative returns, the positive returns in the unrelated sectors (e.g., of beverages and medical supplies) will help offset the negative impact. Similarly, if you are a risk-tolerant investor who would like to invest a small portion of your portfolio in junk bonds, you can find mutual funds that specialize in this area. They invest in a wide variety of such bonds, hence are not affected much—at least not to the extent of your portfolio—by one or two issues that default.

Where diversification benefits fall short is in sector funds. These involve investments in narrow industry groups, such as in financial services, energy, housing, electronics, technology, and precious metals. The most well-known set of sector funds is put out by

Fidelity Investments. Consider as an example this list of sector funds, which Fidelity calls "Select Portfolios," the names of which are self-explanatory:

- Air Transportation
- Banking
- Biotechnology
- Chemicals
- Computers
- Construction & Housing
- Defense
- Electronics
- Energy
- Financial Services
- Health Care
- Insurance
- Pharmaceuticals
- Retailing
- Software/Computer Services
- Technology
- Telecommunications
- Utilities Growth
- Wireless

By putting a lot of your investment money into one or two of these sectors, you run the risk that the portfolio's value will fluctuate a lot. On the "up" side, you would be happy; on the "down" side, you would be sad. For example, in August 2000, Fidelity's Select Technology fund was trading at an NAV of more than $170. As of March 2003 (less than three years later), however, it traded at about $38.50. During that period, the price reached a low of $31, in September 2002. By contrast, the Vanguard 500 Index Trust fell from $140 to $77. Granted, this is a big loss, but not nearly as big as the less-diversified technology fund (which, by the way, is a load fund with an up-front charge of 3%).

In addition to diversification, mutual funds provide access to securities that you ordinarily would not have. You can buy shares in a mutual fund that specializes in, for example, Ginnie Mae bonds (which were discussed in Chapter 3), whose minimum purchase amount can be prohibitively high, at up to $25,000. Or, if you are interested in real estate investments but have no desire (or the income) to invest directly in property, you can buy mutual funds geared toward real estate. Not only would shares in these funds be affordable, they would likely be diversified across different areas and different types of property, as well. In addition, as mentioned previously, easy-to-understand ratings on these and other mutual funds are readily available.

EXCHANGE-TRADED FUNDS

Similar to an index mutual fund, an exchange-traded fund trades just like a stock. It represents a set of securities—a portfolio, if you will—traded on an exchange, mostly the American Stock Exchange (AMEX), just like a single security. Although they are called funds, exchange-traded funds are not mutual funds. Here is a list by category:

- *DIAMONDS*. The Diamond Trust Series is directly tied to the 30 stocks in the Dow Jones Industrials.

- *FITRs*. Fixed-income trust receipts represent various Treasury securities, including Treasury bills, notes, and bonds.

- *HOLDRs*. Marketed by Merrill Lynch as a series of 20-stock portfolios, these groups are like sector funds, in that each HOLDR represents a particular sector, such as telecommunications, biotechnology, the Internet, and so on.

- *IShares MSCI*. Worldwide funds, nearly 80 in all, issued by Barclay's Global Investors, these are both index and sector funds, including ones for both stocks and bonds.

- *QUBES*. Representing the 100 largest capitalized (share price multiplied by shares outstanding) stocks on the National Association of Securities Dealers Automated Quotations (NASDAQ), they are designed to mimic the NASDAQ 100, which serves as a barometer for the stock performance of the high-tech sector.

- *SPDRs*. Standard & Poor's Depository Receipts, informally known as "Spiders," are directly linked to the S&P 500.

- *StreetTRACKS*. Put out by State Street Global Advisors, these nine funds are indexed across the Dow Jones Industrials, the Wilshire Real Estate Investment Trust Index, and a series of domestic and global growth and value indexes, for both large- and small-company stocks.

- *VIPERS*. These index participation receipts represent index funds marketed by Vanguard.

At first glance, exchange-traded funds appear to have significant advantages over mutual funds. For one, you can trade them just like a stock, which is not possible with a mutual fund, and unless you cash out your shares, you do not have to pay capital gains taxes. In addition, if you are risk-tolerant, you can sell the fund short; that is, you can bet that it will decline in value by selling shares now with the opportunity to buy back the shares at a lower price later. The difference is your profit.

That said, it is not yet clear that exchange-trade funds will replace mutual funds. Exchange-trade funds appear more suited to the active trader—someone who likes to buy and sell securities often—than to passive mutual fund index investors. They also carry a disadvantage that no-load and low-load mutual funds do not have: brokerage fees. Every time you trade, you pay a fee. This can be significant compared to the S&P 500 index. On an investment of $10,000, a low brokerage fee of $50 on an exchange-traded fund will take several years before it becomes competitive with the low-fee structure of the Vanguard's 500 Index.

REAL ESTATE INVESTMENT TRUSTS

Real Estate Investment Trusts are generally referred to as *REITs*. They are securities that invest directly in real estate. As stocks do, REITs trade on major exchanges. They come in three forms:

- *Equity REITs*. These REITs both invest in and own property. Their revenues come from the rents of the properties.

- *Mortgage REITs*. These REITs are concerned with property mortgages and the lending of money for them. Their primary source of income is the interest earned off the loans.

- *Hybrid REITs*. These REITs combine the investment approaches of equity and mortgage REITs.

REITs provide the important service of allowing individuals and institutions relatively easy access to the real estate market. They also have tax advantages and offer high-dividend yields.

SOME THINGS TO AVOID

There are several things to avoid in mutual fund investing. Do not hold many mutual funds; do not put too much into sector funds; tiptoe around IPO funds, especially if you are risk-averse; and be wary of funds that charge big loads and have big expenses.

- **Avoid investing in too many funds.** Situations in which investors own twenty or more mutual funds are not uncommon. Unless you are investing in sector funds or in very special situations (such as mutual funds by country), you do not need to own more than five to ten, and often fewer. For example, it does not make much sense to own both Fidelity's Magellan (which is an actively managed and large stock fund) and SPDRs, because these two funds invest in many of the same stocks and both are very strongly associated with the S&P 500. One will do the job.

Similarly, why invest in a sector fund for technology and the exchange-traded NASDAQ 100? The NASDAQ 100 is loaded with technology-type stocks, and it's closely linked to large-capitalization stocks, such as Cisco Systems, Intel, and Microsoft, which are usually grouped as technology-based funds. For example, witness the large fall in the NAS-DAQ index, from well over 4000 in August of 2000 to about 1250 by March 2003—a drop that parallels the steep drop in the Fidelity Select Technology fund as well as the steep drop in the stock prices of each of these companies. Once again, pick one, but not both.

In addition, mutual funds are notorious for being overdiversified. This means they invest in too many securities. Why is that not a good thing? Because the more securities a fund manager buys, the more likely it is that the fund manager is buying nonperforming securities or ones that neither increase return nor reduce risk. The point is that your portfolio can be well diversified with a few broad-based funds. There is no benefit to overdoing it.

• **Avoid putting too much of your investments into sector funds.** It is common for investors to seek out what is "hot," those individual securities and sectors that seem to have good upward momentum. This is why hot sector funds are popular. By investing in several of these funds, you might begin to believe that your portfolio is reasonably diversified, but it's not. Although you would be investing in funds that have many holdings, the holdings may be strongly correlated with each other. In short, although you might not be putting a lot of eggs in one basket, the baskets are similar and few in number.

• **Avoid—or at least tiptoe around—IPO funds.** If you think it is tough to guess which IPO is going to be the next big winner, you are right. If you think that an IPO fund, because it is bigger and more diversified than anything you could build, will enable you to uncover the next Cisco or Microsoft, you are probably wrong. In terms of return and risk, your money is likely put to better use elsewhere. Concisely stated, recall the fable of the hare (the IPO fund) versus the tortoise (SPDRs).

• **Avoid or be wary of funds that have large loads and big expenses.** It is tempting to conclude that you always get what you pay for, but with respect to mutual funds, that is not always the case, and some professional analysts would say that it is not usually the case. There is no strong evidence that actively managed, large-load funds with large expense ratios can outperform mutual funds tied to a broad market index.

SUMMARY

Mutual funds and exchange-traded funds are portfolios of investments whose shares you can buy. There are thousands of these funds of every size, shape, and feature, from high-risk, aggressive growth funds to almost risk-free money market funds.

One of the principal advantages of fund investing is gaining access to a broadly diversified group of investments at a relatively low cost. That cost is measured, in the case of mutual funds, by net asset value per share, in the case of exchange-traded funds, by the price per share, just like a stock.

When picking mutual funds, try to find highly rated, broadly diversified, no-load funds that show strong returns, low risk, and have low management fees.

OPTIONS

In 2003, Alan Greenspan, then the head of the Federal Reserve System, the U.S. central bank, said that the use of *derivatives* has been good for the economy. What did Greenspan mean? What are derivatives? Welcome to the most complex and dynamic market in finance, derivatives, of which options are a category. Just a glance at the key terms is enough to make you frown.

If you are not interested in active investing, you can safely skip this chapter. If you are interested in active investing, you would be wise to learn about the rudiments of derivatives in general and options in particular. Why? Simply put, they can help you reduce the risk of your investments.

To allay any initial anxiety, you do not need a degree in finance to understand and use derivatives. You do not even need to be well versed in math, if it happens that the word "derivative" brings back unpleasant memories of algebra, geometry, and calculus. Simply stated, a derivative is a financial instrument whose value is based on, or derived from, another financial instrument, such as a stock or a bond.

In this chapter, we are going to cover one type of derivative, an *option*. An option is an agreement—a contract, if you prefer—between you and another investor that gives you the right to buy or sell a security, but with one important exception: you are under no obligation to do so. The choice is yours, as the word "option" indicates.

Most investors end up doing nothing with their options. They allow them to expire worthless. Put simply, your decision to either buy or sell hinges on a simple concept: "return to risk." Do it only if it improves the return to risk of your investments.

WHY OPTIONS CAN BE GOOD FOR YOUR INVESTMENT PORTFOLIO

How can options help improve the return-to-risk performance of your investments? At a minimum, by protecting your investments against unfavorable price swings, options can help reduce the chance that your returns will be less than you had expected. They do this principally by reducing risk, but they can also help increase returns. They especially come in handy with stocks because stock prices fluctuate a lot more than, for example, bond prices.

Some stocks (such as those in the technology sector) are, by any reasonable standard, quite risky. Their prices are volatile, often realizing big increases in the short term, quickly followed by sharp declines as investors sell the stocks to take profits. A technology stock that has enjoyed a recent surge in price might still have significant long-term price appreciation potential but not without a lot of price fluctuation along the way. Options can help reduce the impact of these fluctuations (think of how taking motion sickness medicine reduces dizziness). For our purposes, we will keep the discussion centered on stocks, and in this respect, options are derived from stocks, and their values are derived from the values of stocks.

TYPES AND FEATURES OF OPTIONS

There are two basic kinds of options, a call and a put:

- A *call* gives you the right to buy stock. In other words, you have the right to "call in" from another investor up to the number of shares of stock the contract allows.

- A *put* gives you the right to sell stock. In other words, it gives you the right to "put to" another investor up to the number of shares of stock the contract calls for. Just knowing about a call and a put will go a long way toward helping you understand options and how to use them profitably.

Once again, as the word "option" implies, you are under no obligation to do anything. Keep in mind, however, that the option has an expiration date. In the event you do nothing by the time the expiration date is passed, the option becomes worthless. If you decide to execute the option either to *call* in shares from or *put* shares to another investor, then you would be said to be exercising your option.

The options market is different from the stock and bond markets. Options have traded in the United States for more than 100 years and trace

their origin back to the Greeks. But in April 1973, the opening of listed options offered by the Chicago Board Options Exchange (CBOE) changed the market forever. Options were standardized into contracts for 100 shares of an underlying stock with fixed expiration dates and exercise prices, also called *strike* or *striking prices*; that is, the prices at which you can call in shares from another investor or put shares to another investor, set at regular intervals. These features made options easier to trade.

Demand for options has grown fast. The average number of equity (i.e., stock) contracts handled daily by the CBOE alone has more than doubled from about 350,000 in just the last seven years alone. On March 20, 2003, for example, the volume of various stock options jumped to more than 1.3 million. Consider, too, that the options were available only for stocks of a limited number of corporations.

Options come in two forms, American and European; they differ in terms of when they can be exercised:

- *American options* may be exercised, or closed out, at any time prior to the expiration date and are almost exclusively available in the United States.

- A *European option* can only be closed out on the expiration date; a few European-style options are available in the United States as well.

HOW OPTIONS CAN REDUCE RISK: A CASE STUDY

To show you how options can reduce risk, let us say you bought 100 shares of IBM at $55 (which you could have done in October 2002) and watched it jump to $85 in three months (which it did). After checking financial ratios and other pertinent information, you feel that the company's stock price still has room to grow, but you are also concerned that such a strong run up in price in such a short period might be the catalyst to drive the stock price down to $75. What can you do? To protect your position, you can decide to buy one put contract at a strike (i.e., exercise) price of $85. One contract is good for 100 shares of stock. Assume this costs you $4 per share. Thus, the put costs you $400, plus brokerage fees, which we will ignore here for simplicity.

You have now protected your gains. How? If IBM's stock price were to drop to $75 (which it actually did), the put increases in value, because you bought it at the strike price of $85. The put would be worth at least $10 ($85 minus $75) times the number of shares in each contract. Because each contract is good for 100 shares, the put would be worth $1,000 ($85 minus $75 multiplied by 100 shares), and maybe more, depending on the amount of time left before the options expire. Thus, as the price of the stock falls, the price of the puts *rises*, helping to reduce your potential loss of profit.

In this example, the $1,000 loss in profits is offset by a $600 gain in the value of the puts. The $600 is the difference between the $400 you paid for the put and its current value of $1,000. Although overall you have lost some profit, you reduced the loss by $600. This is another illustration of how options can help reduce your investment risk.

That said, now that you have reduced your investment risk, you still have to decide what you want to do. Assume that IBM's stock price hovers around $75, at least until the expiration date. You have three choices:

- **Sell the put.** You can sell the put back into the market on or before the date it expires, for $1,000. Your profit from selling the put would be $600 ($1,000 minus $400, though this ignores brokerage fees). With this move, you would also keep your shares.

- **Exercise your option.** You can exercise your options by selling the shares for $85, the strike price at which you bought the put. In doing so, it will cost you the $400 you paid for the option. The bottom line is that you will have sold your IBM stock for $81 per share, or the $85 price per share of stock minus the $4 price of the put. Although $81 is less than $85, it is, obviously, more than $75, the price without the option. By the way, be not concerned about to whom you are selling, or putting, the shares. Your broker will handle that for you. It will be no one you know, and there is no easy way to find out.

- **Let the option expire.** If you let the options expire, you will keep your original shares, but you will lose the $400 that you paid for the option.

Note that the first two choices leave you equally well off financially. The first choice leaves you with $600, which is $6 ($10 minus $4) multiplied by 100 shares. It is no coincidence that $75 plus $6 is $81, the bottom-line price in the case of the second choice.

What will you do if the stock price rises above $85? The higher it gets, the less your puts will be worth, because your exercise price is $85. If, by all indications, the stock price is going to stay well north of $85, say around $92, you may decide to sell the puts well before expiration. Given the rise in price to $92, however, you will not get $4 for the puts, but something less, say, $2, and even less if the puts are close to the expiration date. In this case, you would sell the puts for $2 multiplied by 100 shares, or $200. This amounts to a loss of $200 ($400 minus $200), which would be more than made up in the $7 gain ($92 minus $85) in the price of the stock. Overall, you would be ahead by $500 ($700 minus $200).

KEEP IN MIND THAT OPTIONS EXPIRE

We need to mention two things about the expiration date. First, as a rule, the longer the time remaining before the option expires, the higher the price (also called the *premium*). Time affords the opportunity for the option premium to move in a favorable direction, up or down. As your option gets close to expiration, however, there is little time left for any news or market action to affect the stock price, and in turn the option premium. If this were the last day you could exercise your options, and the stock price is holding steady at $75, then the put premium would be at least $10, and maybe just a bit more, say $10.25. If you had another month, or even longer, to go, then the price would be higher, say, $11; and if market sentiment about the stock and the overall stock market were negative at the time, then it could be somewhat higher still.

Second, the expiration date for options is the third Friday of every month. If in a newspaper or on the Internet you saw "Mar-03" next to the premium of $4, then you would have until just before 4:00 P.M. (technically, with options, you have about another ten minutes past 4:00 P.M.) on the third Friday in March 2003, which was March 21, to decide whether to exercise your options, sell your options, or do nothing. In this case, of the three choices

indicated above, we recommend either the first or second.

OPTIONS CAN HELP IMPROVE YOUR RATE OF RETURN ON INVESTMENTS

The IBM example showed you how an option can reduce risk. In addition, as mentioned previously, an option can also help you improve your rate of return. For example, think about your odds of winning when you buy stock. To keep things simple, you have one chance in three:

• You win if the stock price increases.

• You neither gain nor lose if the stock price stays the same.

• You lose if the stock price moves down.

Can you improve your odds? Yes, you can. You can sell, or *write*, a call option. When you do so, you give other investors the right (but not the obligation) to buy your stock. However, the other investors can do so only if they give you some money, a premium. After all, if other investors think your stock is great, you might as well make them pay for the right to buy your shares. The premium is determined by the demand for, and supply of, the stock, from which the call option is derived (the concept of a derivative).

As soon as you receive your money, and it is yours forever, your odds of winning rise to at least two in three:

• You win if the price of the underlying stock moves up.

• You also win if the stock's price does not change because you have received some money for selling the call.

Actually, depending on how much you got, you might still win if the price of the stock falls by only a small amount, say a few dollars. If the stock price falls a lot, you will lose, but not as much as if you had not sold the call option.

To illustrate, let us say that you write a call on IBM at a strike price of $85. Assume the call premium is $5. Because one contract is good for 100 shares, you get $500. Assuming you want to keep the shares, you hope, at least until the option expires, that IBM's stock price neither rises nor falls much. Why? If it rises by just a few dollars, say to $88, then it is unlikely your 100 shares will be called in, or sold. (Unlike buying an option, you are obligated to do something when you sell an option.) This is because it will not be profitable for another investor to exercise the call until IBM's stock price rises above $90, or a price above $85 plus the call premium of $5. If another investor were to call in your shares at $88, he or she would be buying instantly into a loss, because the 100 shares would have actually cost $90 (the strike price of $85 plus the $5 premium).

If IBM's stock price behaves as you hope, you get to keep your shares along with the $500. You have now improved your return without taking on more risk. You are ahead by $500, which is certainly a better deal than if you had done nothing at all.

Keep in mind that until the option expires, writing the call prevents you from enjoying further increases in the price of the stock. In addition, if you want to hold the stock in the event that the stock price jumps into the $90 range, you can buy the options back, but doing so will very likely cost you more money than you initially received. Nonetheless, at a minimum, you will have improved your profit position and reduced your risk, all of which help ensure a sound sleep.

The previous example concerned what is referred to as a *covered* call, which simply means that you were covered with the shares you own. If you did not own the shares, you would be said to be writing the calls *naked*. Be warned that writing naked calls does *not* reduce your risk. It increases it by a lot.

Exhibit 5–1 gives the advantages and disadvantages of either writing calls or buying puts.

EXHIBIT 5–1. WRITING CALLS AND BUYING PUTS

Action	Advantages	Disadvantages
Buy put	Keep your shares unless you put/sell them to someone else	Lose some money, especially if stock price rises
Write covered call	Money in your pocket	Could lose out on further price increase and/or lose shares

To reiterate, when buying a put, you get the opportunity, in the event the stock price falls, to sell the shares (put them) to someone else. Moreover, in contrast to writing a call, you do not have to worry about losing your shares; however, the move will cost you some money. Either way, though, you will be reducing your risk compared to the alternative of doing nothing. When writing a covered call, you get money up front that is yours forever. Just be aware that in the event the stock price rises, you run the risk of losing your shares, and in turn losing the opportunity to sell your stock at yet a higher price.

Given the advantages and disadvantages of a call and a put, you might be wondering whether you could improve your position by doing both, that is, buying puts and writing covered calls at the same time at the same exercise price and expiration date. The answer is yes. Such a position is called a straddle. Although you will have additional brokerage fees to pay, by writing one covered call at $85 and buying one put at $85, you would lock in your profits no matter what occurs.

There is one more situation in which buying an option can help reduce your risk: short selling. Here you have a case of "sell high, buy low," rather than the more typical "buy low, sell high." Although the previous example suggested that you would be taking on more risk by buying a call option, you can also use them to reduce risk. For example, if you are selling IBM's stock short, and therefore speculating that the price might drop, you are exposing yourself to the possibility that the stock price will rise. The higher it rises, the bigger your loss. You can hedge this possibility by buying calls. If the stock price rises, your implied loss on the stock is offset, at least partially, by the rising value of the calls.

SPECULATING WITH CALLS AND PUTS: TAKING ON HIGH RISK

The discussion so far has been about reducing your risk, also called *hedging* your risk. It has dealt with protecting profits, or alternatively, minimizing your losses. These illustrations also highlight two sides of the market. While you are trying to hedge your risk, another investor is taking on more risk. In effect, the other investor is a risk-tolerant *speculator* who is betting that you and the market are underestimating the stock price movement, whether up or down. In either case, you are protecting your profits, but if the swing in stock prices turns out to be greater than you and others expected, the speculator will profit.

In the IBM example, a speculator who feels that IBM's stock price was rising too far, too fast, might decide to buy puts in the hope that the price will decline. Such a move is equivalent in spirit to selling the stock short, or betting that the share price will decline. In this case, the speculator (who does not own the shares) buys the puts at $4 and hopes that the underlying stock price will fall by a lot. If it does, there will be an increase in the put premium and, in turn, the realization of profit.

For example, assume the put premium rose to $10, meaning the speculator's profit would be $6 multiplied by the number of shares. If the investor bought ten contracts, the profit is $6000 (ignoring brokerage fees). Note that because the speculator does not hold the shares, he or she cannot put the shares to another party. If the stock price does not fall, or if it falls only by a small amount, then the investor can either sell the options at whatever price the market values them or allow them to expire worthless.

For the speculator, buying puts offers advantages over shorting stock. The most attractive feature is that the speculator's losses are limited to the cost of the puts. With short selling, the loss mounts as the stock price rises, a scary situation. For example, in the case of IBM, if the speculator shorts the stock at $85 and it rises to $125, the speculator is out $40 per share ($125 minus $85); the situation would get progressively worse if the stock price continued its upward march. In addition, the short seller has to pay any cash dividends that come due while shorting the stock. Furthermore, given the complexity of the short position, the short seller may have to make a good-faith deposit to the brokerage firm that equals the value of the shares sold short.

The primary disadvantage of buying puts is the time element. If the expiration date is in the near future, the short seller might not have enough time to profit from the purchase of the puts. A similar expiration date does not hold when shorting.

In the opposite case, the investor who believes that IBM's stock price is undervalued can buy calls. Once again we will use $85 as the strike (i.e., exercise) price, and assume that $5 is the call premium and ignore brokerage costs. This amounts to speculating that IBM's share price will rise well above $85. If it does rise to $95, for example, then the call buyer has two choices for taking profits:

- **Sell the calls.** The speculator can sell the calls at approximately $10 per share, or $95 minus $85, the strike price. If the investor had bought ten calls, the profit would be $95 minus $85 minus the $5 call premium multiplied by the 1,000 shares, or $5,000.

- **Exercise the options.** The speculator can call in the shares at $85 and either hold them or

sell them outright at $95. If sold outright, then the 1,000 shares are called in at $85 per share. The profit will be:

$$\$95 \times 1{,}000 \text{ shares} - \$85 \times 1{,}000$$
$$\text{shares} - \$5 \times 1{,}000 \text{ shares}$$
$$(\$95{,}000 - \$85{,}000 - \$5{,}000 = \$5{,}000)$$

In either case, the profit is the same. However, in the first case, the investor has to spend only $5,000, or the ten calls multiplied by the call premium of $5. In the second case, the investor has to spend $85,000 when calling in the shares, or the 1,000 shares multiplied by $85. This is a lot more money than $5,000, but it does give the investor a chance to hold onto the shares, which could be a good move if there is a lot of near-term momentum in the stock price. For most investors, though, $85,000 is a lot of money, and without the call options, they would not be able to take advantage of a potentially profitable situation.

When it comes to speculation, going "naked," whether writing calls or writing puts, is one of the most risky moves you can make. In the case of writing calls, you are speculating that the price of the stock will not rise. To return to the IBM example, if you write ten naked calls and if the stock price never rises much above $85, you earn a profit of $5 multiplied by the 1,000 shares implied in the ten contracts, or $5,000. However, if the stock price rises to $95, you run the big risk of having the shares called in when you do not own them. The result could be that you will be forced to buy them at $95 per share and sell them at $85 per share, leaving you with a gain of $5 per share from the call premium, or $5,000, but a loss of $10 per share on the stock, or $10,000. Overall, your loss is $5,000 ($10,000 minus $5,000).

In the case of writing puts, you are speculating that the price of the stock will not fall. Using the IBM example and the $4 premium for puts, if you wrote ten puts at $85, and the stock price never fell much, or even rose, then you would profit to the tune of the $4 times the 1,000 shares, or $4,000. However, if the stock price fell to $75, you then would run the big risk of 1,000 shares being put to you at $85 when they are worth only $75, for a loss of $4 from the put premium minus the $10 loss on the stock multiplied by 1,000, $6,000. The only consolation is that the price of the shares you now hold might reverse course and rise, but now must do so to $81 just for you to break even. Of the four choices—buying calls, selling calls, buying puts, and selling puts—the more conservative moves are buying puts when you own the stock and writing covered calls. Money managers, financial advisors, and portfolio specialists routinely sell covered calls to increase income and ultimately rates of return.

You should be aware, though, that just the opposite is the case when buying and writing options for speculation. The risk is sometimes several times that of the stock itself, which is why brokers often require that you have collateral, especially with naked calls and puts. The same is true with a margin account, where you borrow the money you are going to invest (discussed in Chapter 1). Reinforcing this requirement is the observation that only a relatively small percentage of speculative calls and puts prove to be profitable.

Although buying calls and puts for speculation is risky, it can be attractive, especially if you do not have a lot of cash. In the IBM example, you might not be able to afford 1,000 shares at $85 per share, or $85,000, but you might

be able to buy ten calls at a price per share of $5, or a total cost of $5,000, which is much more affordable. An advantage of this move, as opposed to buying the shares outright, is that the most you will lose is $5,000, assuming the options expire worthless because the stock price never increased.

The same applies to a put. If you expect a stock price to decline and you buy one or more puts, the most you can lose is the cost of the puts. The alternative to buying puts is to sell short. Recall that short selling means borrowing the shares, selling them, and then hoping the stock price falls so that you can buy them back at a lower price. If the price does fall and you buy back the shares, the difference between what you sold them for and what you paid for them is your profit.

What happens, though, if the stock price rises, and keeps rising for an extended period? You stand to lose a lot; in fact, your losses are theoretically infinite in a world of rising stock prices. By buying puts, you are effectively limiting your loss to the cost of the puts. If the underlying stock price rises, the worst that can happen is that your options expire worthless.

The disadvantage of puts is the fixed amount of time available for the underlying stock price to fall. It could well be that your prediction is directionally correct; however, the price decline begins after the puts have expired, so the more time you give yourself, the bigger the premium will be.

Throughout these illustrations, we have discussed both the underlying stock price and the option price, or premium. But we have not discussed what it means if you choose an exercise price at, below, or above the actual stock price. Let us take a look at calls first. If you either buy or sell (write) calls at a strike price that equals the actual stock price, you would be said, in option parlance, to be *at the money*. If you either buy or sell calls at an exercise price that is less than the actual stock price, you would be said to be *in the money*. If you buy or sell calls at an exercise price that is greater than the actual stock price, you would be said to be *out of the money*.

In the IBM example, if the actual stock price were $87 and you bought ten calls at an exercise price of $85, you would be *in the money* by $2. This difference of $2 is also referred to as the intrinsic value. Conversely, if you bought the calls at an exercise price of $90, you would be *out of the money*. There is no intrinsic value for an *out-of-the-money* option.

In the case of puts, the at-the-money logic holds, but for the other two, it reverses. An exercise price that is less than the actual stock price would be said to be out of the money. If you buy or sell puts at an exercise price that is greater than the actual stock price, you would be said to be in the money. Assume IBM's stock price is $87. If you bought ten puts at an exercise price of $90, you would be in the money, with an intrinsic value of $3.

READING OPTIONS TABLES: READ THE FINE PRINT

Before going deeper into options, let us pause and place calls, puts, strike prices, and expiration dates into perspective with an illustration. Referring back to Chapter 2, we will use GSD, Inc., whose symbol is GASD. Assume that the closing price for the stock, as of August 25, was $15, and that the expiration date for September is the 17th. With those parameters in mind, take a look at Exhibit 5–2.

Here's how to read the table:

- The first column lists GASD's closing price for the previous day, followed by four strike (exercise) prices: $5, $10, $15, and $20. The $5 increment is a common listing.

- The second column lists the expiration month (in this case, the third Friday of September, the 17th, and the third Friday of October, the 15th).

- The third and fifth columns give the call and put premiums, or option prices, relative to each strike price. With respect to the calls, note that at $15, GASD is deep in the money at striking prices of $5 and $10, is at the money at $15, and out of the money at $20. The opposite reasoning applies to the puts.

- The fourth and sixth columns provide the volume, or number of contracts. Note that most of the activity was at $15.

EXHIBIT 5–2. READING AN OPTIONS TABLE					
GASD 15 Stk	Exp.	Pr.	Call Vol.	Pr.	Put Vol.
5	Sep	10.90	21	.20	0
10	Sep	6.10	62	.90	37
15	Oct	1.30	172	2.05	210
20	Oct	.40	42	5.90	59

PRICING OPTIONS: EASIER DONE THAN SAID

The previous illustrations of in-the-money and out-of-the-money options provide us with an introduction to the pricing of options. There are actual formulas for determining the price of options, the most well known of which is the *Black-Scholes options pricing model*. The formulas generally depend on six criteria, posed in the form of questions:

- **Is the option in the money, and if so, by how much?** The deeper in the money it is, or the bigger the actual stock price is compared to the exercise, or strike, price, the bigger the option's premium will be.

- **How much time is left before the option expires worthless?** The more time left, the higher the option's premium will be.

- **How much does the price of the underlying stock fluctuate (often called volatility)?** The more it fluctuates, the higher the option price will be.

- **What is the underlying stock's current price?** The higher the stock price, the higher the option price will be.

- **What is happening with interest rates?** Rising interest rates tend to increase option prices.

- **Does the underlying stock pay a dividend?** If it does, the option price tends to fall because the stock looks increasingly attractive.

Let us go back to the IBM example to illustrate each of these influences, beginning with the stock price at $85, the exercise price at $85, and the put premium at $4. In the case of the first criterion, if IBM's stock price quickly falls to $75, the put option will now be in the money. The deeper it goes into the money, the higher the premium will be. In this case, it would rise from $4 to about $11.

Although the stock price decreased by $10 ($75 minus $85), the option premium only increased by $7 ($11 minus $4). Why did the option premium not increase by $10? This is a feature of options pricing known as *delta*. It is also referred to as a *hedge ratio*, given that options can be used to hedge (reduce) risk. Delta is the change in the price of the option relative to the change in the price of the underlying stock. The options market treats in-the-money options differently from out-of-money options. As a rule, the deeper in the money the option is, the smaller the delta will be.

In the example, we went from an at-the-money put option, or an exercise price that equals the stock price at $85, to an in-the-money put option, where the stock price, at $75, was less than the exercise price. This is a delta of 0.70 ($7 divided by $10). Deltas tend to get somewhat smaller the deeper in the money the option gets. The change in the delta divided by the change in the underlying stock price is what is known as *gamma*.

The same logic, only in reverse, applies to calls. All you need to remember is that the more the stock price rises, the deeper in the money the call is, the higher the call premium will be, and the smaller delta will get.

IS TIME YOUR ALLY OR YOUR ENEMY?

The previous illustration assumed that you still had some time left before the option expired. If there were a lot of time left, say, at least six months, the put premium, based on the stock price of $75, would be higher than $11. If the company were not doing well and the market's momentum was on the downside, a lot of time left would provide an opportunity for the stock price to fall more, leading to an even higher put price. But, if there were not much time left, the option price would be less than $11, much closer to the difference between the strike price and the stock price. For example, if the stock and exercise prices were both at $85, with one week before expiration, the put premium would probably be no more than $1, and very likely less.

There is a feature in the options market that allows you to hold an option for a considerable time. It is called a *LEAP*, which stands for long-term equity anticipation. With LEAPs, you can "go long" for more than nine months and up to 39 months. If you do it with deep-in-the-money call options, you are effectively practicing a buy-and-hold strategy advocated by many financial planners and Wall Street specialists. More important, you are giving yourself plenty of time for the options to work in your favor.

If you buy a short-term call, you run the risk that an unfavorable short-term development for a company (for example, a promising drug that proves ineffective in trials) could push the stock price down, and therefore the option price. You would probably end up with a loss.

If you had more time, though, the stock price could recover, and along with it the option premium. In addition, stock prices tend to show an upward movement over time. This makes sense, because as an economy grows, so will the sectors that support it. If there is a bias to the up side, then going long for a long period is a sensible strategy, and LEAPs could conceivably be part of that strategy.

For example, say you are interested in technology stocks, but are low on cash. You observe that technology stocks, especially in the computer industry and semiconductor sector (the "brains" of computers and other high-tech

gadgets), go through so-called boom and bust periods, leading to wide swings in stock prices. From your research, you find that technology firms are currently in the throes of a severe downturn, and their stock prices are depressed. Moreover, it is unclear when the next upturn will occur, but when it does, their stock prices could jump, and you do not want to miss a profitable opportunity. So if you do not have the cash to buy many shares, if a margin account—one in which you borrow money to invest—is something you wish to avoid, and if near-term uncertainty is too high to speculate with short-term options, what should you do?

In this example, you could buy in-the-money LEAPs in technology firms, such as Cisco Systems, Dell, Intel, and Microsoft. If the LEAPs do not expire for at least two years, you increase your chances that your investments will grow during the next technology upturn. Keep in mind, though, that as the time left before the options expire decreases, the option premium will tend to decrease as well. The change in the price of an option divided by the decrease in the time before the expiration date is what is known as *theta*. As a buyer of a call option, you want the theta to be small; that is, you do not want the price to decrease much as the option moves closer to expiration.

VOLATILITY: A FANCY WORD FOR PRICE FLUCTUATIONS

The computer and semiconductor sectors are good examples to explain the concept of volatility—wide swings in stock prices. It is not uncommon for the risk in these sectors to be as much as ten times greater than the risk of the overall stock market, as measured by the S&P 500. That is a lot of risk by any standard, and that risk has a big impact on the call and put premiums of these firms.

Given their wide swings, there are periods when the stock prices can experience tremendous upswings, easily increasing by ten or more points in one week. The same, and more, can happen on the downside. The result is that the call and put premiums, both in the money and out of the money, will be much higher than for firms in a more stable and predictable industry, such as in mature pharmaceutical companies. Their stock prices tend to be much more stable because the products of the companies undergo less rapid change than those of technology-based firms.

For example, in March 2003, Pfizer (a company well known for developing and marketing pharmaceuticals for a wide variety of ailments) had a stock price of about $31. With an expiration date of January 2005 and a strike price of $30, the corresponding LEAP was priced at about $6. By contrast, Novellus (a company in the semiconductor equipment market, whose stock was trading at almost the same price as Pfizer's at the time) had a LEAP with the same strike price and expiration date priced at about $10. The big difference between these two stocks is in the volatility, or risk. Making an investment in Novellus stock is about seven times riskier than making one in Pfizer stock.

As another comparison, let us look at a financial company, Citigroup. Its risk is significantly higher than Pfizer's because financial companies tend to be more sensitive to changes in economic activity than pharmaceutical companies. Citigroup enjoyed a stock price in March 2003 of about $37, or about $6

more per share than Novellus. The price of the comparable Citigroup LEAP, however, was only about $10, the *same* as the LEAP on Novellus. So despite Citigroup's significantly higher stock price, and an underlying risk structure that is higher than Pfizer's, the LEAP price was only equal to Novellus', clearly the stock with the highest level of volatility among the three.

The same logic holds for puts, only on the other side of the strike price of $30. In the case of Pfizer, as of March 2003, the call premium was about $4. For Novellus, it was about $8.50. Once again, we see the impact of Novellus' higher volatility on the put premium.

BIGGER WILL MEAN MORE EXPENSIVE

The bigger the underlying stock price, the bigger the option premium will be. It is that simple. The reason is because the potential loss from, say, a 10% adverse price change in the stock is larger for a stock at $100—a reduction per share of $10 (0.10 multiplied by $100)—than for a stock priced at $8—a reduction of $0.80, or 0.10 multiplied by $8. No doubt you would feel the loss of $10 per share a lot more than $0.80 per share.

Recall for a moment the discussion about the impact of time on option prices. We said that the more time available before the option expires, the higher the premium will be. This is because more time allows the underlying stock price to change, thus changing the option price; and the higher the stock price rises, the more you can expect to pay for the option.

IT IS IN YOUR INTEREST TO FOLLOW INTEREST RATES

Buying stock can tie up a lot of money. Is there an alternative strategy? Yes, there is. You could, for example, buy a LEAP, as explained in the section on "Is Time Your Ally or Your Enemy?," rather than buy 1,000 shares in a company. Going back to the example involving Pfizer, you could buy 1,000 shares at $31 per share, which would cost you $31,000. Alternatively, you could refer to Chapter 2 on money market investments and decide to buy ten LEAPs at $6,000 ($6 per every share of stock that the ten LEAPs represent) and invest the remaining $25,000, or $31,000 minus $6,000, in either U.S. Treasury bills or certificates of deposit, or both. The point is that as interest rates rise this move looks increasingly attractive. Thus, the LEAPs, or call premiums in general, will rise in value. Just the opposite will tend to happen when interest rates fall. When they do, holding stocks looks like the better deal because there is not much to be earned at low interest rates.

NOT ALL MOVES PAY DIVIDENDS

The previous discussion showed how rising interest rates tend to boost the price of options. The opposite holds for dividends. Although rising dividends (especially a large and unexpected boost in them) could conceivably lead to higher stock prices, they probably will not yield much in the way of rising option prices. As dividends on the underlying stock rise, you have an incentive to buy the stock, not the option.

Recall that the definition of an option is a contract that gives you the right (but not the obligation) to buy or sell stock. Because an option does not mean ownership in a company the way stock does, you do not receive any of the dividends associated with the underlying stock. So while the shareholders go about their merry way collecting dividends off the stock, your only hope of a gain is a rise in the price of the call option.

Interestingly, because dividend payments are technically similar to selling shares (a way to get cash), they tend, on average, to put downward pressure on the stock's price. And if a company decides to cut or suspend its dividend, then the market would tend to interpret this as a negative sign, which would send the stock price down. This implies that the dividend decision can work in favor of an investor who has bought puts for speculation. The farther the stock price falls, the more the put premium rises, leading to greater profit.

MORE ON OPTIONS PRICING

There are some secondary influences on the price of options. One is when a company divides its existing stock into more shares, called a stock split. Using the IBM example, if the company announced a two-for-one split at $85, the stock price would be cut in half to $42.50. The call option that was selling at $5 would now be selling for $2.50. But now you would have two of them, not just one. If you held ten calls before the split, you would now have twenty.

Another influence deals with bear markets. Overall, bear market investors (i.e., investors who take advantage of price declines in stocks) may be better off buying puts than selling short. As a result, the price of puts during bear markets tends to rise. There are several reasons for this:

- First (as already explained), by buying puts, you limit your loss to the amount you have spent on the puts. Given that puts involve less money than selling the underlying stock short—ten puts is a smaller financial move than selling 1,000 shares short—they offer more financial leverage than the short position.

- In addition, when you sell shares of a dividend-paying stock short, you have to pay, directly from your pocket, any dividends that the company issues. With put options, there is no such obligation.

The one big disadvantage of puts, as mentioned, is the time limit. Paying a series of put premiums while waiting for the share price to drop may not be cheap, especially if the puts are in the money.

There is one more principle to consider in this discussion, that of put-call parity, which will help to explain a bit more about pricing puts. The put-call parity principle is all about the relationship between calls and puts for the same stock. It is the relationship between the values of puts and calls in a way that prevents an investor from profiting between the two. It is not unlike a stock that is traded on two different exchanges. If you know the buying price in one market, you will know the selling price in the other. Any opportunities to profit between the two should not systematically exist; otherwise, you could buy in one market, sell in the other market, and earn virtually risk-free profit.

OPTION MARKETS

A stock option will trade in one of five secondary markets: the Chicago Board Options Exchange, the American, the Philadelphia, the Pacific, and the New York. Most of the activity (well over two-thirds) is in the Chicago and American markets.

As in stock markets, these markets provide you with one indispensable ingredient for trading options: liquidity. Either through a broker or via the Internet, you can buy and sell very quickly and smoothly.

Associated with the markets is the Options Clearing Corporation. It stands as the go-between among the buyers and sellers of options to make sure that all transactions are carried out. For example, again using the IBM example, assume you buy a call that costs you $5 at a strike price of $85, and that the price of the stock jumps to $95, leading you to exercise your option and call in the 100 shares. How does the process work? First, you inform your broker that you want to exercise your option. The broker then informs the Options Clearing Corporation, which then randomly selects a broker holding the same written contract. To honor the contract, the broker randomly selects another investor who has written the options. Once the writer receives an "assignment notice," it is virtually impossible to offset or eliminate it. The investor has no choice but to sell the shares to you at $85 dollars (keeping in mind that the final cost of the stock will be the $85 per share cost plus the $5 per share option premium plus brokerage charges).

OPTIONS COME IN INDICES, TOO

Stock option indices are available across a variety of market measures (as discussed in Chapter 2), such as:

- Dow Jones Industrials
- Standard & Poor's 100
- Standard & Poor's 500
- New York Stock Exchange
- Russell 2000
- NASDAQ 100
- Value Line

Stock-index options allow you to trade on overall market movements in the same way you trade on movements of individual stocks. If you are bullish about stock investments, rather than trying to pick which stocks will increase in price, you can buy a call on, say, the S&P 100. Similarly, if you are bearish, you can buy a put.

What do you do if you want to exercise your option? How can you take possession of an index, which is abstract? The answer is simple: you receive cash. In fact, all settlements are in cash. Assume you hold an S&P 500 option with a strike price of 800 and you decide to exercise your option at the time the S&P 500 reaches 850. You will receive a cash payment that equals $100 for every point the index is over the strike price of 800. In this case, this translates to $100 multiplied by 50, or $5,000.

Moreover, one of the big advantages of index options is reducing portfolio risk. If you were going long on a portfolio of, say, all 30 Dow Jones Industrial stocks, buying put contracts on the S&P 100, or any index that is closely

associated with these Dow 30 stocks, would be a good strategy. The same would hold if you were selling short, only this time you would want to buy calls.

SOME THINGS TO AVOID

You should avoid at least three things: speculating with out-of-the-money options, speculating in short-term options, and going naked.

- **Avoid speculating with out-of-the-money options.** Speculating with out-of-the-money options is not likely to get the average investor (most investors) very far. Although they are cheaper than in-the-money options, they tend to be riskier, and in many cases, much more so. The reason the price is cheaper is because the odds of the underlying stock price reaching the level at which it is equal to the strike price are low. Thus, the odds are against you, especially with short-term options.

Returning to the illustration involving Pfizer, the premium for the call contract at a strike price of $35 and due to expire in April of 2003—at the time of this writing, about one month—was about $0.10. At first glance, this might seem like a steal, but actually it is not. Barring some major and unexpected breakthrough in drug development, it is highly unlikely that the stock price would have time to move significantly higher than its current price, at the time, about $32. Note the word "unexpected." It is difficult to defend an option-picking, and ultimately stock-picking, strategy based on unsystematic events.

- **Avoid speculating in short-term options.** Your options may be in the money but you are not giving them enough time to earn profits. Unless an unusual and unexpected event comes along, it is very unlikely that you will be able to profit from these moves.

For example, you might be guessing that a company's earnings per share are going to be disappointing to most investors. The announcement of the earnings is due in two weeks, so you purchase short-term puts on the company. The company's performance indeed turns out to be disappointing, but the CEO assures that the problem is short-term and that the company will do well in coming quarters. As a result, the stock price does not drop much, and you are left with either selling the options at a loss or waiting to see if there is a movement in stock price that might help you eke out a small profit—an unlikely scenario.

- **Avoid naked options.** These are some of the highest-risk investments that you will encounter. They are only for the most risk-tolerant investors. To repeat, writing naked calls subjects you to the possibility that you will have to buy instantly into a loss. Writing naked puts may mean you have to come face to face with shares that are not worth very much.

SUMMARY

Although the world of options may sound complex, for our purposes, it is about one thing: reducing risk. To reiterate, options are contracts that give you the right, but not the obligation, to buy or sell stock. Whether the strategy is to protect your profits or to help reduce the risk of an aggressive position, there are numerous simple and sophisticated ways to help you do this.

The workhorses in the options area are calls and puts. Calls allow you to "call in," or buy, shares from another investor. Puts allow you to "put" your shares, or sell them, to another investor.

On one side of the table are investors who want to reduce their investment risk. They buy puts and calls to hedge their risks. On the other side are investors who think that these investors may have underestimated their positions. They buy puts and calls for speculative purposes.

If you are an index investor, you can buy index options, whether for hedging or speculative purposes. The big difference between a stock option and an index option is that all index options are settled in cash.

As some guidelines for pricing options, bear in mind that the premium will rise the deeper in the money the option, the more time left before expiration, the more volatile the underlying security, and the higher the price of the underlying security.

COMMODITIES

Commodities are the raw materials used to produce a wide variety of everyday products. Just a few examples include barley and bran, beef and pork, corn oil and lard, cotton and wool, aluminum and copper, and silver and gold. Trading commodities affects each one of us every day, because the prices determined in the trading pits affect our daily cost of living. For example, as car and truck drivers know well, fluctuations in the world price of oil determine how much they pay for gasoline at the pump. Similarly, as farmers know, the price of corn affects how much we pay for bacon—hogs eat corn—and breakfast cereals at the supermarket.

Although commodities sound easier to understand than stocks, bonds, and options, they are not less risky. As you read this chapter, you will find that they tend to be more risky than most other securities. Trading them is fast-paced, carried on mainly by professionals. Individual investors play in these markets, but not many survive. So if you are not risk-tolerant, investing in commodities is probably not for you.

Although you may not hear much about commodities, they are traded worldwide, even more so than the stocks of U.S. corporations or bonds issued by the U.S. Treasury. The price

for one ounce of gold may be quoted on the Commodity Exchange (COMEX) in New York, but every trader in the pit keeps an eye on prices in London, Geneva, and Hong Kong. The point is that there are no isolated commodity markets; commodities affect everyone, so you will benefit from knowing how these markets work, whether you invest in them or sit on the sidelines.

There are actually two commodities markets: the *spot market*, also known as the cash market, and the *futures market*. We'll begin the discussion with the spot market.

THE SPOT MARKET: CASH ON THE SPOT

To glean something about the spot market, let us turn to agriculture and assume a miller buys 5,000 bushels of wheat to be processed into flour. He buys on the spot market, so-called because the transaction is settled on the spot. In other words, the miller arranges for delivery of 5,000 bushels of wheat at today's price. By the way, 5,000 bushels is considered to be one contract, similar to 100 shares making up one call/put option (from Chapter 5). Here are some examples of commodity contracts:

- Coffee: 37,500 pounds
- Cotton: 50,000 pounds
- Frozen orange juice: 15,000 pounds
- Gasoline: 42,000 gallons

- Lumber: 110,000 board feet
- Pork bellies: 40,000 pounds
- Soybean meal: 100 tons
- Sugar: 112,000 pounds

The reason for these large numbers is because it is not profitable to trade a few bushels, a few gallons, or a few pounds at a time. Thus, the contracts are in terms of large quantities of each commodity. Incidentally, various exchanges handle certain commodities. As a guide, we have the following:

- **Chicago Board of Trade**: Corn, oats, soybeans, soybean oil, soybean meal, and wheat

- **Chicago Mercantile Exchange**: Cattle, hogs, pork bellies, lumber, and dairy products

- **Cocoa, Sugar, and Coffee Exchange**: Cocoa, sugar, and coffee

- **New York Commodity Exchange**: Gold and silver

- **New York Mercantile Exchange**: Crude oil, heating oil, gasoline, natural gas, platinum, and propane

Back to the miller. How much does he pay for the wheat? The price, based on the listing at the Chicago Board of Trade, depends on how much wheat is available (i.e., supply) and how much the miller and all the other users of wheat want to buy (i.e., demand). In early 2003, $3.50 per bushel was a going rate. The factors that determine the price will change minute by minute, according to the weather, politics, currency exchange values, and an almost limitless number of other variables. Prices represent the sum total of all opinions from both sides of market, the buyers and sellers. If you are a seller, the higher the price, the better. Conversely, as a buyer, the lower the price, the better. The so-called clearing price, where the exchange takes place, will be somewhere in between a very high price and a very low one.

To give you an analogy, the spot market is like a loading dock, a place where goods are picked up and delivered. For example, if you are interested in hogs, you could pick up some pork bellies (which are, literally, the bellies of hogs) to make bacon. With the rest of the hog, you could make hams and pork loins. All three parts of the hog are traded on the spot market. If your interest lies elsewhere, say in gold, you would not have a lot to pick up, because gold is indeed a rare material. Even more rare—about ten times so—is platinum, which is why these metals are considered "precious" and why their price per ounce is so high. Although a huge volume of business takes place on the spot markets, these transactions have little appeal to the investor looking for action. That is found in the commodity futures markets.

THE FUTURES MARKET: THE CRYSTAL-BALL APPROACH TO INVESTING

As the word "futures" indicates, this market involves the trading of commodities to be delivered at a future date but at a specified price determined today. This is called a *futures contract*. It is akin to an options contract but with one major difference: an options contract does not obligate you to make or take delivery, whereas a futures contract does. Delivery, though, rarely occurs because investors liquidate their holdings before delivery by arranging an offsetting transaction. The offset means that the investor offsets whatever was the beginning position—a buy with a sell, or a sell with a buy.

Commodity futures began as an effort to reduce the buyer's risk of having to deal with wide swings in raw materials prices. Before futures contracts were invented, buyers and seller used (and still use) *forward contracts*, which are created when you buy a commodity— or any asset—for future delivery. The price at the time of delivery is fixed, but you do not have to pay for the items until they are delivered. Everything is negotiated—price, quantity, quality, location, and date of delivery—to meet the needs of both the buyer and seller. Thus, each forward contract is unique.

Futures are one step better than forward contracts because they are standardized to increase liquidity, which enhances their marketability. Because they are marketable, futures are traded on exchanges. Futures allow buyers to reduce (or hedge) their risk, as in the options market (covered in Chapter 5). Futures are not a means to generate profits as much as a recipe to avoid continually having to pay higher-than-expected prices for commodities.

Returning for a moment to the example on wheat, the miller knows the price at the moment—$3.50—but not what it will be in, say, six months. For example, it might be $4. Although an increase of $0.50 does not sound like much, you have to remember to consider the high volume, meaning, in this case, that $0.50 represents an increase of $2,500:

$$\$4 \times 5,000 \text{ bushels} = \$20,000$$
$$\$3.50 \times 5,000 \text{ bushels} = \$17,500$$
$$\$20,000 - \$17,500 = \$2,500$$

In percentage terms, this increase is 14%. (This increase in price is called a premium because the price exceeds the spot price.) If the miller is unable to raise the price of flour by at least this much, then this period's profits will suffer; in fact, the profits in the previous period, when the price was $3.50, might well turn to losses in the next period. However, if the price per bushel drops, the miller could reap big profits, depending on the price he and the baker, to whom he sells the flour, agreed on.

Millers, and most commodity users, prefer not to engage in the business of guessing what might happen to the price of wheat. They are in the business of producing flour, not in predicting prices. So they hedge against the risk of rising commodity prices. The miller first buys a futures contract, one good for 5,000 bushels of wheat to be delivered in six months. When the six months are up, the miller enters the spot market and buys 5,000 bushels of wheat. He also sells a contract to close out his "buy" position in the futures market, in effect, canceling out his original buy contract.

Does the miller gain or lose? If the spot price for the wheat is higher than he expected, he *loses* because he pays more for the grain than he anticipated. Offsetting the higher price, however, just like in the case of options, he *profits* from an equal rise in the value of the contract he bought six months previously. The value of the contract rises because the price of wheat rises. Thus, he *breaks even* on the cost of the wheat he needs to produce flour. Here is the illustration in numbers. Assume the miller buys a futures contract for $3.50 per bushel, but the cash price six months from now rises to $4 per bushel, with the futures price increasing to $4.25 per bushel:

• **Current date**: Buy futures contract at $3.50/bushel.

• **Six months later**: Cash price at $4/bushel and futures price at $4.25 bushel. Sell futures contract at $4.25/bushel and collect profit of $0.75/bushel, or $4.25/bushel minus $3.50/bushel.

• **Profit**: Cash price paid is $4/bushel, $0.50 more than expected. Total gain from hedging: $0.25/bushel, or $0.75/bushel minus $0.50/bushel (assuming no commission costs) multiplied by 5,000 bushels, or $1,250.

Without the hedge, the miller would have been forced to pay $2,500 more than expected, or $0.50 multiplied by 5,000 bushels. The illustration shows how the miller can hedge, or reduce, the risk of facing higher future cash prices for wheat.

Growers also use futures to hedge and reduce their risks. A farmer may sell wheat three, six, or more months ahead of harvest. When he sees a future price that he likes, he can lock in a profit by agreeing to sell his crop at the future price after harvest. He gives up the prospect of selling at an even higher price than the current quoted price for future delivery, but he gains the security of knowing that his wheat will bring a known price and a known profit.

Investing—or Speculating—in Futures Markets

So far, all we have discussed is simple stuff on spot and futures markets. Where does the investor fit in? In the futures market, whereas the growers and producers are the hedgers, the investor is the *speculator*, betting that the hedgers have miscalculated futures prices—whether up or down does not matter. At the outset, there are three things to keep in mind:

• **As a speculator, you have no interest in using the commodities.** You are interested in the market solely because you stand

the chance of earning a fortune (or losing your shirt).

• **Do not underestimate the chance that you could lose big.** Commodity speculators are probably the biggest risk takers of all investors. This is because, as a speculator, you might encounter any of a number of significant, negative, unpredictable events, from unexpected labor problems to unforeseen weather conditions and political instability.

• **Without you and other speculators, the futures market would not exist.** This is because the hedgers would have no one on whom to *lay off*, or transfer, risks.

When speculating on commodities, you can do the same things you do when trading stocks. You can "go long" or "sell short" (as defined in Chapter 2: either "buy low, sell high" or "sell high, buy low"). The process begins by your establishing a margin account, which allows you to borrow money, with a specialized broker who holds a commodities trading license.

You enter an order to enter into a contract, either as a buyer or as a seller, depending on whether you think market prices are headed up or down. The cost of the contract is minimal. You might pay $500 for the right to take a contract for $10,000 on a commodity. The $500 is called the margin, which is essentially a good-faith deposit. It equals the sum of the cash, highly liquid securities (such as U.S. Treasury bills), and the net "paper profits" (gains minus losses on assets you have not sold). This is known as *leverage*, which means using a little bit of money for the chance of earning large profits.

You will be charged interest on money you borrow from the brokerage firm at a rate known as the broker loan rate. For example, if you intend to buy one contract of wheat for delivery at some specified future date, you are pursuing the strategy of "buy low, sell high," which is the buyer's position.

In commodities trading many traders sell short. They sell contracts with the expectation of closing them out at lower prices before delivery of wheat or other commodities. For example, a trader who sells wheat short at $3.50 per bushel will profit by buying a closing contract for $3.30 per bushel, a profit of $0.20 per bushel.

How Commodities Trading Works

For each contract you commit to, you pay into your commodity trading account an *initial margin*. If you buy two contracts for wheat, using the numbers from our earlier example, you would put up $1,000, as each contract requires a margin of $500. Your broker then contacts the company's representative on the trading floor of, in this case, the Chicago Board of Trade. Your order is sent to a broker in the trading pit. The trading pit is an octagonally shaped series of stepped ramps that permit each broker to see all the other brokers. If you have seen a trading pit either from the observation window of the visitors gallery or on television, the action appears to be totally chaotic, with traders' arms extended as they shout almost continuously, offering to buy or sell contracts. The shouting is really part of a system called *open outcry*, in which voice bids are confirmed by hand signals, shown in Exhibit 6–1.

As chaotic as it appears, the functions of the traders are actually well organized and highly efficient. The trader who receives your order searches by eye and voice for an offsetting

offer at a mutually agreeable price. Verbal agreements are then confirmed with any of a variety of hand signals. Hand signals assure accuracy, as voice contact is difficult in the hubbub of the pit. Each hand signal represents a specific number that communicates the number of contracts and the price, and traders abbreviate totals to speed things up. The pit trader records the number of contracts, delivery month, price, the number of the clearing firm represented by the pit trader, who is the principal for the opposing trade, and a notation of the time.

Your order, and all others, go to the Clearing Corporation of the Chicago Board of Trade. The Clearing Corporation functions as a huge middleman that helps clear what would otherwise be a really unwieldy market. Think of it this way: at a ballgame, the concession stand helps to serve as a clearinghouse that enables you to buy, for example, the number of hot dogs and drinks that you want. Without the concession stand, you run the risk of having an imbalance between the two: either too many hot dogs per drink or too many drinks per hot dog.

The Clearing Corporation settles the account of each member firm at the end of each trading day by balancing commodities bought with those sold. It also marks to market each of the outstanding positions at the end of the day. When something is *marked to market*, that means that each contract is revalued to the closing price. If the price of wheat went up two cents, then all contracts for wheat are revalued upward by two cents. The Clearing Corporation collects from those traders who have lost during the day and credits the accounts of those traders who have gained. Thus, on the opening of the market the next day, all accounts are cleared and trading begins afresh.

EXHIBIT 6–1. HAND SIGNALS USED TO CONFIRM VOICE BIDS

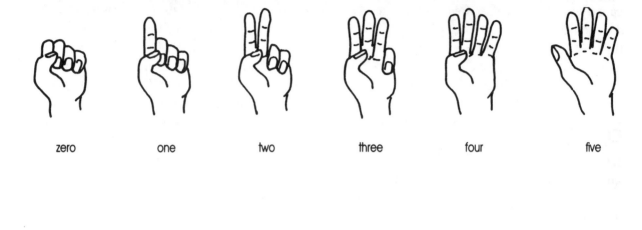

zero   one   two   three   four   five

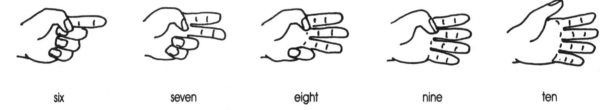

six   seven   eight   nine   ten

Hand signals are used to confirm voice bids in the open outcry system. A bid of $3.21 would be signaled by a sequence of hand signals for the numbers 3, 2, and 1.

The Clearing Corporation maintains tight control over margins as prices fluctuate to make sure enough money remains on hand at all times to assure that contracts will be settled. If your trade shows a decline in price, your broker may contact you, asking you to put up more margin. Instead of putting up more cash, you have the option of entering an offsetting trade to cancel your position, but this would create a loss for you.

The trading floor of the Chicago Board of Trade also functions as an information center. Any information that could affect the prices of commodities is displayed on the trading floor on reader boards or computer screens. Such information may include:

- Weather reports from growing regions

- Market reports from exchanges in other parts of the United States or in other countries

- Crop estimates from the U.S. Department of Agriculture

- Reports of commodities in storage carried over from a previous harvest

- Other similar news that could affect traders' perceptions of future price movements

Although prices appear on quotation boards within sight of the pit traders, the commodities exchange itself takes no action to influence prices. These prices constitute the market, and they are flashed to floor traders and to other markets within and outside the United States. A trade at a higher price is called an *uptick*; a trade at a lower price is called a *downtick*. Many farmers receive price quotations via radio or by computer through modems and cable connections.

COMMODITIES SPECULATION IS RISKY BUSINESS—BUT WITH RISK COMES REWARD

As mentioned, commodities speculators are faced with some of the biggest risks of all investors. The risks can be many times greater than trading stocks, which generally carry a risk index of around 20. For example, between 1996 and 2003, the risk index of gold was about 185, or nine times that of stocks. Unfortunately, the index price of gold dropped over this period from about 133 to 54, a loss of about 12% per year. It is little wonder, then, that the majority of trading accounts do not make much money. In fact, theoretically, the commodities trading market represents what some call a "zero-sum game." For every dollar gained, a dollar is lost. Winners can come out with a profit of $1 only if a loser sustains a $1 loss, and this assumes a "commissionless" world. With unavoidable commission costs on both the buy and sell sides, the outcome is a negative-sum game, in that winners win by the amount losers lose, plus commissions.

And commissions are not cheap. A full-service broker may charge between $50 and $60 for each contract on a round-trip trade, that is, a buy followed by an offsetting sell, or a short sale followed by an offsetting buy. Round-trip trades are typical because nearly all trades are offset to avoid the problems of actually delivering 5,000 bushels of wheat or some

other commodity. A full-service broker can help a new investor get started by offering advice, expertise, and education; but keep in mind that most full-service brokers are salespeople first. Investors pay for this support with higher commissions.

Discount brokers may charge $20 to $30 for each contract on a round-trip. Thus, to reduce commission costs, traders actively seek out discount brokers to handle trades. However, discount brokers cannot give investment advice, so only seasoned traders should use discount brokers.

Commission caveats in mind, the bottom line is that successful trades can produce huge returns. For example, you might speculate on a $10,000 contract with as little as $500, which is a margin of 5% on a $10,000 contract (0.05 multiplied by $10,000). If the contract price increases to $11,000, your position has now improved by $1,000, or $11,000 minus $10,000. The gain of $1,000 might not sound like a lot, but bear in mind that you only put up $500. Wouldn't you like to begin with $500 and end up, say, three months later, with $1,500, or $500 plus $1,000? This is a return of 200%, which is terrific. That said, earning such returns depends on two criteria: coming up with a successful plan and having the perseverance to stick to it. Neither one is easy.

What is easy—but should be avoided—is trading on emotion, which includes relying on hot tips to using a variety of appealing but untested techniques (and in some cases, tested techniques that have no potential). Probably the biggest mistake investors make, especially those just starting out, is trading too often and with too little money. In addition, it is easy, in the heat of the moment, to lose your composure and decide to make a big bet.

Either way, you might lose. If your bet is wrong, you lose your money, and even if you are right, you win big, and probably set yourself up for an even bigger loss down the road when another appealing opportunity presents itself. In any event, you need to begin with at least $10,000—preferably much more than that—because you want to give yourself as much cushion as possible to handle unexpected price movements.

If you are interested in commodity trading, you will probably want to check the Goldman Sachs Commodity Index. As of early 2003, it was made up of:

• Six energy components, comprising about 68%

• Nine agricultural products, comprising about 17%

• Three livestock components, comprising about 7%

• Five industrial metals, comprising about 6%

• Two precious metals, comprising about 2%

Between 1998 and early 2003, the index had doubled in value, from about 125 to 250, a gain of about 16% per year, with a risk not much different from that of stocks, given the diversified commodities components.

There are strategies to reduce risk. One is called spread trading, which is similar to the straddle position in options. In this case, you attempt to take advantage of different markets or different products. Spread trading calls for simultaneously buying one contract and selling another contract related to the first. For example, you might buy one wheat contract (e.g., 5,000 bushels) for September at $3.58 per bushel and sell a December

wheat contract for $3.61. That difference is known as the spread.

Several weeks later, the price for September wheat may have risen to $3.64, and December wheat to $3.64. This strategy is known as a time spread. Thus, you stand to gain $0.06 per bushel on the September contract and to lose $0.03 per bushel on the December contract for an overall profit of $0.03 per bushel, or $150 ($0.03 times 5,000 bushels) on one contract, minus commissions. In a spread, a trader usually wins on one contract and loses on the other. The speculator profits when the amount gained on the win exceeds the loss, plus commissions.

There are also spreads across commodities, akin to diversification. They involve buying a contract for one grain (for example, wheat) while simultaneously selling a contract for a different grain (such as corn). The trader attempts to profit from different price movements of the different grains. In addition, the differing expiration dates may add another degree of risk reduction.

BEING ARTFUL ABOUT INVESTMENTS

We need to take a quick tour of investments in the art world, perhaps better categorized as "collectibles," from antiques and one-of-a-kind cars to fancy jewelry, rare paintings, and sculptures. At first glance, the performance of eBay (the Internet-based company that serves as a clearinghouse for collectibles) should be enough to get you interested, if you are not already. eBay's stock price has increased, between late 1998 and early 2003, by more than 70% per year—this is a phenomenal rate of return. Sotheby's, an upscale and well-known auction house in New York City, also has its own Website that you can search: http://search.sothebys.com.

Tempting as this realm of investments might be, however, the best advice is to look before you leap. Consider:

• Are you interested in the item?

• Is there a market for the item?

• What will you do if it does not sell?

• Does it require special storage?

• Does it require insurance?

The first question is really getting at two things: your knowledge of the item and its usefulness. For example, diamonds may be a girl's best friend, but what do you really know about them? Do you know how diamonds are cut and how that can affect their value? Do you know how to value a diamond?

You might be holding a one-of-a-kind fishing lure or a pro football helmet in mint condition, but the market for those items may be quite thin. Likewise, things like Beanie Babies, pet rocks, and Pokemon have faddish appeal, but have generally no inherent long-term value. So if you buy when the fad is fading, you may get stuck with something you have no use for. And things like special furniture, rare automobiles, and unusual paintings may require storage and insurance costs that eat away at possible returns.

A variety of collectibles, such as coins, stamps, antiques, and the like, tend to have return and risk profiles similar to those found in other commodities. Simply put, investments

in collectibles are risky. As a result, if you are at least moderately risk-averse, you need to be especially careful about investing in them.

SOME THINGS TO AVOID

If you are risk-averse to any significant degree, you should avoid investing in commodities. It is not for the cash-poor, either. Even if you have a lot of cash, do not be tempted to make big bets, even in the precious metals market. In addition, your cash position may enable you to buy rare and expensive artwork and various collectibles, but make sure you enjoy these items, too, because they do not usually have return and risk features that can compete with stocks and bonds.

• **Avoid speculating if you're risk-averse.** If you are even moderately risk-averse, investing in commodities and futures contracts is not for you. Review your responses to the quiz in Chapter 1. Consider investing in this area only if you get a high score. As a rule, if stock investing makes you nervous, then investing in commodities and options, with initial margins, will likely make you a nervous wreck.

• **Avoid speculating if you're cash-poor.** Some investment guides say you need a minimum of $10,000 to play the commodities and futures market. We think you need ten times this amount! Fortunes are won and lost on big bets here, because the markets are quite volatile.

• **Avoid making big bets.** First study these markets carefully to identify a profitable method—which in and of itself is no easy task. If and when you find one, stick to it, and try to avoid big bets. It is easy to get caught up in the emotion of a sudden and unexpected market movement, up or down. Suddenly, you might find yourself with the opportunity to make a big move, one that may not be in line with your trading strategy. Avoid this move. Even if it turns out to be profitable, it will tempt you the next time it is available. Keep in mind the fable of the hare versus the tortoise. Being a tortoise in the futures market is still fast-paced.

- **Avoid investing in precious metals.** All that glitters is not necessarily gold. Beware of loading up on gold and precious metals as investments. For example, gold may have a natural value, and it is a beautiful metal, but it does not provide good returns. The only time gold and other precious metals tend to be good investments is during inflation and political turmoil. Given that paper assets (especially bonds) have uncertain values during times of jumps in prices, and when the geopolitical landscape appears increasingly confrontational and combative, investors naturally gravitate toward hard assets with intrinsic values. Investors in gold stand to benefit. But such events tend to be aberrations. For example, between 1981 and 2001, while stocks and bonds earned annual returns averaging about 15% and 12%, respectively, gold lost 1.8%.

- **Avoid investing in too many collectibles.** The risk is not for the faint of heart in this investment arena. Make sure you enjoy your collections, rather than considering collectibles as something that can compete on a return-to-risk basis with bonds and stocks. Moreover, collectibles may not be the inflation hedge that investors think. In addition, you face the added risk of buying a fake or a forgery.

SUMMARY

Commodities are the raw materials—from grains to precious metals—used to produce many everyday items. They actively trade in markets around the world. Although the rates of return from investing in commodities can be high, so can the risks. Simply put, trading commodities is not for the faint of heart. It is not uncommon for most commodities traders to lose money. So if you decide to invest in commodities, proceed with extreme caution.

FINANCIAL FUTURES

If you understand options and commodities, which we covered in Chapters 5 and 6, then you are ready for *financial futures*. Like options, financial futures are derivatives. Thus, they are contracts, but their focus is not on individual stocks, as discussed in Chapter 5, but on currencies, stock market indices, and interest rates (which also encompass bond market indices). That is the extent of the difference. Otherwise their purpose is the same: to reduce risk. Risk-averse investors attempt to lay off risk to speculators who are searching for big investment gains (i.e., rates of return). These speculators are betting that they can squeeze some profits from the actions of risk-averse investors.

CURRENCY FUTURES

A currency, of course, represents a nation's money. It is separated into two groups, hard and soft:

- A hard currency—such as the U.S. dollar, the euro, and the Japanese yen—is readily converted to other currencies.

- A soft currency—such as Thailand's baht or the Brazilian real—is not.

Hard currencies trade around the world, and they change in value relative to each other all the time.

Many forces can affect currency value, but they are reflected in terms of supply and demand. For instance, because the United States, as a result of its huge appetite for oil and the goods of other countries, ran negative trade balances for years, many U.S. dollars ended up in foreign hands. The payment for Middle East oil, in particular, helped spawn a dollar-type currency known as the *eurodollar*, which is a dollar-denominated deposit in a bank outside the United States. In fact, the U.S. dollar is a means for all countries to pay for Middle East oil.

The fluctuations in currency values have major implications for countries. For example, during the early 1990s, the sheer volume of U.S. dollars held in various banks, investment companies, and in individual accounts outside the United States depressed the price of the dollar compared to most world currencies. This made investing in the U.S. dollar relatively cheap. A good example of this can be found in the actions of Japanese investors. From the mid-1980s until the early 1990s, the yen made tremendous strides against the U.S. dollar, from 250 yen per dollar to less than 100 yen. This gain in the yen paved the way for Japanese investment in the stocks, bonds, and real estate of the United States.

As this was occurring, there was tremendous speculation among traders in both currencies.

Some were betting that the yen would continue gaining; others bet the opposite. In addition, speculation was rampant as to when the respective central banks in each country would intervene and try to stem the dollar's fall. To do this, the Federal Reserve System would enter into the currency markets and buy U.S. dollars with yen. As it did so, the value of the dollar would strengthen somewhat against the yen.

From the preceding discussion, it should be easy to see where you can earn profits. If you thought the yen would continue to strengthen, you would hold your position or even add to it. If not, then you would sell your position. For example, if you bought $10,000 worth of yen at 120 yen per dollar, you would be holding 1.2 million yen:

$$\$10,000 \times 120 \text{ yen per dollar}$$
$$= 1.2 \text{ million yen}$$

If you bet that the exchange rate would fall to 100 yen per dollar, and it did, then you would be able to exchange 1 million yen for your original $10,000 and have another 200,000 yen left over. Converting these yen to dollars would give you another $2,000:

$$200,000 \text{ yen} \div 100 \text{ yen per dollar}$$

Thus, your profit would have been $2,000, minus conversion fees.

Why Invest in Currency Futures?

Where do futures fit in the topic of currencies? Although currencies are never consumed like wheat, corn, and pork bellies, fluctuations in their values can make trading goods in other countries risky. Just like the miller buying wheat, if you have to buy raw materials and other inputs from other countries (as many

must do), and you fear having to pay higher prices in the future, you will want to hedge your risk. It also works from the other direction. If you sell products to other countries, you fear that your home currency might change adversely against the foreign currency, thereby sapping your profits.

An example will clarify this. Assume you are employed by Coca-Cola to sell beverages in European markets. Because the company is based in the United States, the sales you generate in euros, for example, have to be converted to dollars so that they match the company's U.S. sales. Your next major delivery is scheduled three months from now, but you are concerned that the value of the dollar against the euro could change significantly. If the euro declines, more euros would be required in the conversion to dollars, reducing—perhaps even wiping out—your profits. This is called *foreign currency exchange risk*, and it makes managers nervous and shareholders jittery.

To protect the company's profits, you can use a futures contract. By agreeing to sell euros (which is the same as taking a short position) at a specified date, called the *settlement date*, you will protect your profits in the event that the euro declines against the dollar, not unlike a put contract on stock that you own. Of course, some profit will be lost to commission costs, but this is a small price to pay for a good night's rest.

Euro futures are primarily traded on the Chicago Mercantile Exchange. As with bushels of wheat, gallons of gasoline, and pounds of sugar, standard contract specifications exist. Here are the standard contract specifications, or trading units, for seven currencies:

Brazilian real	100,000
Canadian dollar	100,000
Euro	125,000
E-mini euro	62,500
Japanese yen	12,500,000
Mexican peso	500,000
Swiss franc	125,000

International currency futures may also include groups of currencies. Perhaps the most well known is the United States Dollar Index. It consists of the following seven currencies: Australian dollar, Canadian dollar, euro, pound sterling, Swedish krona, Swiss franc, and the yen. The index is constructed such that as the U.S. dollar appreciates, the index rises. As a result, a position that is long means that the foreign currencies will decline if the dollar appreciates; hence, you will need a long position in the dollar index futures contract to hedge the risk. This position is sometimes referred to as a long-long hedge, and it may be used by both firms and investors exposed to foreign currency exchange risk.

As always, when one group is hedging, another is speculating. As an example of speculating, let us say you are bullish on the euro against the U.S. dollar. In other words, you expect the euro to appreciate against the dollar. So you buy one contract at the market price of, say, $1.0613 per euro. One month later, let us say that your bet is right, and the value is at $1.0763 per euro. (Note that it now costs *more* to convert dollars to euros, which implies that the euro has appreciated.) This moves you to close out your position by selling your contract. Your profit is $0.015, or $1.0763 minus $1.0613. Given the contract size of 125,000 euros, your total profit is: $0.015 times 125,000, or $1,875, minus commission costs.

If your initial margin was 5%, or about $6,633 (which is 5% of $1.0613 × 125,000), your return would be about 28% in one month, or $1,875 divided by $6,633.

You can find up-to-the-minute information on currencies from your broker or from various Internet sources. Daily currency quotes are also available in *The Wall Street Journal* and *The Financial Times*. When following the quotes, note the words *open interest*. They refer to the number of futures contracts, or any options contracts for that matter, that are traded but not yet liquidated. An illustration of the euro compared to the dollar, as represented in financial newspapers, is provided in Exhibit 7–1.

EXHIBIT 7–1. EURO/U.S. DOLLAR: E125,000—DOLLAR PER EURO

	Open	High	Low	Settle	Chg	Open Int
June	1.07	1.072	1.069	1.071	0.002	60,000
Sept	1.09	1.093	1.087	1.059	0.007	2,600

Here's how to read the information provided in Exhibit 7–1. The title identifies the size of the contract—125,000 euros—and the price in terms of U.S. dollars. The first line of the table indicates the previous day's opening price, the high, the low, the settle/close price, the change, and the open interest. For June contracts, the opening price was $1.07 per euro, with a daily high of $1.072 and low of $1.069. The settle price, or the representative price around the close, was $1.071. The daily change was $0.002. Finally, the number of outstanding contracts was 60,000. September's numbers were very similar, except the number of outstanding contracts—at 2,600—was much smaller. These numbers provide you with a rough guide to help you understand tracking currency trading.

STOCK INDEX AND INTEREST RATE FUTURES: FOR INVESTORS WHO APPRECIATE INTANGIBLES

In addition to currency futures, there are stock indices and interest rate futures. Portfolio managers (including managers of stock portfolios, mutual funds, pensions, and bond funds) use them to hedge (i.e., reduce) risks. To explain, a portfolio manager may own shares of many companies that are part of the S&P 500 Index. To hedge the risk of a major loss in portfolio value (such as the one that occurred in September 2001 and in September 2002), the portfolio manager may sell S&P futures contracts. (The value of these contracts rises as the S&P 500 falls.) In the event that the S&P 500 declines, and with it the value of the portfolio, the loss is offset (at least partially) by the now-higher value of the S&P 500 futures contracts.

The next two sections of this chapter first take a closer look at stock index futures and then interest rate futures.

Stock Index Futures: What Does the Crystal Ball Reveal?

As we saw in Chapter 2, there are many different indices that measure movements of the stock markets, from the Dow Jones Industrial Average (which is really not an index and which tracks only 30 stocks) to the S&P 500 (with 500 stocks) to the Russell 2000 (with 2,000 stocks). To determine the price of a financial futures stock index, you need to multiply the index in question by one of the following numbers: 1, 5, 10, 20, 50, 100, 250, 500, or 1,000. For example, if it is the Dow Jones, the multiple is 10; if it is the S&P 500, the multiple is 250; if it is the Russell 2000, it is 500.

The most popular index in the world is the S&P 500. Investors use it in three ways: to hedge, speculate, and arbitrage. We've already discussed hedging and speculating; *arbitrage* is a profit arising usually from going long and selling short at the same time on the same investment. Unlike a commodity, which is tangible and deliverable, a stock index future is not. Thus, a stock index future is settled in cash.

Hedging. As an example of hedging, let us say you are holding a portfolio of ten stocks, each of which closely tracks the S&P 500. The stocks that belong to the Dow Jones Industrials, for example, are usually part of the S&P 500. You are concerned about an upcoming economics report on the strength of the U.S. economy. To protect your portfolio from a drop in the market, you decide to sell short S&P 500 index futures equal to the value of your portfolio. This move is sometimes called a *futures overlay*. Assume now that your fears are realized: the report indicates that economic growth is slipping. Consequently, the S&P 500 drops from, say, 850 to 824.5 (i.e., a drop of 3%), leading to a loss in your portfolio of almost 4%. (Note that your portfolio contains only ten stocks, so, because of its small size, it tends to be more sensitive to market movements than the S&P 500.) As this loss occurred, however, the value of your S&P 500 futures index increased by 3%, helping to stem your loss. You close out the futures position and take your gains, minus commission costs.

Alternatively, could you sell your stocks, take your gains, and get right back into the market as soon as it improves? Yes, of course, but it might not have the intended outcome. First, market timing is difficult. If the economic report turns out to be better than you expected, the market might jump, and you would lose out on a profitable opportunity. Second, because of brokerage commissions and taxes, frequent trading of stocks tends to be less profitable than you might think.

But let us say you were betting that the economic report would be more positive than hedgers expected, which would tend to pull up the S&P 500 over 850, or that it would be more negative, shoving it below 824.5. This is to say that you may go either long or short, depending on your perception of the market:

- If you buy a *long* futures contract, you expect the market to rise. At some future time, you hope to close out your position at a higher price and pocket a profit.

- If you sell a futures contract *short*, such as when you hedged your portfolio, you expect the market to decline. Later, you expect to buy back the S&P 500 futures contract at a lower price and pocket the difference.

Speculating. As a speculator, because the S&P 500 tracks the overall stock market so closely, you may effectively buy the market by investing in S&P 500 futures contracts. Instead of tracking individual stocks (such as the ten stocks in the hedging example), you track the S&P 500, which is a measure of the overall market. At the same time, the small amount of initial margin required, which is about 3% of a contract's value, helps keep you liquid.

To participate in the S&P 500 futures market, you would first need to set up a trading account with a broker, one who specializes in financial futures. You must deposit cash or cash-equivalent securities, such as U.S. Treasury bills (T-bills), in the account as a margin (that is, as a good-faith deposit guaranteeing performance). Most traders elect to deposit readily marketable securities

(such as U.S. Treasury bills) because they continue to earn interest, which cash on deposit does not.

The price at the time you buy or sell a contract is known as the entry price. At the end of the day, the contract will be marked to market; that is, it will be adjusted to the closing price of the S&P 500. Your profit or loss will be the difference between your entry price and the closing price each day:

- If the S&P 500 continues to rise from your entry price, you may withdraw cash from the trading account.

- However, if the index *declines* and the value of the contract falls below the margin maintenance level, your broker will call for more margin, in which case you must either deposit more cash in your trading account or liquidate your position at a loss.

Contracts are limited to quarters ending in March, June, September, and December. The last day of trading is the Thursday before the third Friday of each contract month, and settlement is at the opening on Friday. Contracts expiring at the close of the trading quarter may be paid off in cash at the special opening quotation on the Friday after the last day of trading, or they can be rolled over into a new contract at the investor's option.

Returning to the example, suppose you decide to buy one contract at 850. Multiply this by $250 (which, as mentioned, is standard for the S&P 500):

$$850 \times \$250 = \$212,500$$

You promise to pay an initial margin requirement of, say, 3%, indicating that you have to put up $6,375 (which is 3% of $212,500). Assume that the 3% drop does not occur.

Instead, the S&P 500 rises to 860. You give your broker an order to sell your futures contract, which is now worth $250 times 860, or $215,000. Your bet leads to a profit of $2,500, minus commission costs. While $2,500 might not sound like a lot, keep in mind you earned it by putting up only $6,375. Even after accounting for brokerage costs of, say, $100, your $2,400 gain amounts to a return of over 37% (i.e., $2,400 divided by $6,375). Moreover, you earned the return in only a few days. Think about how many investors dream about 37% per year!

Instead of the S&P 500, you could have used a more specialized index. For example, if you felt that technology stocks would be the major beneficiaries of good economic news, you would be better off betting on the NASDAQ 100, which is dominated by big technology companies (such as Intel and Microsoft). Given the volatility inherent in these stocks, on a good day, you could be up more than the ten points registered by the S&P 500, which is a broader based index that is not as "tech-heavy" as the NASDAQ 100. For example, whereas on March 13, 2003, the S&P 500 increased by 3.4%, the NASDAQ increased 5.7%. Moreover, if you feel that the major beneficiaries would be small-cap stocks, then the Russell 2000 (which measures small-cap stock performance) should be your index of choice.

Arbitrage. Essentially, arbitrage is "risk-free" profit. You are simply taking advantage of price disparities. Suppose once again that the S&P 500 is at 850 and that the June futures contract, which is three months later, is at 864. To profit from this difference, as an arbitrageur (as you would be called), you would set up a long position in the S&P 500 by buying the 500 stocks in the same proportions as

represented in the index. Simultaneously, you would go short on the S&P 500 futures contract. These long and short positions lock in the profits equal to the difference between 864 and 850. Moreover, because you would be holding the S&P 500 stocks, you would get the added bonus of the dividends paid by S&P 500 companies.

Be aware, however, that buying all the stocks in the S&P 500 is expensive and costly in terms of brokerage fees. Therefore, you would be better served by going long on the Dow Jones Industrials and selling short the Dow Jones futures contract. Better yet, the Chicago Board of Trade now offers something called mini-Dow contracts, which are half the size of the regular Dow, as well as mini-S&P and mini-NASDAQ futures, which are one-fifth the size of their regular S&P 500 and NASDAQ indices. These futures contracts can help you efficiently manage your cash. Incidentally, by understanding these long-short positions, you can begin to understand a method by which index arbitrageurs execute their trades: *program trading.* As defined by the New York Stock Exchange, it is the simultaneous purchase or sale of at least 15 stocks having a market value of at least $1 million.

In addition to mini-indices, Merrill Lynch has recently developed an index called *TRAKRS.* These are unique futures contracts linked to a broad-based group of stocks, bonds, and currencies that were designed to reduce the perceived complexities of futures trading. You can go long in TRAKRS without having to leverage (or margin) your account. Thus, you need not be concerned with margin calls and their consequences (e.g., having to come up with more cash, being closed out at a loss, etc.) and they require less leverage when shorted. In addition, the multiple on

TRAKRS is $1, so the index is very accessible to individual investors, unlike some of the traditional indices with large multiples. Moreover, if you hold your TRAKRS contract for more than six months, any capital gain will be treated as long term, unlike the twelve-month period for traditional investments.

You can track index futures quotes from a variety of sources, including the financial sections of newspapers and the Internet. Exhibit 7–2 shows an example for the S&P 500 index future.

Here's how to read the information provided in Exhibit 7–2. The first line indicates that the index trades on the Chicago Mercantile Exchange (CME) at a multiple of $250. To clarify, one contract at the June open price of $850.80 was worth:

$$850.80 \times \$250 = \$212,700$$

The high and low prices of the previous day are also shown for June, as well as the approximate closing price. The change indicates the difference from the previous day's settle price. The number of outstanding contracts closes out the line. The next line, for September 2003, gives about the same values, but the number of outstanding contracts is much smaller.

Interest Rate Futures: Your Interest in the Future

Whereas stock index futures are tied to stocks, interest rate index futures are tied to interest-bearing assets (sometimes called fixed-income assets), such as U.S. Treasury bills, U.S. Treasury notes, U.S. Treasury bonds, mortgage-backed bonds, and municipal bonds. In terms of open interest, most of the activity occurs in the following areas:

- Short-term interest rate index futures in the eurodollar market, which deals with dollar-denominated deposits in banks outside the United States

- Long-term interest rate futures in ten-year Treasury notes and U.S. Treasury bonds

U.S. Treasury bill futures contracts have been around since 1976, begun by the International Monetary Market (IMM), which is a division of the Chicago Mercantile Exchange. The purpose, naturally, was to hedge interest rate risks. The 91-day Treasury bill futures contract offers traders an opportunity to buy or sell for future delivery a Treasury bill with 91 days to maturity and a face value of $1 million. The basis for trading is an index that is calculated by subtracting the interest rate from 100. For example, if an interest rate were 3%, then the index would be 97 (100 minus 3).

EXHIBIT 7–2. READING S&P 500 INDEX FUTURES					
S&P 500 Index (CME)—$250 × index					
	Open	High	Low	Settle	Change	Open Interest
June	850.80	859.30	856.00	858.00	660	600,100
Sept	884.50	888.50	861.00	870.00	770	8,250

The same inverse relationship between Treasury bill (or note or bond) price and interest rates holds for interest rate futures:

- If the interest rate on Treasury bills climbs, the price of the Treasury bill futures contract falls.

- When the interest rate falls, the price of the futures contract rises.

The closer to maturity the Treasury bill and its corresponding interest futures contracts get, the closer they become in value. (Recall from Chapter 2 that Treasury bills are sold at a discount; that is, at 3%, you would pay $9,708.74 for a one-year T-bill, which would grow to $10,000.) On the futures' closing date, the futures contract becomes a cash position and the prices of the Treasury bills and the contract are identical. During the interim, changes in the Treasury bill futures contract reflect market interest rate changes and the increasing value of the underlying Treasury bill as it accrues interest.

Although the Federal Reserve System (the nation's central bank) auctions Treasury bills weekly for the U.S. Treasury Department, the futures contracts mature in the contract months of March, June, September, and December. The delivery date is three successive business days, beginning the day after the last day of trading for a specific maturity. Fortunately, brokers dealing with interest rate futures publish a calendar with last trading and delivery dates clearly marked. The overwhelming majority of futures contract traders offset their positions to simplify the transactions, rather than take delivery of the underlying bills, although delivery is possible. Treasury bill futures contracts may run as long as two years to maturity to provide a longer period for hedging.

U.S. Treasury note and bond futures contracts tend to be more complex than their Treasury bill counterparts. Their varying maturities and coupon rates make their pricing more difficult. The Treasury bond futures contract is normally for $100,000 face value (although a smaller one is available from the Commodity Board of Trade) of the bonds. However, the interest rate rule, in which bond prices and interest rates are inversely related, still applies.

Although Treasury note and bond futures contracts are referred to as interest rate futures, this is a misnomer, because the focus is really on the price, not the interest rate. The yield is for reference only. The Chicago Board of Trade uses conversion factors to adjust for differences in maturities and coupon payments. The inverse relationship between a bond's price and the interest rate still holds, however. So if you were to take a long position in a Treasury bond futures contract—say, three months before settlement, with a yield of 4.69%—and the actual yield at time of settlement was 4.37%, you would have made a good decision. The lower yield implies that the price of the Treasury bond has increased, which is exactly what you want when taking a long position.

It is easy to find quotes on Treasury bill, note, and bond interest rate futures, and, in turn, to monitor trading activity. The example shown in Exhibit 7–3 is similar to what you'll find in financial newspapers, such as *The Wall Street Journal*. It includes the listing for both Treasury bonds and Treasury notes:

Here's how to read the information provided in Exhibit 7–3. In the section on Treasury bonds, the top half of the table, the first line shows that the bonds are traded at the Chicago Board of Trade at a contract value of $100,000.

The fractions are in thirty-seconds. Thus, 110-03, which is the opening price for the June contract, is 110 3/32, or 110.09375. Each point is $1,000 of face value, which means that 110.09375 converts to $110,093.75.

In addition to the opening price, the second line also contains the high, low, and closing (settle) price for the previous day, as well as the change and the number of contracts outstanding. At 1/32, note that the change implies 0.03125. Multiplying this number by $1,000 gives the dollar change: $31.25. The third line gives the numbers for September.

As we saw in Chapter 3 on bonds, the Treasury note is very similar to the Treasury bond, differing only in years to maturity. Thus, for the bottom half of the table, the data come from the Chicago Board of Trade, the contract value is $100,000, and the fractions are in thirty-seconds.

Eurodollar futures contracts (which are the "deepest" financial futures contract available) began trading on the International Monetary Exchange in 1981. The contract has maturities that go out as far as ten years, with a face value of $1 million. Contracts mature in March, June, September, and December. The last day of trading is the second London business day prior to the third Wednesday of the delivery month. Because eurodollar deposits cannot be delivered, cash settlements are available unless contracts are offset. Eurodollar futures contracts also trade on the Singapore International Monetary Exchange, permitting trading 24 hours a day. Eurodollar contracts have been so successful that they have been extended to Euro-LIBOR (i.e., the euro), euroswiss, and euroyen. In fact, the eurocurrency contracts have taken considerable market share away from Treasury bills, for two reasons:

EXHIBIT 7–3.   READING THE FUTURES MARKET LISTINGS FOR TREASURY BONDS AND NOTES

Treasury Bonds
(CBT)—$100,000; pts 32nds of 100%

	Open	High	Low	Settle	Change	Open Interest
June	110-03	110-18	110-01	111-11	1	370,450
Sept	110-01	110-14	110-01	110-04	1	22,339

Treasury Notes
(CBT)—$100,000; pts 32nds of 100%

	Open	High	Low	Settle	Change	Open Interest
June	112-18	12-31	12-035	12-175	1.5	748,600
Sept	111-18	111-22	102-18	11-165	2.0	15,844

- Corporate and banking transactions are tied to what is called the *LIBOR*, or the London Interbank Offer Rate, which is a short-term interest rate.

- Unlike Treasury bond futures, Treasury bill futures are rarely used for speculation. The minimum price change, or "tick," for a eurodollar contract is one-fourth of a basis point (i.e., 0.0025), and it equals $6.25. To help you understand how to track trading in Treasury bill and eurodollar futures, Exhibit 7–4 provides representative listings.

Here's how to read the information provided in Exhibit 7–4. The first line of the Treasury bills indicates that you are looking at the three-month bill, traded on the Chicago Mercantile Exchange (CME). The contract value is $1 million and the trades are in basis points, where a basis point is one-hundredth of a point, or 0.01.

The second line gives the typical information: open, high, low, closing price, and change. Remember that the index values are based on 100 minus the interest rate. The line ends with the open interest. The same interpretations apply to the eurodollar.

SOME THINGS TO AVOID

Speculating in financial futures is one of the riskiest moves you can make. In terms of things to avoid, this is one of the most notable. Simply put, do not speculate in these areas unless you are very risk-tolerant. Furthermore, do not invest without a lot of cash and securities; be careful about making bets against the market; beware of precious metals; and stay away from speculating with interest rate futures.

- **Avoid speculating with stock index futures.** Steer clear of stock index futures. To reap gains in this area, you must be adept at predicting market movements. Few investors have this ability.

- **Avoid speculating on interest rate futures.** Like stock market movements, interest rates are tough to predict. Few can do it well. (If you can predict the future of interest rates, you have no need to read this book—unless you're doing so for sheer pleasure.) The only exception is when interest rates appear to be at a historical high or low. For example, back in the early 1980s, Treasury bill rates rose to as high as 15%—an amount way above the

EXHIBIT 7–4.   READING U.S. TREASURY BILL AND EURODOLLAR FUTURES

13-Week Treasury Bills (CME)—$1,000,000; pts of 100

	Open	High	Low	Settle	Change	Open Interest
June	97.90	97.91	97.90	97.90	2.2	2,010

Eurodollar (CME)—$1,000,000; pts of 100%

	Open	High	Low	Settle	Change	Open Interest
June	97.77	97.79	97.75	97.77	2.4	700,518

long-term average of about 3.5%. As another illustration, throughout much of 2002 and 2003, interest rates were very low. Treasury bill yields were around 1.3%; 5-year Treasury note rates were under 3%; and 30-year Treasury bond rates were less than 5%.

When interest rates are high, you would want to buy Treasury futures, because as interest rates eventually fall, the futures price will rise. Depending on the kind of bet you want to make, you could profit handsomely. Conversely, at historically low interest rates, you would want to do the opposite: namely, sell Treasury futures. As interest rates eventually rise, the prices of the Treasuries will fall, leading to some nice profits.

Remember, though, these historical highs and lows are exceptions, not rules. In the end, you would be well advised to shy away from speculating on interest rate futures.

SUMMARY

Financial futures are designed to reduce risk, whether in currencies, stock indices, or interest rates. That said, the risk-averse actions of conservative investors create profitable opportunities for risk-taking speculators. For example, the U.S. dollar, as a hard currency, attracts a lot of attention from both hedgers and speculators.

The most popular stock index future is the S&P 500. The deepest interest rate futures are found on Treasury bonds and eurodollars. Speculating in these areas is very risky, because you are making short-term bets on financial market movements, and stock prices and interest rates are tough to forecast accurately, especially in the short run.

PART

2

DO YOU WANT TO PICK YOUR OWN SECURITIES?

A LOOK AT TECHNICAL ANALYSIS AND FUNDAMENTAL ANALYSIS

KEY TERMS

technical analysis, fundamental analysis, expected return, moving average, breakout, support level, resistance level, filter rule, whipsaw, buy-and-hold strategy, earnings per share, operating profit, dividend payout, current ratio, cash flow per share, efficient markets theory, weak form, semistrong form, strong form

Part 1 of this book provided an overview of stocks, bonds, and derivatives, essentially laying the foundation for financial decision making. Part 2, which encompasses Chapters 8 through 11, is concerned with how to build on this foundation—that is, how to use the information you've learned so far. For instance, do you know when a security might be cheap? Do you know why? These chapters will help you answer these and related questions.

This chapter is also designed to help you answer another important question: Do you want to pick securities yourself or pay someone to pick them for you? Alternatively, do you consider yourself an active investor or a passive one? If you have decided that you neither want to pick your own securities nor pay someone to do it for you, then you should read this chapter for perspective only.

In this chapter, we will cover some tools of the trade. In doing so, we will confine our discussion to stocks and bonds, which are the securities of choice for most investors. Of these two, we will spend more time on stocks because their prices are harder to deal with than bond prices.

In the world of finance, the tools we will investigate are separated into two well-known groups, technical analysis and fundamental analysis:

- *Technical analysis* is concerned with analyzing past price and volume data, usually by using charts and graphs. The first half of this chapter discusses technical analysis.

- *Fundamental analysis* deals with variables that measure performance, such as income and debt variables. The second half of this chapter addresses fundamental analysis.

Regardless of which group appeals to you, the bottom line is that each set of tools is designed to do one thing: predict prices. The objective is to find a set of tools that can help you accurately estimate the rate of return that you can expect from an investment. In finance, this rate of return is referred to as *expected return*. In the end, you will be looking for stocks and bonds that you expect will provide high returns at risk levels that you can tolerate. This last point helps put into perspective the quiz you took in Chapter 1 on assessing your risk tolerance.

TECHNICAL ANALYSIS: HOW TECHNICAL DO YOU WANT TO BE?

Technical analysts (also known as technicians) examine the technical elements of the market in search of clues to future action. They are the gurus of market activity indicators. You will often hear the stock or bond market described as "oversold" or "overbought." You will also hear comparisons between the number of stocks "up" and the number of stocks "down" for the day. All of these are considered market timing signals designed to help you decide when to buy securities and when to sell them.

For example, when the general level of short-term interest rates has declined, stock prices generally rise. Given this relationship, in the tradition of "buy low, sell high," it is worth exploring when the decline starts and how much of a stock rise can be expected. A technician might, for example, focus on interest-rate-sensitive stocks, which are likely to show the largest price increases. The information can then be charted and used to predict future stock price trends. In this manner, technical analysis can help you determine an expected return for an individual stock or bond or for the respective markets. The period could be for the next day, the next month, or the next year.

Technicians operate on the assumption that the market takes into account all information, and they presume that market participants are aware of all relevant and fundamental information; that is, no analyst has an advantage over others through knowing something the others do not.

Technicians agree that markets undeniably display patterns that can lead to profitable opportunities, and they use a variety of indicators or characteristics of the market that reflect specific aspects of market activity. Two of the most-often-used indicators are the daily summaries of a major average, such as the Dow Jones Industrial Average, and daily volume.

The aforementioned charts are important to technicians. In their quest for the perfect indicator, charts help display discernible patterns that might signal a rise in a stock's or bond's price a few days before the price actually rises. The technician can then buy the security, wait for it to rise, and sell it at a profit at the new, higher price. No such reliable indicator appears to exist, however, but that does not stop technicians from continuing to search for them.

Because a single indicator can seldom be counted on for its predictive value, technicians look for combinations of indicators to help them predict changes in direction more reliably and consistently. It is not uncommon for technicians to use many different indicators for predicting, for example, which stocks to buy and sell. Because of the competitive nature of the business, however, they tend to keep their methods and indicators under wraps. Newsletters publish predictions of stock, bond, and market activity based on technical analysis, but the systems that underlie these are never revealed.

Constructing Stock Price Charts for Technical Analysis of the Markets

Because much of technical analysis involves graphics, knowing how to construct a chart will aid your understanding of technical analysis and help you to interpret results. For example, Exhibit 8–1 shows a chart of IBM's stock price from around September 2002 through August 2003. What does this chart reveal?

The vertical axis in Exhibit 8–1 displays IBM's stock price for the period; the horizontal axis gives the dates. There are two lines of interest here. First, focus on the one that shows the greater fluctuations—this is the actual price line. You can see that IBM's stock price fell from about $80 in June to about $55 in October. From there, the price jumped to over $85 by the end of November before settling into a trading range from about $77 to $87.

How could you have identified buy and sell signals? One popular way is to use a *moving average* (the "50-day MA" in Exhibit 8–1). To explain, statisticians use a variety of averages or "indications of central tendency." A simple mean is the one familiar to most people. To figure a simple mean, you add up the numbers to be averaged and divide the total by the number of entries. A moving average is one that moves with time. Each day, a new data point is added, and the earliest point is removed. Intervening points between earliest date and the most recent date are averaged and plotted at the most recent date.

Technically, a moving average smoothes the data, removing the daily rises and drops to allow the underlying movement to be seen; it eliminates the so-called noise in an array of data. Moving averages may cover 5 days, 13 weeks, 200 days, or any other period. A long period tends to remove more of the rises and

EXHIBIT 8–1.   CHARTING IBM

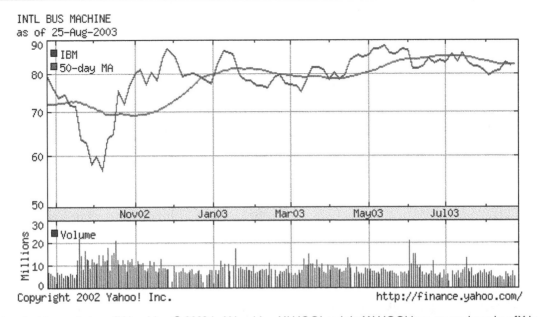

dips from the data, but many weeks may need to be studied to see any important change in direction. A shorter period smoothes the data but may still move up and down in a pattern that could hide an underlying trend.

To construct a moving average, pick a period and average each of the groups of prices as the period moves. Exhibit 8–2 uses a 10-week mean, and averages weekly closing prices of a generic stock. Adding the first 10 weekly numbers produces a total of 451.50. Dividing this number by the 10 data entries yields the first 10-week mean of 45.15. To construct a moving average, drop the top (i.e., earliest) number and add the next (i.e., the latest) number in the array. The total of numbers from week 2 through week 11 is 457.63, for a 10-week mean of 45.76.

The moving average proceeds one week at a time by repeating the process. Exhibit 8–2 shows how these 10-week averages move with a line connecting data points. Exhibit 8–3 shows a plot of the results. Note how the moving average smoothes the actual weekly price line, as represented by the Fund Price Line.

The problem with the common mean as a moving average is the need to add all of the numbers each day or week to compute the total from which the average is figured. (A computer, of course, can simplify the process.) Despite its cumbersome construction, the moving average is frequently used for up to a 52-week analysis of stock prices.

Returning to Exhibit 8–1, you can see how the smoother line, which represents a 50-day moving average on IBM's stock price, puts IBM's stock price into perspective, and it helps identify potential buy and sell signals. For example, the price line is below the moving average line through most of September and October with a range of $55 to $70.

Signals and Patterns to Watch for in Technical Analysis Charts

By October 2002 in the IBM example shown in Exhibit 8–1, the moving average line had clearly flattened and the price line had moved through it. This is usually an indication of a buy signal, called a *breakout*; and so it was in this case. In less than a month, you could have bought IBM stock at about $70 per share and sold at about $82 a share, for an excellent gain in a short period, a gain that could easily have been greater if you had made the purchase a week earlier.

But unless you sold very soon after the price crossed $80, much of your profit would have been short-lived, for the stock price sharply reversed itself for the next three months, dropping below the moving average line to $77 by March 2003.

Actually, a sell signal occurred soon after the price hit about $85 at the end of November. In December, the price line moved down through the moving average, suggesting that it might be time to sell the stock.

There are other signals to use as well, as shown in Exhibit 8–4; specifically, patterns indicating support and resistance levels are shown in Exhibit 8–4, charts 8–4a through 8–4j. The point here is that prices can trade in a range. The low end of the range is called the *support level*; the high end is called the *resistance level*.

Prices within a trading range move from a price support level at the bottom end of the range to a price resistance level at the upper

EXHIBIT 8–2.   COMPUTING A SIMPLE MOVING AVERAGE

Week No.	Stock Price	10-week Average	10-week Mean	Week No.	Stock Price	10-week Average	10-week Mean
1	42.11			32	56.75	543.25	54.33
2	43.38			33	57.00	548.25	54.83
3	44.00			34	58.13	554.13	55.41
4	45.50			35	59.25	560.38	56.04
5	45.13			36	60.00	566.88	56.69
6	44.63			37	61.13	574.25	57.43
7	44.50			38	61.25	581.00	58.10
8	46.50			39	61.25	586.25	58.63
9	47.75			40	60.75	592.00	59.20
10	48.00	451.50	45.15	41	60.00	595.50	59.55
11	48.25	457.63	45.76	42	59.75	598.50	59.85
12	49.25	463.50	46.35	43	59.13	600.63	60.06
13	49.38	468.88	46.89	44	57.75	600.25	60.03
14	48.75	472.13	47.21	45	57.25	598.25	59.83
15	48.50	475.50	47.55	46	58.50	596.75	59.68
16	49.63	480.50	48.05	47	57.13	592.75	59.28
17	50.50	486.50	48.65	48	54.75	586.25	58.63
18	51.00	491.00	49.10	49	54.00	579.00	57.90
19	51.75	495.00	49.50	50	53.25	571.50	57.15
20	52.00	499.00	49.90	51	52.00	563.50	56.35
21	52.00	502.75	50.28	52	50.50	554.25	55.43
22	51.75	505.25	50.53	53	49.88	545.00	54.50
23	52.00	507.88	50.79	54	49.00	536.25	53.63
24	52.25	511.38	51.14	55	50.75	529.75	52.98
25	53.00	515.88	51.59	56	50.00	521.25	52.13
26	53.50	519.75	51.98	57	47.25	511.38	51.14
27	53.75	523.00	52.30	58	46.75	503.38	50.34
28	54.50	526.50	52.65	59	44.50	493.88	49.39
29	56.00	530.75	53.08	60	46.00	486.63	48.66
30	55.00	533.75	53.38	61	44.75	479.38	47.94
31	56.50	538.25	53.83	62	43.00	471.88	47.19

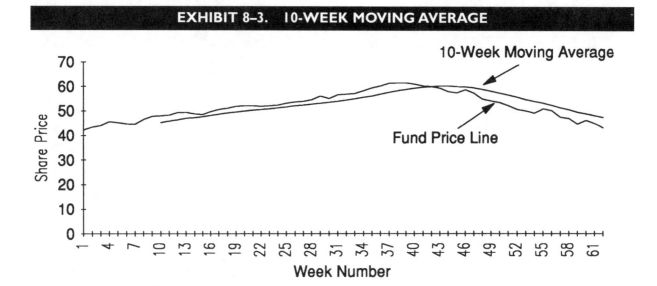

EXHIBIT 8–3. 10-WEEK MOVING AVERAGE

end of the range. When investors see the price reaching the resistance level, they may sell shares, knowing that the stock has retreated when it reached that level in the past. But when the stock price reaches the lower support level, investors may buy shares with the expectation that at some point it will reverse and climb to the resistance level again, where they can earn a profit by selling.

A stock that continues to trade within a fairly narrow range is not likely to generate any excitement until it breaks out. Note that at the right end of chart 8–4a in Exhibit 8–4, once again we have a breakout; once a stock breaks out of a trading range, it tends to continue until it establishes a new and higher trading range. Technicians have discovered that once a stock breaks out of a trading range in either direction, something is propelling it up or down, and that the forces that led to the breakout are likely to continue affecting the stock.

An opposite pattern appears in chart 8–4b in Exhibit 8–4, with a breakout to lower prices. If an investor is holding stock, he or she would likely sell at a breakout. Thus, if a stock price breaks below the support level, chances are it will continue dropping, possibly until it establishes a new and lower trading range, where a new support level would be reached. Break-outs tend to occur at major changes in volume, either up or down.

Reversals can assume different patterns. A reversal occurs when a pattern of upward movement changes to a downward movement, as in the following examples:

• When a stock's price moves steadily upward then suddenly drops and keeps on dropping, as in chart 8–4c in Exhibit 8–4. This is called a panic reversal. Such a pattern may have been apparent after the sharp market drop in October 1987 or the market drop that followed the terrorist attacks on September 11, 2001.

• A more likely reversal pattern is shown in chart 8–4d. Prices may be rising, but the daily incremental rise begins to taper off until it stops rising and gradually begins to lose in price. This is known as the round-top reversal.

EXHIBIT 8-4. CHARTS USED IN TECHNICAL ANALYSIS

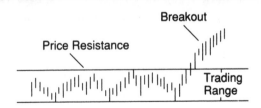

8-4a Price Resistance

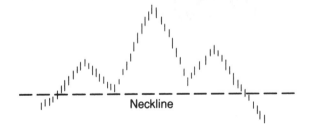

8-4f Head-and-shoulders Reversal

8-4b Price Support

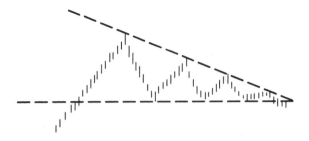

8-4g Descending Triangle Reversal

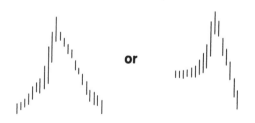

or

8-4c Panic Reversal

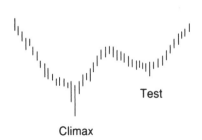

8-4h Selling Climax Reversal

8-4d Round-top Reversal

8-4i Round-bottom Reversal

8-4e Double-top Reversal

8-4j Double-bottom Reversal

- A double-top reversal, shown in chart 8–4e, can easily confuse technicians, as the direction of prices changes often.

- Similar confusing signals can result from the head-and-shoulders reversal, shown in chart 8–4f. In a true head-and-shoulders reversal, the middle hump (i.e., the "head") must rise higher than the "shoulders" on either side. The two bottoms between the head and shoulders tend to be similar, and a breakout occurs when prices drop below the level of the two bottoms. Then it's time to sell.

- The descending triangle reversal, shown in chart 8–4g, displays two significant characteristics. First, the intermediate lows of each cycle reach about the same level. Second, the high points of each cycle are successively lower. When prices drop below the level of the intermediate low, it is time to sell.

- Instead of a spiky top, a selling climax reversal may appear, as in chart 8–4h. Typically, a selling climax reversal occurs on high volume when shareholders dump shares at any price to avoid losing even more value. And, just as typically, prices tend to rise from that low point. Later, prices may drop again, and a test to see if prices drop to the former low level may occur.

- The round-bottom, shown in chart 8–4i, is the reverse of the round-top.

- The double-bottom, shown in chart 8–4j, is the reverse of the double-top, and it's just as confusing to technicians as the round-bottom.

Other Major Market Indicators

There are a number of other market indicators you should familiarize yourself with. They are described in brief in the following sections.

Trends. Trends that appear in the charts are major market indicators. Instead of a horizontal trading range, where prices bounce off the support level at the bottom and off the resistance level at the top, share prices may move about an inclining or declining trend line. Trends are extremely important because they may last for several years, as in the 1990s, for example, when annual stock market returns of 20% and higher were not uncommon.

Penetrations. These can be another important market indicator. You may hear about the Dow Theory from time to time, one of the oldest technical systems in use, as it is widely followed. It aims only to indicate primary trend direction; it is not used to forecast either the duration or height of an upward trend or the duration or depth of a downward trend. The theory uses variations in the Dow Jones averages as basic indicators. An upward (i.e., bullish) trend may appear to signal a rising market if each succeeding high is higher than the preceding high. A penetration occurs when the Dow Jones Industrial Average closing price exceeds the previous high closing price. An important element of the Dow Theory, however, is confirmation. A new upward trend is not confirmed until the Dow also penetrates its previous high closing price. Similar definitions on the downside confirm a bearish trend.

The logic behind the Dow Theory is that for a bull market to continue and reach new highs, the prices of stocks of manufacturers must be bid up. Similar interest would bid up the prices of the stocks of transportation companies, railroads, trucking companies, and airlines. They need to move together to establish a true bull market. If manufacturers are making products but not selling and transporting them, the bull market is weakly based, hence the need for confirmation.

A variation on the Dow Theory is the *filter rule*. It states that if the price of a security rises by a certain amount, say 10%, you should buy the security and hold it until its price drops from a subsequent high. You should then sell the security and take a short position in it until the price rises again by 10%.

Short-interest Charts. Only a technician's creativity limits the use of various chart indicators. A short-interest chart follows the number of issues sold short, as short sellers (sellers of borrowed stock) believe the market is headed down. Short sellers must buy the stock back at some point, however, and some technicians see this as a bullish indicator.

Sentiment Indices. A sentiment index surveys the opinions of a sample of financial newsletter writers. When a majority of the writers are forecasting a bull market, a contrarian may take a bearish position that the majority is always wrong. A contrarian is an investor who invests in stocks when others are selling, and vice versa. The sentiment index has at times also proved to be a reasonably accurate indicator of market directions.

Odd-lot Indices. An odd-lot index relies on the collective action of small investors. Market watchers believe that small investors—those with too little money to buy in round lots (100 shares)—tend to be wrong most of the time. Thus, when many odd-lotters enter the market, indicated by the daily report of odd-lot trading, professionals and technicians believe the market will reverse and head down.

Market Timing. Market timing with moving averages compares daily prices with a long-term moving average. Numerous financial newsletters chart moving averages and announce timing changes according to their unique combination of charted data. The typical move occurs when a stock, mutual fund, or index penetrates a 33-, 39-, or 52-week moving average. Various systems may be used. For example, a 52-week moving average of the Dow or the S&P 500 may be charted against a single mutual fund. Or a composite group of mutual funds may be charted as a 39- or 52-week moving average, and a single fund several individual funds compared to it.

The Confidence Index. The confidence index is used to glean the temperament of the market. It is the ratio of blue-chip grade bond yields to low-grade ones. It tends to reveal to what extent investors would like to take chances with their investments. As bondholders become more confident in the strength of the economy, their risk aversion lessens, and they tend to switch from high-grade bonds to low-grade ones.

Trend-following System. A trend-following system calls for moving into and out of a mutual fund according to specific rules. "Moving in" means to invest cash in mutual fund shares; "moving out" means to redeem shares in mutual funds. You can move out of one fund and into another within the same family of funds. A family of funds is two groups of funds managed by the same fund distribution corporation, such as the Vanguard Group.

Mutual funds, rather than individual stocks, are the typical vehicle for moving in or moving out because movements in or out cost less in brokers' fees than timing individual stocks. If no-load mutual funds are the vehicles, moves may cost nothing. As an example, look at the moving average above the daily or weekly closing prices for Mutual Fund A in Exhibit 8–5, the Fund Price Line. Because the moving average lags the changes in share prices, gradual changes have minimal effects. As long as closing share prices remain below the moving average, investors remain out of the market. Typically, they will have parked their money in a money market fund because these funds maintain a constant share value. Thus, the investor incurs no risk of losing capital.

When the closing price moves up and penetrates the moving average, investors move money from the money market fund into the mutual fund. When the mutual fund's price line penetrates the moving average, share prices are expected to continue moving up. Investors remain invested in the mutual fund for as long as the daily or weekly closing share prices remain above the moving average. But, if the market slows and reverses, the closing share price line penetrates the moving average. At that point, the investor moves from the mutual fund back to the money market fund. In a price-reversal, trend-following market-timing system, investors do not get out at the top and they do not get in at the bottom; they pick up most of the move in both directions.

Whipsaws. A single moving average can generate *whipsaws*, when the closing price penetrates the moving average on an up move and then drops back. On an upward penetration, the investor moves money from a money market fund to a stock mutual fund. A day or a few days later, share prices drop back and the investor switches back to the money market fund, usually at a loss.

Market timers have developed different tactics to reduce the occurrence of whipsaws, even though they have not completely beaten them. One tactic is to use more than one moving average. If mutual fund prices penetrate a reference moving average to the upside, an investor might not switch until the upward trend is confirmed by a similar move of the Dow Jones Industrial Average and its moving average, similar to the Dow Theory confirmation; or a buffer band might enlarge the neutral zone. A penetration must move past the moving average by a small margin, such as 1.5% of the value of the moving average. A similar buffer zone protects the moving average on the lower side. A 3% buffer zone

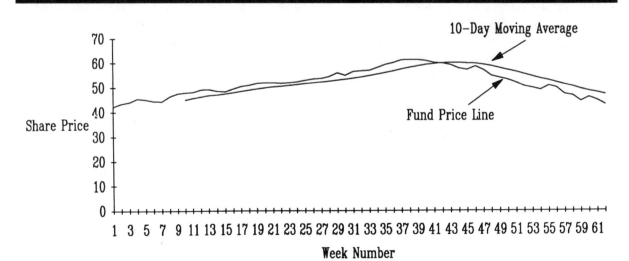

EXHIBIT 8–5.   SAMPLE 10-DAY MOVING AVERAGE

10–Day Moving Average

Share Price

Fund Price Line

Week Number

means penetrations must be stronger than when the difference is a single line. A strong penetration is less likely to be reversed quickly than one that barely makes it past the moving average.

Keep in mind that moving average timing systems typically underperform a *buy-and-hold strategy* during long-term bull markets. A buy-and-hold strategy calls for buying stocks or mutual funds and holding them for years through ups and downs. Timing works best in a market that moves up and down in broad, medium-term cycles in the order of four to five years from crest to crest. (A cycle is one complete move up and then back down to near the original starting level.) By moving out of a stock mutual fund into a money market fund in response to a timing signal, an investor avoids the loss of capital in the stock fund and earns interest on the money parked in the money market fund. When the trend swings upward again, the investor moves back into the stock fund at a lower share price and holds until the moving average timing system signals another switch into the money market fund.

A timing system has the advantage in this case because losses hurt more than gains can remedy. If a mutual fund loses 50% of its value in a decline, it must gain 100% to reach its former level. For example, suppose Fund M drops in share price from $10 per share to $5 per share. It has lost 50% of its value. But the share price must double or gain 100% to reach its former level of $10 per share.

FUNDAMENTAL ANALYSIS: BACK TO THE BASICS

Unlike technical analysis, fundamental analysis does not rely on charting, nor is it con-cerned with moving averages, filter rules, breakouts, and the like. Instead, fundamental analysis involves three steps, in the following order:

1. Analysis of the overall economy
2. Analysis of individual industries
3. Analysis of companies within selected industries

Analyzing the Overall Economy

Because up to 50% of the variability of a company's earnings can be linked to overall economic activity, an analysis of the economy should precede all other industry and company analysis. Specifically, the focus should be on the business environment, such as the outlook for profits, consumer confidence, and business sentiment. For example, if a downturn in economic activity is occurring (commonly known as a recession), stocks and bonds will be heavily affected: stock prices will drop, in anticipation of poor corporate performance. In turn, downgrades of bonds— both corporate and municipal—are inevitable.

To illustrate, as economic growth slumped during the early years of the twenty-first century, the S&P 500 fell with it, declining by more than 14% per year. Meanwhile, many corporations suffered bond rating downgrades, into the noninvestment grade classifications (recall from Chapter 3, this means below Baa/BBB/BBB), making it more difficult for them to raise capital.

Conversely, if economic growth is robust and the future bright, stocks and bonds will respond accordingly. As evidence, the United States enjoyed strong economic growth during most of the 1990s, resulting in big gains in stocks. In fact, from the mid-1990s through

1999, the annual return on the S&P 500 was close to 30%, fantastic by historical standards of around 11%.

Analyzing Individual Industries

Your interest in certain stocks and bonds should be heavily influenced by current and expected economic conditions. This is the basis of industry analysis:

- Some industries find their fortunes tied closely to business cycles, for example, the auto and steel industries. In boom years, their sales are brisk and their stock prices rise. In down years, their sales are slow and their stock prices fall.

- Other industries are "defensive" in nature, for example, mass merchandise firms, which often experience an increase in sales during recessions, as consumers become more cautious about their spending.

- Still other industries appear to be only loosely connected to overall activity; for example, the pharmaceutical sector will likely sell many of its products regardless of economic conditions, because for many individuals their products are a necessity.

Analyzing Specific Companies

Company analysis is next in the process. It calls for a thorough understanding of the company, emphasizing the company's product and its performance to determine its value as a possible investment. This requires a lot of data. Fortunately, the emergence of the Internet has made the collection and analysis of the data easier than ever before. In addition, reporting organizations (such as Moody Investor Services, the Standard & Poor's Corporation, and Value Line) continue their excellent work.

Before you tackle the job of analyzing a company's financials (i.e., reports of sales, earnings, liabilities, balance sheet, and profits), you need to examine what a company does and how well it does it. Begin by asking: Is it a manufacturing company or a service-oriented company?

- **Manufacturing companies** make products, such as beverages, cars, computers, medical devices, appliances, and nuts and bolts. They turn raw materials, or small parts and subassemblies, into finished goods for sale.

- **Service-oriented companies** make nothing; they serve the public with something it wants or needs. McDonald's serves hamburgers; Wal-Mart sells goods; doctors and dentists offer health services; schools provide education. All are part of the service economy.

Note that governments provide services, too, but unlike corporations, they issue no stocks. However, they do sell billions of dollars worth of bonds and debt instruments. The interest paid on various kinds of bonds reflects how efficiently various governments provide services, and you should understand the government or agency that issues bonds before you loan them your money.

Learning about a company is not difficult. Various sources of data and general information about a company are readily available, as described below.

Newspapers and Magazines. Business periodicals regularly publish articles about individual companies. Profiles of major companies appear in *BusinessWeek, Fortune, Forbes, The New York Times*, and many other publications. If you are researching a particular company, go to your library to check various publication indices to find magazine articles that may have appeared.

Annual Reports. These are issued by the company and usually include lengthy descriptions of a company's activities, along with colorful photographs of facilities and products. Annual reports are also sources of recent financial data. Current stockholders receive an annual report automatically. If you are interested, send a postcard to the company or telephone to request a copy. Companies are pleased to send non-shareholders copies of their annual reports.

Annual Meetings. These are a good source of information, and they are not limited to shareholders. Some companies stage extensive public relations events to advise attendees about operations, and display their activities and results with slides or movies.

Internet. The World Wide Web on the Internet provides loads of financial information about companies, from current stock prices and bond ratings to the latest internal news. At company Websites, financial reports are usually available as well, and in some cases go back several years. In addition, you can often easily find condensed financial information, such as stock price highs and lows, value ratios (price-earnings, price-book, and price-sales), debt ratios, and the like.

Television. The rise in televised reports and analyses of stock and bond market activity has led to readily available condensed financial reporting on company fundamentals, such as sales growth, *earnings per share*, and to what extent investors were pleased with the company's performance.

Analysts' Reports. These reports from brokerage company analysts often provide a depth of analysis not easily found elsewhere. They can be obtained on request if you are an active client of the brokerage firm that produced the reports, but are not so readily available to the public at large.

Subscription Information. This can be obtained from Standard & Poor's and Value Line, for example. Value Line, in particular, offers clear, condensed financial information.

When reading about a company, you should ask at least three questions:

1. **What industry is the company in?** This question is concerned with the state of the industry:

   • Is it a growth industry?

   • Is it a mature industry?

   • Is it in a declining industry?

For example, railroads were once the dominant form of transportation and dominated early measures of the Dow Jones Industrial Average. But their fortunes began to decline noticeably following World War II, when motor and air transport made serious inroads to the transportation market. Obviously, you want to find a sector that is growing.

2. **Where is the company positioned within the industry?** This question is concerned with market dominance:

   • Is the company an industry leader, known for innovative products that are in constant demand? Or is it a laggard, with products and services that seem out of touch with current trends?

   • Are its products patented and protected from competition? Or are other companies positioned to become viable competitors?

   • Will the company be able to maintain (if not expand) its market share? Or is it vulnerable to decline?

3. **What is the company's specialty?** This question concerns two things: the necessity of the product or service and its life cycle. You want a company to be specializing in a "must-have" product or service that is not considered a short-term trend or fad, and one that the competition cannot easily duplicate.

For example, consider the rapidly changing technology sector. A must-have product in one period soon thereafter can easily become the next "toaster"—a product once considered innovative that can now easily be reproduced by many companies. Similarly, so-called generic drugs often become effective substitutes for previously patented, innovative treatments for human ailments once the patents run out.

Once you are satisfied you have the answers to these three questions, you will be in a position to examine a company's financial performance, as represented by its income statement and balance sheet, to which we now turn.

WHERE TO FIND FINANCIAL INFORMATION: READING INCOME STATEMENTS AND BALANCE SHEETS

A company's income statement and balance sheet represent the keys to financial performance. The next two sections of this chapter describe each, with examples to illustrate and clarify.

The Income Statement: How to Read and Understand It

A simplified income statement is provided in Exhibit 8–6. Revenues and other income are reported at the top. Costs and expenses follow.

Gross profit, or profit before taxes, paves the way for the bottom line, net profit. Let us examine in more detail the parts of the income statement shown in this exhibit.

The bottom line (both literally and figuratively) is net profit, sometimes called net income, and often called earnings. Note that revenues do not necessarily represent sales alone, although distributing a variety of products is this sample company's primary activity. Interest from cash invested is another source of revenue, along with rents, royalties on subsidiary rights sales, and unspecified income that could include tie-ins to books, toys, and other products (such as T-shirts based on toy characters). All of these are part of total revenue.

EXHIBIT 8–6.   INCOME STATEMENT

ABC Distributing Co.
Income Statement
Year ending December 31

Revenues		
Sales	$9,780*	
Rights	42	
Interest	30	
Other income	28	
		$9,880
Costs and Expenses		
Cost of goods sold	$4,840	
Operating profit		$5,040
Sales expenses	1,525	
General admin. expenses	430	
Interest on debt	1,920	
Depreciation	104	
Miscellaneous expenses	40	
	$4,019	
Gross Profit (before taxes)		$1,021
Federal taxes	$549	
State & local taxes	39	
	$588	
Net Profit (earnings)		$433

*000 omitted in all amounts.

Costs usually break down into the following components:

- **Cost of goods sold** for ABC Distributing Co. (our example company) comprises the production costs of products purchased from manufacturers. Subtracting the cost of goods sold from total revenues yields an important number known as *operating profit*, or the profit on sales before selling and general administration costs are deducted.

- **Sales expenses** include salaries and travel expenses for salespeople, warehousing of the products, rent for wholly owned store outlets, and similar expenses.

- **General administration expenses** include staff salaries plus accounting and other overhead costs that cannot be attributed to specific product lines.

- **Interest on debt** is the cost for money borrowed by selling bonds.

- **Depreciation** is the amount deducted to recover the annual cost of previous capital expenditures.

- **Miscellaneous expenses** are a catchall for many identified costs too small to warrant a line of their own.

Before-tax profits (or losses) fall out after deducting all costs from total revenues. Federal, state, and local taxes are deducted from the before-tax total to leave the net profit, or earnings.

The Balance Sheet: How to Read and Understand It

Like our sample income statement, the sample balance sheet shown in Exhibit 8–7 is greatly simplified, to introduce you to the basics of what you need to know to be able to read and understand the information provided on this document. This example includes a list of assets owned by ABC Distributing Co. and an offsetting list of liabilities and stockholders' equity. The two lists must balance—that is, they must add up to equal dollar amounts. In analyzing a company's balance sheet, it is important to relate current assets and liabilities to long-term assets and liabilities.

Current assets are those assets expected to be sold or converted into cash within the next twelve months. Current liabilities are those expected to be paid within the next year. Long-term refers to assets and liabilities with an expected life in excess of twelve months. On the asset side, here are some quick definitions of each of the elements listed under the assets of the sample balance sheet shown in Exhibit 8–7:

- **Cash.** This is exactly what you think it is: cash in a checking account at a bank.

- **Securities.** An element of the sample income statement in Exhibit 8–6 shows interest on investments, and these investments by ABC Distributing Co. are U.S. Treasury bills, which are noted among the current assets in Exhibit 8–7. Rather than keep large amounts of cash in a checking account drawing no interest, the company's financial officer invested excess cash in T-bills to earn income from the asset. Treasury bills, of course, are highly liquid, meaning readily convertible to cash. (A category often used in balance sheets is called cash equivalents; it includes very marketable short-term assets easily converted to cash.)

- **Accounts receivable.** These represent sales that have not yet been paid for by customers.

- **Inventory.** This is a major asset for a product distributor, as it represents the stock of unsold goods stored in a warehouse. It also includes products in various stages of production, known as work-in-progress. The inventory is valued at the products' production or purchase cost.

• **Prepaid royalties.** These are early payments to owners of protected property for rights to produce and sell a product.

• **Other current assets.** This is a catchall category for small asset items, such as office supplies and equipment.

Using the Income Statement and Balance Sheet to Evaluate a Company's Financial Condition

An analyst examining the income statement and balance sheet in a company's annual report will look for telltale signs of the company's financial condition. A number of the important points are described in the following sections. Using these and other fundamentals, an analyst can draw a broad range of impressions and conclusions from the raw numbers presented in a company's financial statements. Numbers are not absolute, however; judgment and experience are critical to the analyst's conclusions, and there is no substitute for either when appraising the potential value of stocks.

Earnings. If a company produces a profit, obviously, that is good. How good? To answer this question, two signs are watched closely: earnings per share and earnings as a percentage of revenues.

EXHIBIT 8–7.   BALANCE SHEET

ABC Distributing Co.
Balance Sheet
Year ending December 31

Assets			Liabilities		
Current assets			Current liabilities		
Cash in bank	$306*		Accounts payable	$1,670	
Securities (T-bills)	375		Loans & notes payable	3,100	
Accounts receivable	1,680		Royalties payable	680	
Inventories	9,337		Other	375	
Prepaid royalties	50		Total current liabilities	$5,825	
Other current assets	33		Long-term bonds	1,752	
Total current assets	$11,781	$11,781	Total liabilities	$7,577	7,577
Long-term assets			Stockholders' equity		
Plant & equipment	430		Common stock	4,600	
Investment property	100		Retained earnings	124	
Total long-term assets	$530	530	Total stockholders' equity	$4,724	4,724
			Total liabilities and		
Total assets		$12,311	stockholders' equity		$12,301

* 000 omitted in all amounts.

For instance, say ABC Distributing Co. has 500,000 shares of stock outstanding. Earnings per share (or net profit per share), as shown on the income statement in Exhibit 8–6, are earnings divided by shares. In ABC's case, this is:

$$\$433,000 \text{ in earnings} \div 500,000 \text{ shares} = \$0.87 \text{ per share}$$

If an analyst figures that a stock in the distributing industry is conservatively priced at 10 to 15 times earnings, the stock of ABC Distributing might be fully priced at $8.66 to $12 per share. ("Fully priced" is a euphemism for a stock price that will probably not rise until earnings rise.) Second, in the case of ABC Distributing, net earnings of $433,000 represents 4.4% of gross revenues, probably a bit better than the industry average.

Return on Equity. This is calculated using figures from both the income statement and the balance sheet. Again, take the net earnings and divide by stockholders' equity (listed among the liabilities on ABC's balance sheet, shown in Exhibit 8–7) to get the average return on the equity invested by shareholders. In ABC's case, this is:

$$\$433,000 \text{ net earnings} \div \$4,724,000 \text{ in} \\ \text{stockholders' equity} = 9.17\% \text{ average ROE}$$

A 10% to 15% return on equity can be considered a likely target.

Growth. A major characteristic of growth companies is that they "plow back" earnings to expand business. How did ABC Distributing do for the year in question? One measure is the retention rate, which is the amount of net earnings the company retained for growth. To calculate the retention rate, you deduct dividends from net earnings and divide that number by net earnings. But ABC Distributing, like many growth companies, did not pay dividends to stockholders, therefore its retention rate is 100%.

Now let's suppose that ABC had paid dividends, say $100,000, to shareholders. What would the hypothetical retention rate have been? To find this number, simply find the net earnings on the income statement in Exhibit 8–6, subtract the amount of dividends, and divide that number by net earnings:

$$\$433,000 - \$100,000 = \$333,000 \\ \$333,000 \div \$433,000 = 77\% \text{ retention rate}$$

Of course, not all net profits are likely to be reinvested for growth; a major portion of after-tax profits may go for paying off portions of the debt principal.

Dividend Payout Percentage. Because many investors expect some immediate return, they may look at how much a company pays out in dividends. The percentage of net earnings paid in dividends is called the *dividend payout.* In the case of ABC Distributing, no dividends were paid, so the dividend payout was 0%.

Assuming a $100,000 hypothetical dividend payment, the dividend payout would be calculated by dividing the amount of dividends paid by net earnings:

$$\$100,000 \div \$433,000 = 23\% \text{ dividend} \\ \text{payout percentage rate}$$

This is low by many standards, but it's not unusual for a company dedicated to growth. A mature company with stable earnings might pay as much as 50% of its earnings to shareholders as dividends.

Reinvestment Rate. Another measure of how much a company is plowing back for growth is the reinvestment rate, calculated by taking the return on equity (which was calculated by taking net earnings and dividing it by stockholders' equity) and multiplying it by the retention rate. For ABC Distributing, this would be:

$$9.17\% \times 1.00 = 9.17\%$$

The 1.00 represents the 100% retention rate. And a 9.17% reinvestment rate is an average figure.

Current Ratio. The relationship of current assets to current liabilities is a widely watched figure known as the *current ratio*. It is obtained by dividing current assets by current liabilities (both of which are found, of course, on the company's balance sheet, shown in Exhibit 8–7). For ABC Distributing, this is:

$$\$11,781,000 \div \$5,825,000 = 2.022$$

A current ratio of 2.0 or greater is considered good—in other words, ABC has twice as many assets as liabilities. Inventories, which are part of current assets, tend to raise the current ratio for distributors because inventory amounts to a large value.

Long-term Debt Ratio. Strong balance sheets are those with high percentages of equity (i.e., shareholder ownership) and small percentages of long-term debt. A common sign of balance sheet strength is the long-term debt ratio, or long-term debt (found on a company's balance sheet)—in Exhibit 8–7, this is listed as long-term bonds, because this is the type of security ABC has invested in—divided by total liabilities (also found on the balance sheet). For ABC Distributing, this figure is:

$$\$1,752,000 \div \$7,577,000 = 23.12\%$$

A 50-50 ratio (i.e., 50% debt and 50% equity) is a common goal, because a heavy debt load leaves a company vulnerable to low sales, as in a recession.

Long-term Debt/Stockholders' Equity Ratio. Another measure of long-term debt is its relationship to stockholders' equity. Conservative financing calls for equity to equal or exceed long-term debt. For ABC Distributing, calculate this percentage by dividing the amount of long-term bonds by stockholders' equity, both of which are found on the company's balance sheet. From Exhibit 8-7 we derive this equation:

$$\$1,752,000 \div \$4,724,000 = 37.09\%$$

The 37.09% is the ratio. Although no cause for alarm, this figure does suggest a bent toward aggressive financing. A number closer to zero is preferred.

Cash Flow. Almost as important as net earnings is how much cash flows into the company. Even if a company is profitable, it cannot continue without a positive cash flow. Depreciation figures heavily into cash flow calculations, as it is a nontaxable source of cash. The formula for cash flow is net earnings plus depreciation (both found on the income statement in Exhibit 8–6). For ABC Distributing, this is:

$$\$433,000 + \$104,000 = \$537,000$$
$$\text{in cash flow}$$

Higher cash flows result from previous investment in depreciable assets. This rate of cash flow for ABC is not a particularly strong number, as suggested by the cash flow per share, calculated next.

Cash Flow per Share. The *cash flow per share* is another meaningful number for analysts. This number reflects how much cash is flowing into the company for each share of stock outstanding, calculated simply by taking the cash flow amount (calculated by adding net earnings and depreciation, as just described) and dividing it by the number of shares outstanding. For ABC Distributing, this would be:

$$\$537,000 \div 500,000 \text{ shares}$$
$$= \$1.07 \text{ per share}$$

Although $1.07 is not a bad number, a higher one would be preferred—for example, at least $3, which would reflect a cash flow of $1,500,000. Cash flow per share is only important as it relates to previous years' results. It depends on the number of shares, which puts cash flow on a relative basis.

Book Value per Share. Another simple evaluation is determined by dividing the stockholders' equity (which can be found on the balance sheet in Exhibit 8–7) by the number of shares outstanding (which are available from annual reports as well as Internet sources). For ABC Distributing, this would be:

$$\$4,724,000 \div 500,000 = \$9.45 \text{ per share}$$

The higher this value, the more likely it is that the company's stock is undervalued.

Additional Evaluation Criteria. As a further guide, you might want to screen stocks using the following criteria:

- **Strong sales/revenue growth.** Look for companies whose sales growth has been at least 10%. This criterion shows support for the industry the company is in as well as its position within the industry. For example, a company in a declining industry will have a difficult time generating annual revenue growth of at least 10%.

- **Earnings per share.** Check to make sure that earnings per share have been steadily increasing, and preferably at double-digit rates. If the company's revenue growth (above) is strong and the company is well managed, earnings per share should be significant and growing.

- **Cash.** Make sure the company has plenty of cash and/or other highly marketable securities (called cash equivalents). You want the company to be a strong cash generator, because lots of cash protects a company through hard times and gives it the financial means to expand into other markets through acquisitions of other companies.

- **Little to no debt.** Finally, the less debt the company has, the less burdened it is with having to make timely payments of interest and principal.

OTHER PERSPECTIVES ON ANALYZING THE MARKETS

Technical and fundamental analyses provide direction on evaluating securities. How good is this direction? Will it help you earn big profits? Many researchers think not, and they have a powerful concept to support them, called the *efficient markets theory*. It says that all relevant information is almost instantaneously incorporated into the prices of stocks and bonds. The implication is that securities are neither underpriced nor overpriced, and so no unusually large profits are systematically possible. Thus, you cannot beat the market. The theory can be broken down into three forms:

- *Weak form.* Past price and volume data cannot be systematically used to outperform a strategy of investing in a broad market index, such as the S&P 500.

- *Semistrong form.* Public information cannot be systematically used to outperform a broad market index.

- *Strong form.* Insider information cannot be systematically used to beat a broad market index.

The first two are especially relevant. The implication of the weak form says that technical analysis is essentially useless. Past price and volume data are not going to help you outperform the market. You might earn profits from it, but you would be better off buying index funds, especially after adjusting for commission costs, taxes, and risk.

Fundamental analysis fares no better. According to the semistrong version, knowing about, for example, earnings per share, the dividend payout ratio, and cash flow is not going to help you beat the market. Although you will undoubtedly earn profits, they will be less than your gains from index funds, after adjusting for commission costs, taxes, and risk.

What is the reasoning behind these statements and their implications? In a word, it is about incentives. The desire to earn big returns as quickly as possible virtually assures that big returns will not be available. As soon as a profitable opportunity presents itself, investors virtually fall over each other trying to take advantage of it. The implication is that market incorporates new information so quickly that the average investor cannot, on average, hope to take advantage of it. To what extent this holds has been fiercely debated, and we postpone further discussion on this debate until Chapter 9.

SOME THINGS TO AVOID

Regardless of your belief in either technical or fundamental analysis, you should avoid the following: trying to time stock markets, companies with no earnings, companies accused of accounting fraud, and companies in financial distress.

- **Avoid trying to time the market.** By trying to time markets, we mean trying to determine the optimal time to "buy low, sell high"; or, if you are interested in short selling, to "sell high, buy low." Because all investors, to one degree or another, are interested in getting in and out of the market at the "right" times, market fluctuations—sometimes big fluctuations—are inevitable.

Consequently, it becomes difficult, almost impossible, to predict when prices have "bottomed" and "topped." The best advice, especially when going long, might well be to stick it out through thick and thin. That way, you are bound not to miss any big rallies, which tend to be short and unpredictable. Moreover, by trying to time markets, you will undoubtedly be trading more, which has implications for brokerage fees and taxes. To paraphrase a familiar cliché, remember that frequent trading can be bad for your wealth.

- **Avoid companies with no earnings.** Stay away from companies that are long on promise but short on performance. This often happens with IPOs (initial public offerings). A stock will be touted as having great potential, and buyers often quickly snap up shares, hoping the stock will become the "next Microsoft" or the "next Cisco," two stocks that had great runs during the 1990s. It is not unusual, though, for the companies to show not a shred of profits.

Such was the case during the Internet boom of the late 1990s. Companies with little or no earnings had stocks that were bid to spectacular heights, to the hundreds of dollars, only to drop precipitously once company earnings fell short of expectations. Many companies had management teams with great ideas but were unable to deliver on them. The result was no earnings; and without earnings, there was no cash. A firm without cash is like a car without gas. Here are a few examples of stock prices, adjusted for stock splits, of companies fueled by the emergence of the Internet. They still exist, but their future is uncertain.

CMGI
High: $138 (April 1999)
Current: $0.80 (March 2003)

DoubleClick
High: $127 (April 1999)
Current: $7.70 (March 2003)

Red Hat
High: $106 (December 1999)
Current: $5.40 (March 2003)

On the upside, the rates of return were almost unbelievable by historical standards. For example, the annual rate of return on CMGI between January 1995 and December 1999 was more than 350%! Over this period, $1,000 invested in the company would have earned nearly $2 million. On the downside, the $2 million would have dropped to virtually zero, as the company's stock price plummeted to below $1. A similar story holds for the other two stocks, just not as eye-popping. Again, these are three stocks that survived—so far. Hundreds more did not.

- **Avoid companies charged with accounting fraud.** Investors show no mercy to companies accused of "cooking the books," so do not assume that investors will buy the stock once the necessary "corrections" have been made. The stock may remain out of favor for years.

- **Avoid companies in financial distress.** It could be tempting to chase the stocks of companies that are financially distressed to the point of bankruptcy. The thinking is that a new, better company will emerge and the stock will recover. Although this is always a possibility, you would likely do better by searching elsewhere.

SUMMARY

When selecting securities, you will find that the tools of the trade fall into two categories: technical analysis and fundamental analysis. Technical analysis deals with an examination of past price and volume data. It relies heavily on the use of charts to display patterns that analysts believe may signal profitable trading opportunities. These patterns include breakouts, panic reversals, and head and shoulders.

Fundamental analysis is concerned with company performance, as represented by income statement and balance sheet data, such as earnings, cash flow, and the dividend payout. The idea is to invest in companies that show consistently strong performance.

In addition to these two main tool groups is the theory of efficient markets, which asserts that, compared to the performance of a broad market index, neither technical nor fundamental analysis is very profitable. The weak form states that technical analysis cannot be used to systematically beat the market. The semistrong form states that fundamental analysis cannot be systematically used to beat the market. The strng form takes the same position with respect to inside information.

MORE ON TECHNICAL
AND FUNDAMENTAL ANALYSIS

KEY TERMS

mean reversion, January effect, earnings surprise, PEG ratio, behavioral finance

In Chapter 8, we discussed technical and fundamental analysis. Recall that technical analysis argues that significant profits can be found by analyzing patterns in historical price and volume data, and that moving averages, filter rules, and other technical tools can help you form good trading strategies. Weak-form efficiency, in contrast, argues that technical analysis is essentially useless, that you would be better off investing in index mutual funds.

Fundamental analysis asserts that bargains can be found by looking at a company's fundamental financial position: measures of its sales, profits, cash, and debt. Semistrong form efficiency, however, states that such information has already been incorporated into the prices of securities. Thus, you will find no bargains this way. The implication is, once again, that you would be better off investing in index mutual funds than using fundamental analysis.

In this chapter, we provide a survey of the evidence, to determine where market efficiency appears to hold up and where it does not. We hope to provide you (especially if active investing interests you) with ideas on

selecting securities. The objective is to find stocks and bonds that offer good value, that is, securities with above-average returns to risk.

EVALUATING MARKET EFFICIENCY FROM A TECHNICAL ANALYSIS VIEW

Are markets really efficient? At a broad level, the answer is yes. There is a lot of evidence that financial markets rapidly absorb new information very quickly. That said, it is not clear that prices perfectly reflect that information. First, let's explore where market efficiency seems to hold up.

Evidence Supporting Weak-form Efficiency

Let's consider technical analysis first, which means that we will explore the evidence that markets are weak-form-efficient. Following are descriptions of various technical analysis methods that offer such evidence.

Odd-Lot Theory. This theory suggests that odd-lot selling should be interpreted as a "buy" signal because so-called odd-lotters do not know what they are doing. Likewise, odd-lot buying should be interpreted as a sell signal. The rule, though, seems to have difficulty identifying major turning points. Without the turning points, you have little to go on when trying to decide when to buy and/or sell. Moreover, the odd-lot index can be quite volatile, which adds to the risk of making a wrong decision.

Trends in Historical Security Prices. Looking at the relationship over time between stock prices suggests that the price in one period is related to the price in the previous period, especially over the long run (more than one year). However, for shorter periods, such as per day, week, or month (which are the periods that technicians like to focus on), evidence of the relationship has been difficult to find.

Price-Volume Signals. The idea here is that a period of rising prices combined with large volume suggests pent-up demand for stocks. Thus, prices should continue to rise until there is a drop in prices on large volume, a sell signal. It appears that these movements contain no useful information about future prices. In the end, you are likely to end up with a lot of unsuccessful trades that carry commission costs far in excess of that of a naïve buy-and-hold strategy.

Runs Test. It is conceivable that stock and bond prices fluctuate randomly but still occasionally follow trends that price-volume signals and historical trends cannot pick up. That is, prices might move unpredictably most of the time but then move predictably the rest of the time. This is a *run*. It begins with a change of sign in a series of numbers; in this case, it would be the price of the stock. Tests of whether you can profit from runs suggest that you would be better off looking elsewhere.

Head-and-shoulders Method. It is not unusual for the head-and-shoulders formation to occur but without penetration of the prices, and it is not easy to identify the potential for failed outcomes.

Where Technical Analysis Appears Useful

The areas in which technical analysis might be beneficial, at least to some degree, are described in the following sections.

Filter Rules. Although commission costs can eat into profits, especially if trading is done through a full-service broker, there is evidence that small filter rules (e.g., around 1%) can help you earn above-average returns. In fact, one study found this was true even with large commission costs.

As always, though, you need to be careful. It seems that filter rules work better for some stocks than for others, and the higher the commission cost, the more likely that you would be better off just buying an index fund.

Moving Averages. Several studies have found that moving averages have some usefulness in identifying when to buy and sell securities, even after accounting for commissions. Proceed with caution here, too, however. Profits are not straightforward because the rules appear to also identify buy and sell signals that lead to losses.

Price Momentum. Do hot stocks stay hot, and do cold stocks stay cold? According to the *price momentum hypothesis*, they do. This hypothesis is based on the simple idea that recent trends in past prices will continue. There is systematic evidence supporting the idea, making it seem as though investors are *under*reacting to new information. So, if a stock is hot, you should

buy it; otherwise avoid it. Be careful, and
read on.

Mean Reversion. Stocks and bonds can sometimes get on one-way streets. At times it seems,
no matter what the announcement, some
stocks continue their upward march, while
others continue to flounder. In short, some
are in favor, some are not. However, sooner
or later, the process reverses, and the stock
prices head toward a long-term average. This
is called *mean reversion*.

For example, during the mid- to late 1990s,
Internet stocks (including those without any
earnings, i.e., profits) were the rage, with
prices leaping into the hundreds within weeks
after being issued. Other more staid stocks,
sometimes referred to as "old-economy"
stocks, showed little or no gain despite the
fact they had positive earnings. But soon
after the dawn of the new century, the process
had reversed itself, and with a vengeance for
Internet stocks. In the meantime, the out-of-
favor staid stocks became favorable again.

In other words, the process of mean reversion
tends to support a contrarian investment strategy in which you should avoid in-favor stocks
for out-of-favor stocks. Moreover, from a fun-
damentalist viewpoint, out-of-favor stocks
should be more attractively priced, with lower
price-earnings and price-book ratios than their
counterparts. A number of academic studies
have tended to support mean reversion as a
way to earn above-average profits, especially
over three to five years.

National Elections. There is a fair amount of
evidence indicating that stock and bond markets move according to which political party
controls the White House and Congress. There
are two patterns worth exploring:

- It would seem that investors prefer Republicans
to Democrats, because Republicans tend to be
more "pro business" than Democrats. However,
evidence indicates that stock markets tend to do
better with Democrats, a phenomenon that has
occurred for decades.

- One study found that much was to be
gained by investing in small-cap stocks
when Democrats controlled both Congress
and the presidency, but large-cap stocks
should be the choice whenever the president
and Congress were not from the same party.

January Effect. Historically, at particular times
of the year, stock markets do better than at
other times, a pattern that has repeated itself
for decades. For example, January has tradi-
tionally been one of the best months to be
invested in stocks. The *January effect* is the
term used to describe this decades-long strong
performance of stocks in the first month of
the year. Even accounting for the poor results
during January 2000 and 2003, since 1971,
the Dow Jones Industrials were up nearly
2% in January, which converts to an annual
return of over 25%.

Perhaps in anticipation of the January effect,
December has proven to be another good
month, up nearly 1.6%. There is evidence
that the January effect is alive and well in
foreign markets, too, and may be even
stronger there. Evidence of the effect has
been found in Australia, Austria, Belgium,
Canada, France, Germany, Italy, Japan, the
Netherlands, Singapore, Switzerland, and
the United Kingdom.

Other Seasonal Effects. The best three months
to be in stocks are November, December, and
January. In addition to the nearly 2% and 1.6%
returns for January and December, stocks have
been up by about 1.2% in November, perhaps

due to mean reversion from the worst three months to be in stocks: August, September, and October.

Although October is infamous as the month during which the two big stock market crashes occurred, in 1929 and 1987, September is, in fact, the worst month for stocks. Between 1950 and 2003, it is the only month with a negative average return. Note that following the terrorist attacks of September 11, 2001, the U.S. stock markets were shut for the remainder of the week in order to forestall what undoubtedly would have been panic selling. In the end, the S&P 500 was down by 8% for the month; in September 2002, the S&P 500 was down by 11%.

By combining these effects, it is safe to conclude that you would be wise to be in stocks from the end of October through the end of April. For a number of decades, the rate of return from stocks between these two months has averaged about 7%. By contrast, during the period from May through October, stocks have earned only about 1%.

Day-of-the-Week Effects. Monday tends to be a poor day for stocks, whereas Wednesday and Friday tend to be good days. Tuesday and Thursday tend to be mixed. Evidence also suggests that when Friday is negative, Monday is even more so. The only month in which stocks finish on a positive note on Mondays is in January. The only consolation about the first day of the week is that the biggest drop in stocks prices on Mondays tends to occur in the opening hour or so of trading. Trading then tends to finish on a more upbeat note.

EVALUATING MARKET EFFICIENCY FROM A FUNDAMENTAL ANALYSIS VIEW

As mentioned in Chapter 8, fundamental analysis deals with a company's performance from the economic environment in which it operates to its performance as reflected in its financial statements. Because the concern is now with fundamental analysis, semistrong form efficiency applies.

Evidence Supporting Semistrong Market Efficiency

We begin with the evidence that favors the theory, described in the following sections.

Media Reports of Company (and Stock) Performance. As noted earlier in this chapter, you can easily obtain investment advice from television, newspapers, and magazines, but studies indicate that not much is to be gained by doing so. For example, the evidence suggests that televised reports of current business conditions—which often feature financial analysts offering their insights into market conditions and recommending securities— are unlikely to help you earn above-average profits. In one such report, you would have had to buy and sell the recommended stocks the same day.

When it comes to print media recommendations, although the historical return to risk for many of the companies is impressive, the information does not seem to have any predictable content. As a result, investing in the published recommendations is unlikely to lead to superior performance.

News of Company Acquisitions. When Company A plans to acquire Company B, it offers to do so for a price above Company B's current stock price. (This is to entice Company B's shareholders into agreeing to the acquisition.) Can you take advantage of this rise in price of Company B's stock? Because the price increase is virtually instantaneous, you probably will not be able to do so.

Announcement of a Change in Economic Policy. The nation's central bank, the Federal Reserve System, sometimes tries to effect major changes in interest rates, either to stimulate or reign in aggregate spending. Would following the bank's actions improve the likelihood of earning big profits? The answer is no. On the contrary, it seems that markets do a good job of anticipating these changes.

Announcements of Stock Splits and Stock Dividends. Stock splits and stock dividends are essentially payments of more stock to shareholders. Some observers suggest that the announcement of these payments is a sign that good times lie ahead. Others state that the company is making its stock more affordable for the individual investor. Regardless, both explanations suggest that stock prices should rise. Buying stocks of companies that have recently split, however, does not appear to be a good strategy. To profit from stock splits and stock dividends, you need to *anticipate* them, which requires considerable time and effort, more so than may be worthwhile.

Investment Newsletters. More than a million investors reportedly subscribe to newsletters offering advice on buy-sell decisions, market timing, and the outlook for securities. It is far from clear, however, that the subscriptions are collectively worth their prices. One comprehensive study examined the performance of the recommendations for over 100 letters for more than a decade. In terms of return to risk, there was no sign of superior performance. Even if you followed the recommendations of the highest-rated newsletters of the previous year, your risk-adjusted performance would not have beaten the market's performance. Sticking to one newsletter was not helpful, either.

Announcements of Accounting Changes. In terms of financial statement analysis, an announcement of a change in the way companies record their activity could affect earnings. In turn, stock prices would be affected, up or down.

For example, when a firm announces that it is changing its depreciation method, its earnings would be affected; however, there would be no economic consequence. An analysis of accounting changes showed that markets rapidly adjusted to the new information.

Information about Mutual Funds. A vast literature on mutual funds suggests that actively managed funds generally underperform index funds, especially when expenses and load fees are factored in. A summary of the findings is as follows:

- Large funds perform about as well as small funds.

- Fund managers who are very active traders tend to do a bit worse than managers who are less active.

- Few fund managers appear to add much value.

- Load funds appear to underperform no-load funds.

- The majority of funds earn returns no higher than the S&P 500's returns.

Where Fundamental Analysis Appears Useful

There are also examples in which markets may not always be semistrong-efficient. These are described in the following sections.

Earnings Reports. Companies announce their earnings on a quarterly basis. In some cases, companies announce a positive *earnings surprise*. The evidence indicates that markets may be somewhat slow to react to these surprises. In fact, above-average returns may be possible for up to six months after the announcement.

Hot Mutual Funds. Although the weight of the evidence suggests that active mutual fund managers are unable to beat the market, research also indicates there are inefficiencies that you might be able to take advantage of. For one, there appears to be what's called a "hot-hands" effect. Funds that did well one year are likely to continue doing well in the relatively near future—for about a year. One study found that a yearly strategy of investing in the best-performing mutual funds enjoyed average returns that far and away exceeded market returns. However, the hot-hands effect tends to be short-term, and there appears to be no evidence to indicate a long-term hot-hands effect.

Size Effect. Over many years, small firms (also known as small-caps, as measured by the total market value of their stock) experience higher risk-adjusted rates of return than large firms. The January effect, mentioned earlier as an exception to weak-form efficiency, is linked to the size effect. Only small-caps have consistently enjoyed higher returns to risk than the market. Although risk-adjusted returns for large-caps tend to be higher as well, they have been noticeably lower than those of small-caps.

(Incidentally, the link between the January effect and size extends to international markets.)

Value Ratios. There are three rules to keep in mind here:

- **Stocks that have low price-earnings ratios tend to outperform those with high price-earnings ratios.** That said, refrain from being too mechanical with this rule, as you might miss out on some good opportunities. Nonetheless, by being prudent, you will reduce the chance of building a portfolio that is subject to large downswings in price.

- **Stocks with low price-book ratios are worth looking at.** The Standard & Poor's Corporation reportedly uses the price-book ratio in its construction of a value stock index, which can be superior to a growth index.

- **Watch price-sales ratios.** They not only indicate relative value, but sales are less subject to manipulation than earnings are.

Dividend Yield. Companies with high dividend yields are sometimes overlooked, and thus underpriced. Holding stocks with big dividend yields (i.e., 5% and higher) can lead to significant double-digit returns. In this regard, there is a trading strategy known as the "Dogs of the Dow." The idea is to pick the ten stocks with the highest dividend yields and then choose those with the lowest prices. There are a variety of choices here, ranging from the bottom three to the bottom five to all ten.

Price-earnings/Growth Rate. This relationship is commonly referred to as a *PEG ratio*. It is simply a company's price-earnings ratio divided by its expected growth in earnings per share. Stocks with PEG ratios of less than 1 are expected to enjoy above-average rates of return, whereas those above one will likely experience below-average rates of return. There is evidence to support this view.

Growth versus Value Effect. Growth management and value management are two well-recognized investment styles:

• Value managers prefer stocks that have low earnings growth, relatively large dividend yields, and low price-earnings ratios.

• Growth managers lean in the opposite direction.

The evidence clearly shows that, in contract to popular perception, the value strategy is superior to the growth strategy. For decades the difference has been noticeably large, especially between value small-caps and growth small-caps. This growth-value differential extends internationally, as well.

Value Line Effect. As noted in earlier chapters, Value Line is a well-known investment advisory company that evaluates about 1,700 stocks. Studies have suggested that its rating system of 1 through 5, where 1 is best and 5 is worst, can be a valuable way to help screen stocks.

EVALUATING MARKETS ACCORDING TO THE BEHAVIORAL FINANCE THEORY

A theory called *behavioral finance* argues that investors might not be the hard-to-fool profit-seekers that the concept of efficient markets assumes they are. Instead, it maintains that psychology plays a strong role in investment behavior, leading to, for example, investors who overestimate their stock-picking abilities and trade too frequently, or hold losing investments

too long, or sell winning investments too early. This is also evident in the popularity of lotteries, which some people systematically play even though the chance of winning is virtually nil.

Other human factors might also contribute to market inefficiency. Some investors are known to be hampered by what's called hindsight bias, which occurs when they wrongly believe that they could have predicted the correct outcome if only they had more of the correct information, or after the result has been revealed to them. Other investors overreact to "hot" stocks, chasing them without regard to company or industry fundamentals. Witness the Internet investment craze of the 1990s, which imploded when many dot-com stocks went bankrupt after first experiencing meteoric price increases, often with little or no earnings from operations.

The bottom line is that financial markets might not be as efficient as the theory implies. If this is true, then it increases the probability that you will develop and execute an active and successful investment strategy.

SOME THINGS TO AVOID

Several actions to avoid in regard to market efficiency include being too mechanical with one or more rules, frequently changing your buy-sell strategy, investing in companies with a lot of variation in their earnings per share or in companies you know nothing about, applying rules in a blanket fashion, and holding losers too long:

• **Avoid being too mechanical in your approach to investing.** You would be wise not to use only technical analysis with its reliance on charts that don't always display the patterns you are searching for. It is better to blend a rule or two in technical analysis with one or more in fundamental analysis. One study did just that, and the results indicated superior results.

- **Avoid following blanket rules.** Just because a company has, for example, a relatively high price-earning ratio does not necessarily mean its stock is overvalued. You should also check, for example, the PEG ratio, which can be found on the Internet or through investment publications. You should also check the industry the company is in and what its position is. Consider Microsoft during the 1990s, when its price-earnings ratio was often quite high, in excess of 30. Yet quarter after quarter, the company was a cash-generating machine that enjoyed strong sales growth and solid earnings-per-share growth.

- **Avoid changing your investment strategy too often.** Jumping back and forth between trading methods is a mistake that enriches only your broker. Before rushing out to try a new method, first reflect on it, then test how well it works. A mistake that many investors make is to switch strategies frequently. In the end, they often end up with no strategy at all.

- **Avoid investing in companies with variable earnings per share.** Be suspicious of companies whose earnings per share not only fail to display an upward trend, but also are positive for a year or so, then negative, then positive again. It becomes hard to determine what to expect from such companies.

- **Avoid investing in companies you know nothing about.** Be wary about investing in companies you have never heard of or those whose product lines you either do not know or do not understand. This holds even if you are paying someone to invest for you. Many high-tech companies, for example, produce very sophisticated equipment that only a specialized engineer would understand.

- **Avoid holding losers too long.** It can be tempting to hold losing investments for a long time, hoping that somehow their prices will increase again. Perhaps this is due to a psychological need "to be right." In a detailed study of individual investor behavior, this was the conclusion. Apparently, many investors, especially those who trade frequently, tended to hold their losers too long. The result was subpar investment performance. The bottom line is that you need to develop a trading strategy that works and one that you will stick to.

SUMMARY

This chapter discussed the effectiveness of technical and fundamental analysis with respect to the theory of efficient markets. In many instances, the theory seems to hold; that is, neither technical analysis nor fundamental analysis can be used to help you outperform a broad market index, commonly referred to as "beating the market." If you cannot beat the market, then the notion of active investing (in which you choose your own securities) may not be tenable.

However, we were able to uncover some patterns that might help you develop a superior security selection strategy. With respect to technical analysis, these patterns included filter rules, moving averages, and various seasonal effects. With respect to fundamental analysis, we showed that earnings reports, size effects, dividend yields, and value stocks could conceivably serve as the foundation for developing a superior stock selection strategy.

PUTTING IT ALL TOGETHER:

PORTFOLIO ANALYSIS AT A GLANCE

KEY TERMS

portfolio analysis, systematic risk, unsystematic risk, naïve diversification, efficient diversification, correlation, optimal portfolio, beta, American Depository Receipt

Chapters 2 through 7 introduced the securities that dominate financial markets. Chapters 8 and 9 dealt with choosing the securities and developing investment guidelines for buying and selling them. In this chapter, we will discuss putting the securities together to earn the highest possible return for a given level of risk (recall that the concept of *return to risk* was introduced in Chapter 1). This process is called *portfolio analysis*. It consists of three steps: selecting securities, constructing a portfolio of them, and tracking their performance. (For perspective, refer to the quiz in Chapter 1.)

INVESTMENT PORTFOLIOS SHOULD DIFFER AT DIFFERENT AGES

Whether you are an active or a passive investor, you should think about portfolio analysis. The manner in which you construct your portfolio can significantly affect your ability to attain your financial goals. To begin, should age affect your investment decisions? On balance, the answer is probably yes, but much depends on your tolerance for risk and the reason(s)

you are investing. Depending on where you are in your life, the mix of investments can and should vary according to the guidelines shown in Exhibit 10–1 (see page 137).

As you can see, each group listed in Exhibit 10–1 has a different portfolio. The youngest group has the most aggressive portfolio because its members have time to make up for any significant losses. The oldest group has the least aggressive portfolio for the opposite reason. Yet one thing is common across the five portfolios: *diversification*. The purpose is to spread out or reduce the risk as much as possible but without having to sacrifice the rate of return you need to reach your goal. The investments consist of stocks, bonds, REITs, and money market funds, none of which is strongly related to the other. In particular, REITs offer excellent diversification benefits against stocks. They have large dividend yields and solid returns and are an excellent hedge against inflation, and the fluctuations in their rates of return are generally independent of the fluctuations in stock returns.

DIVERSIFYING TO REDUCE RISK

Risk is of two types, *systematic* and *unsystematic*. The difference between the two lies in the fact that systematic risk is not diversifiable, whereas unsystematic risk is. To explain, systematic or predictable risk is rooted in the system. It exists, for instance, because changes in economic activity and in interest rates affect everyone, either directly or indirectly.

Unsystematic risk is unique to the event and, as a result, can be controlled by "not putting all your eggs in one basket."

EXHIBIT 10–1.

Twenties: Life in the fast lane; plenty of time to take chances.

Stocks:	80% (A lot of growth stocks)
Bonds:	5% (Corporate investment-grade and high-yield)
Real Estate:	10% (Real Estate Investment Trusts)
Cash:	5% (Money market account)

Thirties: Life in the passing lane; still some time to take chances.

Stocks:	75% (Growth mixed with growth-income stocks)
Bonds:	10% (Corporate investment-grade and high yield)
Real Estate:	10% (Real Estate Investment Trusts)
Cash:	5% (Money market account)

Forties: Life in the middle lane; turn toward more conservative selections.

Stocks:	70% (Dow 30, S&P 500, index funds)
Bonds:	10% (Treasury and corporate investment-grade)
Real Estate:	15% (Real Estate Investment Trusts)
Cash:	5% (Money market account)

Fifties: Life firmly in the cruising lane; veer more toward conservative selections.

Stocks:	60% (Dow 30, S&P 500, index funds)
Bonds:	15% (Treasury and corporate investment-grade)
Real Estate:	15% (Real Estate Investment Trusts)
Cash:	10% (Money market account)

Sixties and beyond: Life in the slow lane; turn strongly in the direction of stable returns.

Stocks:	40% (Low-risk, high-dividend yielding stocks)
Bonds:	20% (Treasury and corporate investment-grade)
Real Estate:	20% (Real Estate Investment Trusts)
Cash:	20% (Money market account)

Here are some illustrations of unsystematic risks as they apply to investments:

- Accounting scandal
- Unexpected resignation of a CEO
- Labor strife
- Plant explosion
- Unforeseen side effects of a product
- Defective product
- Lawsuit
- Adverse weather

As you can see, each of these examples would affect an individual company, or the companies within the industry, and their stock prices, but not those of other firms. For example, side effects from the use of a drug for anemia would not affect the demand for automobiles or beverages, and thus would not affect the stock prices of the firms in these two industries. Similarly, when the auto industry announces a product recall, the demand for personal computers would not be affected; nor would the demand for textbooks be affected by lawsuits against the tobacco industry. To reiterate, by not loading up your investments in one firm or one sector, you can diversify away from these unique, unsystematic events.

Naïve Diversification

Finance recognizes two kinds of diversification, *naïve* and *efficient*. The first is easier to understand. Naïve diversification deals with selecting securities across a wide variety of different industries. For example, with stocks, you might choose one company each from agriculture, beverages, health care, biotechnology, computer software, homebuilding, and electrical machinery. With bonds, you might buy some from the U.S. Treasury and some

from the auto industry and utilities. Note that no one industry dominates all these securities. The result is reduction in risk. Say, for example, a drought occurs: it will impact agriculture, but not the computer software industry. Likewise, if the homebuilding sector is suffering from a slump, the beverage and biotechnology industries are not likely to be affected.

Naïve diversification is prominent in large portfolios of securities, such as the S&P 500 and most mutual funds. No single stock or bond, for instance, makes up a significant portion of the S&P 500 or these diversified funds. Many mutual funds adhere to a rule that limits the amount that can be invested in a security to 5%. In this way, an unforeseen and negative event, such as a product recall, that affects a company's performance is confined to one security.

Efficient Diversification

Efficient diversification improves upon naïve diversification. It is concerned with reducing risk while preserving portfolio return. To begin, refer back to Chapter 1, to the rules for doubling your money: determine which rate of return you want to aim for, keeping in mind that greater return is possible, on average, only by assuming more risk. You then select securities that you believe will enable you to earn that rate of return. Efficient diversification is designed to help you choose securities that will help you to reduce your risk as much as possible for the rate of return that enables you to reach your goal.

How does it do this? Although it relies on sophisticated computer programming, the key lies within a simple word: *correlation*. Correlation is the degree to which one thing is associated with or related to another thing.

For example, the fortunes of Intel and Microsoft are strongly tied to the personal computer market. Although each company plays a different role (i.e., software and chips, respectively), their rates of return tend to move together; that is, they are *positively correlated*. When Intel's stock price is up because of strong computer sales, Microsoft's will be up as well. The opposite holds, too. When computer sales decline, the revenues of both companies drop, leading to a fall in their respective stock prices, and in turn their respective rates of return. Similarly, in the beverage industry, the revenues of Coca-Cola and PepsiCo would both rise with a broad increase in demand for soft drinks, in turn triggering increases in stock prices of both companies.

For purposes of diversification, however, it is *negative correlation* that is desired, as when comparing, say, Intel's stock returns with those of Procter & Gamble. This is because negative correlation can actually reduce portfolio risk. How? When one company's returns are rising, another company's returns are falling. On balance, however, both sets of return are still positive. By means of negative correlation, you are minimizing the fluctuation in returns in the expected return on the portfolio.

An overlooked aspect of portfolios is that the risk may be higher than you might realize. This is because the risk of a portfolio may be more than the sum of the risks of the individual securities. The amount over and above the sum of the individual risks depends on the degree to which the set of returns are correlated. The more correlated they are, the greater the risk of the portfolio.

OPTIMAL INVESTMENT PORTFOLIOS ARE EFFICIENTLY DIVERSIFIED

An *optimal portfolio* is one that is efficiently diversified. Few portfolios can be considered optimal. Mutual funds certainly are not; in fact, they tend to be overdiversified, which hurts fund performance.

How might you build an optimal portfolio? To begin, you need to understand the securities that interest you. And—it cannot be overemphasized—knowing your risk tolerance is critical. If you want to avoid risk as much as possible, you should be looking at high-grade bonds and low-risk stocks. If you can tolerate more risk, you might think about higher-risk stocks, lower-grade bonds, and perhaps a bit of speculative real estate.

Building an optimal portfolio continues with knowing about the risks of the securities you have chosen. This risk is measured by the up-and-down fluctuations in the returns, called variance, or the degree to which the rates of return on a security vary. This is also called volatility. The more they vary from day to day, week to week, and month to month, the higher the variance. The higher the variance, the more uncertain you will be about the return you will earn from one period to the next. The more uncertain you are, the greater the risk of the security. As an example, let's take a look at the monthly returns of three stocks during 2002, shown in Exhibit 10–2:

- Exxon Mobil (Stock symbol: XOM)

- General Motors (Stock symbol: GM)

- AOL Time Warner (Stock Symbol: AOL).

EXHIBIT 10–2. MONTHLY RETURNS, 2002, FOR EXXON MOBIL, GENERAL MOTORS, AND AOL TIME WARNER			
	XOM	**GM**	**AOL**
January	−0.65%	5.23%	−18.04%
February	5.76%	4.64%	−5.74%
March	6.13%	14.11%	−4.64%
April	−8.35%	6.12%	−19.58%
May	−0.61%	−2.40%	−1.68%
June	2.49%	−14.00%	−21.34%
July	−10.18%	−12.91%	−21.82%
August	−3.56%	4.00%	10.00%
September	−10.01%	−18.71%	−7.51%
October	5.50%	−14.55%	26.07%
November	4.10%	21.17%	10.98%
December	0.38%	−7.15%	−19.98%

Looking carefully at the numbers shown in this exhibit, you should note three points:

• Of the 36 returns, AOL Time Warner has the largest positive one, 26.07%.

• AOL has the most double-digit rates of return, eight. Moreover, it had quite a run of negative returns the first seven months, with four of them averaging about −20% (i.e., −18.04%, −19.58%, −21.34%, and −21.82%). General Motors has six double-digit returns and Exxon Mobil has two.

• AOL Time Warner's returns (in absolute value) are the largest in seven of the twelve months: January, April, June, July, August, October, and December. General Motors has the largest in four of the months: March, May, September, and November; and Exxon Mobil has the largest in one month: February.

On the basis of these results, you can see that AOL Time Warner has the largest fluctuations in the returns. Out of its eight double-digit returns (of which five are negative), six exceed 15%. Thus, its variance is the highest, so its stock would be considered to have the most risk, because the return, from month to month, is not very predictable. From these results, it is difficult to figure out what the next month will bring. Thus, the chance that your prediction will be wrong is high.

By contrast, Exxon Mobil would have the least risk. Although its returns are far from constant, they are not nearly as variable as those of the other companies. In terms of actual variances, we have the following: ExxonMobil, 37; General Motors, 156; and AOL Time Warner, 237. With respect to the twelve months of 2002, AOL Time Warner's stock is considered to have nearly 6.5 times more risk than Exxon Mobil's (237 divided by 37) and about 52%

more risk than General Motors'. (The Appendix gives an illustration on how to compute variance.)

The importance of knowing about the risk you are willing to bear cannot be overstated. Too many investors plunge into stocks without any idea of the risks. As risky a stock as AOL Time Warner has been, it pales in comparison to that of some companies, whose risk, at times, has been more than three times higher.

The point, however, is not that you should never invest in such companies but that you must know your risk tolerance, which takes us back to Chapter 1, in which you were asked to assess your risk tolerance by answering some questions. Remember, the bottom line is "be true to yourself." Do not take unnecessary chances.

Graphing the Relationship between a Portfolio's Expected Return and Its Risk

Let us take a look at a graph, which we call the "portfolio curve," that sums up this discussion; it is shown in Exhibit 10–3. This graph represents the relationship between the expected return on a portfolio and portfolio risk. It has the following characteristics:

- It represents the best that you can do *given what the market offers*. For example, there are some years when strong economic growth and low inflation send stock prices upward. In effect, the market is offering investors big returns. However, as quickly as the gains are earned, they could reverse themselves. The point is, your investment decisions will be strongly influenced by market conditions.

- The curve slopes from left to right to reflect the observation that higher portfolio returns are possible only when taking on more risk. Assuming you build a portfolio that is on the line, higher returns are possible only if you are willing to assume more risk, and your willingness to do so depends on your risk tolerance. Thus, along the curve, "return to risk" takes on added significance.

- The objective is to "get the curve" by reducing your risk as much as possible. The more you reduce the risk, the closer you get to the

EXHIBIT 10–3. PORTFOLIO CURVE

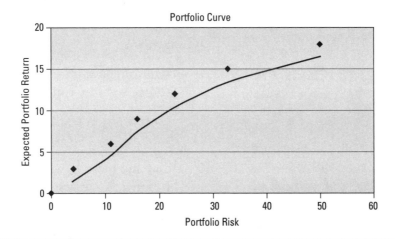

curve, and the closer you get to the curve, the better your portfolio's performance in terms of return to risk. That is the objective.

Combining systematic and unsystematic risks, we conclude that all portfolios that lie on the portfolio curve have had all unsystematic risk diversified away. All that remains is the systematic risk, which is not diversifiable.

The vast majority of portfolios do not appear to lie on or near the portfolio curve. They tend to be somewhere inside it. As you might guess, this has an important implication. The farther the portfolio is from the curve, the less efficient it is, and the less efficient it is, the less likely you will be beating the market.

Where should your portfolio be along the curve? That is up to you. Again, it depends on how much risk you can bear. If you are very risk-averse, then it is in your interest to find portfolios on the curve that have expected returns in the range of 5% to 10%. In this range, the risks, as indicated by the curve, are between about 6% and 16%. If you want higher returns, say around 12%, then according to the curve, you have to be ready to assume more risk, in the range of 20% to 25%. The more risk you are willing to bear, the higher the return you can shoot for.

MEASURING SYSTEMATIC RISK USING BETA

To move closer to a simple and elegant measure of systematic risk, economists have come up with a concept called *beta*. You can get it off the Internet or from print media, such as in Value Line's *Investment Survey*. What does beta mean and how can you use it? Let us address this question as follows:

- Beta is greater than 1: Aggressive security
- Beta equals 1: Moves with the market
- Beta is less than 1: Defensive security

These three categories lead to more questions. For example, what is meant by "aggressive" and "defensive"? The returns from an aggressive stock tend to bounce up and down more than the market's returns, as measured by, for example, the S&P 500 or the Wilshire 5000. To illustrate, when the market's returns increase by 10%, an aggressive stock's returns, on average, will be up by *more than* 10%. By comparison, a defensive security's returns will be up by *less than* 10%. If the security's beta equals 1, then it will have increased, on average, by 10%. As you might infer, if you were very risk-averse, you would tend to invest in defensive securities. If you were risk-tolerant, you would be inclined to invest in aggressive securities.

How can you determine the beta of a stock? Based on historical data, here are some guidelines, as of early 2003, followed by examples:

- Financials (e.g., Citigroup and Merrill Lynch): aggressive

- Technology (e.g., Intel and Microsoft): aggressive

- Traditional Manufacturing (e.g., General Motors and Caterpillar): market mover

- Transportation (e.g., CSX and Roadway): defensive

- Food and beverage (e.g., Safeway, McDonald's, Coca-Cola): defensive

- Medical (e.g., Johnson & Johnson, Medtronic, and Pfizer): defensive

- Energy (e.g., Exxon Mobil and ChevronTexaco): defensive

- Utilities (e.g., Consolidated Edison and DQE): defensive

Of all industries, arguably one of the most notorious for big betas, at least from the 1990s through 2003, is the semiconductor group, led by Intel. This sector makes computer chips and equipment that powers everything from computers to DVD players to cell telephones. The sector is highly cyclical, often going through so-called boom and bust cycles. But as big as Intel's beta is, at 1.80, many companies in this sector have betas as large, if not larger.

Owing to its relatively recent emergence, another sector with big betas, even larger than those of the semiconductor group, is the Internet. As of this writing, it is reasonable to conclude that it is the most aggressive sector. As evidence, the beta of AOL Time Warner is 2.50. The beta of Yahoo!, the Internet search engine provider, is significantly higher, at 3.60. Yet its beta nearly pales in comparison to the whopping beta of the e-business and enterprise software company, CMGI, which is at 5.00! Think about this for a moment. Historically, whenever the S&P 500 or the Wilshire 5000 have shown an upward or downward trend, on average, CMGI's returns have changed by five times the market's returns.

By contrast, the smallest betas are in the energy, beverage, and medical groups. Johnson & Johnson and Coca-Cola register the lowest betas at 0.35, followed by Exxon Mobil at 0.40. Note that these three companies are household names. Unlike the products and services of technology companies, the demand for which can be uncertain if not unpredictable, the demand for gasoline and oil, beverages, and health care is steady and reliable. Thus, the returns on the stocks of these three companies tend to fluctuate far less than those of the overall market.

Rounding out the description is the traditional manufacturing group, led by General Electric, with a beta of nearly 1. Other firms in this group include United Technologies, which is primarily engaged in the production of elevators and aerospace equipment, with a beta of 1.1, the same beta as another aerospace equipment firm, Honeywell.

Note, however, there are exceptions. A traditional manufacturer, Alcoa Aluminum has a large beta, 1.40, in part due to the specialized nature of the aluminum industry. In contrast, the beta of Caterpillar, a maker of earth-moving equipment, is 0.80, suggesting relatively mild fluctuations in returns for a capital-intensive company.

So far, this discussion has focused on betas for stocks. What about the betas for corporate bonds? They are much lower than the betas for stocks, generally in the range of 0.10 to 0.50. By comparison, stock betas on the Dow Jones Industrials, for example, range from about 0.30 to 2.00 and much larger, and it is not unheard of for stocks on the NASDAQ to exceed 3.00. In addition, stocks are traded much more frequently than bonds, which can increase the size of the betas.

Is there an easy way to find expected returns and beta? Yes, there is. Value Line produces both and provides predictions. Then all you need to do is take the high and low annual returns and divide them by the stock's beta. Repeat this for a variety of companies. Finally, choose the stocks that have the highest returns to beta, taking care not to choose more than a few stocks from any one sector or from closely related sectors.

There is one more question that needs to be answered. How can beta help you determine how much to invest in each security? The Appendix outlines a statistically specific way, but to keep things simple here, remember that the bigger the expected return divided by beta, the more you should be inclined to invest in the security.

Concerning how much to invest in each security, be aware of two things. First, while low-beta securities generally have low risk, they sometimes can have a lot of unsystematic risk. So you need to be careful. If the company is not part of either the technology or biotechnology sectors, but rather from a long-established industry, such as food, beverages, metal manufacturing, services or utilities, then there is a high probability that the company's stock is not high-risk. That said, you do have to be careful about these other sectors, or any newly emerging sectors, as well. To that end, you would be wise to check Value Line's ratings. It uses a scale of 1 to 5, where 1 indicates lowest risk and 5 indicates highest risk. A stock with a risk of at least 3 probably carries more risk than a highly risk-averse investor might tolerate.

Second, as a rule, we suggest that you invest no more than 15% in any one security, and you would be wise to keep the maximum at less than this. Although, at times, some securities might rate a higher weight, keep in mind that by investing increasingly in one or a few securities, you run the risk of having an underdiversified portfolio. Keep in mind that most mutual funds adhere to the rule of not investing more than 5% of their assets in a single security.

INVESTING INTERNATIONALLY: LOOKING BEYOND YOUR OWN BACKYARD

There is little to stop you today from taking advantage of opportunities beyond U.S. borders. Evidence suggests that you would, in fact, be wise to do so. Whether the markets are in Canada, Europe, Latin America, Asia, or the Pacific Basin, investing in other countries offers opportunities for further diversifying your portfolio, with a possible bonus of a higher return. Consider that, in terms of stocks, the U.S. market is roughly half of the world market, so why should you believe that the only opportunities to build up your portfolio are at home? More compelling, the stock markets of some countries have been growing more rapidly than those in the United States. For example, while the S&P 500's stock prices crawled along at a rate of under 3% from 1997 through 2002, consider the success of these stock prices in other countries:

- Egypt's jumped by more than 100%.
- Italy's increased by more than 40%.
- Denmark's went up by nearly 40%.
- Australia's increased by more than 20%.

The point is, by expanding your investment horizons, you might be able to uncover some good investment opportunities.

In terms of mutual funds, it has been observed that the return-to-risk benefits of global portfolios significantly exceed those of domestic ones. For example, holders of global portfolios with the same risk as a domestic ones enjoyed returns that were, on average, three percentage points higher. In terms of the doubling rules cited in Chapter 1, such a difference can add up quickly. The same conclusion holds for bonds: the minimum-risk portfolio tends to be in the range of 70% domestic and 30% international.

You can also take advantage of international diversification through *American Depository Receipts (ADRs)*. These are stocks traded on a U.S. exchange but headquartered in another country. There are more than 2,000 ADRs listed on U.S. exchanges. Exhibit 10–4 lists some actively traded ADRs in the United States.

Neither international/global mutual funds nor ADRs are problem-free, however. Countries have their own unique risks, from political uncertainties to poor economic policies. In addition, and no less important, there are exchange-rate risks. You might invest in another country's markets only to lose profits when the foreign currency is converted back into U.S. dollars.

Nevertheless, it appears that optimal portfolios exposed to currency risk do better than those that are "hedged" against the risk. Not only is the risk likely to be lower, but the return is also likely to be higher. Concisely put, international diversification adds value.

Given the depth and breadth of the discussion, a quick summary of guidelines is in order:

- Diversify your portfolio.

- Remember that risk comes in two forms: systematic and unsystematic.

- Unsystematic risk is diversifiable; unsystematic risk is not.

- Buy stocks that have high expected returns to beta, and sell stocks that have low expected returns to beta.

SOME THINGS TO AVOID

There are several things to be circumspect about when putting together your portfolio. If you are at least moderately risk-averse, you will want to avoid investing too much in any one broad area, such as agriculture, manufacturing, mining, or services. You will also want

EXHIBIT 10–4. ACTIVELY TRADED ADRs IN THE UNITED STATES

Company	Industry	Headquarters	Exchange
BP-Amoco	Energy	United Kingdom	NYSE
DeBeers	Mining	South Africa	NASDAQ
Ericsson	Communications	Sweden	NASDAQ
Glaxo Wellcome	Medical	United Kingdom	NYSE
Imperial Oil	Energy	Canada	AMEX
Nokia	Communications	Finland	NYSE
Nortel	Communications	Canada	NYSE
Royal Dutch	Energy	Netherlands	NYSE
Toyota	Auto	Japan	NYSE

to avoid becoming overconfident, as it tends to lead to frequent trading, such as selling "winners" too early, well before their prices have peaked. In addition, avoid becoming emotionally attached to the stocks of particular companies; and when it comes to emotion, stick to your strategy. Regarding mutual funds, be careful about sector funds.

- **Avoid investing too much in one area.** By "area," we mean, for example, manufacturing, agriculture, or technology. Although the companies may well be in different industries (autos, steel, and electrical machinery), their returns might well move together in good times and in bad times.

  For example, from 1998 to early 2000, the Y2K scare (in which people seemed concerned that world economies would shut down when computers failed to make the date switch to the year 2000) moved many consumers and businesses to increase spending on cutting-edge technology, from personal computers and computer networks to DVD player and cellphones, only to cut back dramatically once it was clear there was no such problem. In fact, as pointed out, the technology-laden NASDAQ exchange fell by 78% between March 2000 and October 2002, taking down even some nontechnology stocks.

- **Avoid becoming overly confident.** If you are initially successful, take care not to become overconfident. Doing so often leads to selling winning stocks too early and holding losing stocks too long. This runs counter to the Wall Street rule "ride your winners and sell your losers." The result is subpar portfolio performance, especially compared to a passive strategy of investing in broad market indices. Although financial markets can be quite generous, they can also be brutal and seemingly fickle, especially when your portfolio is losing money.

- **Avoid becoming emotionally attached to your investments.** Extending the previous point, avoid making investments prompted by patriotic causes, loyalty to an employer, or commitment to a particular firm. For example, it is far from clear that the "buy American" campaign from the 1970s and 1980s advanced the stocks of domestic companies. Even more to the point, after adjusting for inflation, you will find that U.S. savings bonds, with their appeal to invest "for the good of the country," have not been a good investment.

- **Avoid changing investing strategies.** If you find a set of rules that work well for you, do not deviate too much from them. Some of the most unsuccessful investors often get caught up in the emotion of the moment— short-term, momentum investing—and end up trading securities without a well-defined approach. The outcome is poor portfolio performance.

- **Avoid investing too heavily in sector mutual funds.** As emphasized earlier, be careful when it comes to investing in sector mutual funds. The securities in these funds are strongly correlated, as their success is tied to a single sector (such as technology, financial services, chemicals, and energy). Unless you can find investments that have low correlations with these funds, you will not have a diversified portfolio. When times are good, you will feel great, but in bad times you will feel terrible.

SUMMARY

Portfolio analysis is about putting together a set of securities that can help you improve your investment returns and reduce your risk. The key begins with diversification. Most portfolios are naïvely diversified; that is, they are invested in securities representing a wide variety of industries. Although this is an important first step, it does not always go far enough. Efficient diversification tries to reduce portfolio risk while preserving portfolio return. It does so by focusing on the correlation (i.e., the degree to which the returns on two securities are related) between each pair of security returns. The rule is, invest in securities whose returns have correlations as low as possible.

Risk comes in two forms, systematic and unsystematic. Systematic risk, which represents risk that affects all securities, is not diversifiable. Conversely, unsystematic risk is diversifiable, and it represents events unique to a firm or sector (such as accounting scandals, product recalls, lawsuits, and adverse weather). Systematic risk is measured by beta. You should choose securities whose returns to risk, as measured by expected rates of return relative to their betas, are high. Choosing securities in this manner, keeping in mind the correlation rule, will help you reduce portfolio risk while preserving portfolio return.

CHAPTER

11

TRACKING YOUR PORTFOLIO

—AND THE ECONOMY

KEY TERMS

Gross domestic product, real GDP, discount rate, dollar-cost averaging, market order, limit order, good 'til canceled order, trailing stop order, wash sale, churning, portfolio beta

From the previous chapters, we can now provide a summary, but along the way we will address a few new topics, such as keeping your eye on the economic landscape, dollar-cost averaging, and tracking your portfolio.

GETTING ON THE RIGHT INVESTING TRACK

Let us begin with a broad summary of the steps to take to get started on the right investment track:

1. Determine your objectives (i.e., whether you need money for retirement, education, property acquisition, etc.).

2. Know how much you will need and how much you can afford to invest.

3. Familiarize yourself with financial markets and what they offer.

4. Assess your tolerance for risk.

5. Remember the principles of compounding and the "doubling rules" (covered in Chapter 1).

6. Keep in mind that return and risk are related.

7. Decide whether you want to be an active or passive investor.

If you want to be a passive investor, here are some guidelines for how you should invest:

- Put your money into a select few index mutual funds and REITs, with percentages for each group (as outlined in Chapter 10). The Vanguard Group is well known in this area, with low-cost funds that replicate, for example, the S&P 500, the Wilshire 5000, Treasury bonds, corporate bonds, and intermediate-term bonds.

- Remember that stocks outperform bonds (especially after adjusting for inflation), so do not overload in bonds.

- Keep in mind that real estate investments (e.g., property and REITs) do well at diversifying portfolios.

- Use a buy-and-hold strategy; trade as little as possible.

- Be tax-savvy (e.g., invest in Roth IRAs, 401(k)s, 529 plans, municipal bonds, etc.).

If you want to pick your own securities—that is, be an active investor—then you should:

- Choose stocks and bonds of companies with strong sales growth, solid EPS (earnings-per-share) growth, and that generate a lot of cash.

- Look for opportunities based on exceptions to market efficiency, such as mean reversion, seasonal effects, and low market value ratios.

- Avoid stocks with large price-earnings, price-book, and price-sales ratios; they may be richly priced.

- Be wary of companies that have issued a lot of debt.

- Adjust stock returns for beta.

- Diversify your holdings by investing in companies whose security returns have low correlations, and by putting some money into real estate and REITS.

- Use derivatives, especially put and call options, to further reduce your portfolio risk.

- Leave emotion out of your decisions to choose and/or hold onto your investments.

- Use a buy-and-hold strategy.

- Use the tax laws to your advantage (e.g., long-term capital gains, municipal bonds, etc.).

KEEPING AN EYE ON THE ECONOMY: A MACROECONOMICS PERSPECTIVE

How is the economy doing? Is consumer and business confidence high or low? What is the Federal Reserve System (i.e., the U.S. central bank) up to? Are Congress and the president thinking about tax cuts? These are all questions you need to consider before making your investments. Granted, you do not want to spend too much time reflecting on these issues, otherwise you might find yourself trapped into trying to "time" the market, which is not a good idea. Still, knowing something about economic conditions can help you decide how to alter your portfolio according to this information.

Tracking Gross Domestic Product Values

The most closely watched measure of economic activity is called the *gross domestic product*, or *GDP*. It deals with the value of everything produced. The more that is produced, the bigger the economy gets. As a rule, the long-term trend in inflation-adjusted GDP (which is often called *real GDP*) is just over 3%. So anytime the economy begins to expand toward this number and beyond, the stock market is going to anticipate the growth and begin to rise. The reason is simple: more production translates to better bottom lines, and stock rises will rise on the good news. Conversely, when real GDP begins to fall (as it did in 1990 and 2000), the stock market declines. If the decline in GDP is protracted, layoffs ensue, pushing down both consumer and business confidence, making things worse as people begin to rein in their spending.

The point of this discussion is to emphasize the advice to "touch up" your portfolio rather than to try to time markets. As economic growth begins to show a sustained increase, and if you are at least moderately risk-averse, then perhaps you want to shift a small portion of your portfolio from bonds to stocks, even to somewhat higher-beta stocks. You would want to do just the opposite during slowdowns in real GDP.

Keeping an Eye on What the Federal Reserve Does

Can you anticipate what is likely to happen economically? To some degree you can. One way is to watch the actions of the Federal Reserve System. As a brief background, the Fed, as it is often called in financial circles and in the media, watches over the nation's money supply: currency, checking accounts, and savings accounts. Through its actions, it can increase or decrease the amounts in those accounts. It does this through its purchases and sales of U.S. Treasury bills. Concisely put, the more bills it buys from investors, the more cash they will have. Investors, in turn, deposit the cash (in the form of checks) into their bank accounts. Banks, noticing the influx of cash, begin to loan the funds, and at increasingly *lower* interest rates. The lower the interest rates go, the more incentive buyers have to get a loan, whether to buy a home, a car, appliances, or other "big-ticket" items. As you and others do so, there is an increase in demand for these products, leading to more production, and eventually higher stock prices.

But trying to figure out what the Fed is up to is not easy. Nonetheless, one of the easiest ways is to watch for changes in the *discount rate*, which is the rate of interest that the Fed charges banks on loans. One study showed that successive decreases in the discount rate signal that the Fed is trying to expand the amount of money and, in turn, drive interest rates down. Successive increases imply just the opposite. The implications are clear. When interest rates are falling, you want to be holding stocks and bonds. You want to be much more cautious, however, when interest rates are rising. To repeat, be careful not to try to time markets; instead, "touch up" your portfolio.

Tracking Your Taxes

Taxes can also impact your portfolio. When John F. Kennedy became president in 1960, income earners in the highest tax brackets found that 92% of their dividends were being taxed away. Naturally, the tendency for any high-income individual was to shy away from stocks. It stands to reason that investors will be more inclined to invest in stocks when they know that they will be able to keep most of their gains, both capital and income. There is a catch here, though. Investors and businesses seem to need to be convinced that the tax rates will be permanent: that the Congress and the president are "serious." Short-term, anecdotal tax cuts (such as increases in rebates and temporary tax reductions) are almost worthless. People will not react much to the added income because they expect the tax cut either to be a one-shot affair or to be repealed.

INVESTING BY DOLLAR-COST AVERAGING: FOR THOSE WHO FEAR INVESTING TOO MUCH AT ONCE

Dollar-cost averaging simply means investing a fixed amount periodically. This approach to investing can help you avoid the risk of investing all of your money when the prices of securities are high, the wrong time for the "buy low, sell high" approach. Perhaps, you don't have a choice; perhaps the best that you can do is to put some of your income every month into a savings plan, in which case you will be automatically dollar-cost averaging. The prices of securities fluctuate. As a result, because you are investing a fixed amount, you will be buying fewer shares when security prices are high and more shares when prices are low, as Exhibit 11–1 illustrates.

You might find the effect of dollar-cost averaging intriguing. Note that the average price in Exhibit 11–1 is $36.67, but the average *cost per share* is $32.73. The difference is due to the fact that you bought more shares at lower prices than you did at higher prices. For example, you bought 18 shares at $20 per share and 12 shares at $30, but only 6 shares at $60.

In the end, you made money because the value of the portfolio is:

$36.67 (the average price) × 66 (the total number of shares purchased) = $2,420.22

However, if you invested only $2,160, there's a positive difference of $260.22:

$2,420.22 − $2,160 = $260.22

This is approximately a 12% return on your investment, which is pretty good.

Be careful, though, about making too much of this example. Dollar-cost averaging is not going to solve all your investment problems. If prices of stocks and bonds are declining, you will be losing money, and it is not uncommon for investors to also lose heart when this occurs. As pointed out throughout this book, you need to stick to your strategy in good times and bad. In fact, if you buy shares during times of steep declines in stock and bond prices, dollar-cost averaging will work even better for you. But if you abandon the effort, dollar-cost averaging will not work.

There is one drawback to dollar-cost averaging. If you are holding a sizeable sum (e.g., from the liquidation of securities, sale of real estate, inheritance, etc.) and you decide to dollar-cost average, you could lose out on the highest rates of return. Given that bull markets tend to outpace bear markets, the lost opportunity could be significant. Nonetheless, in the spirit of dollar-cost averaging, it is probably not a bad idea to keep a little bit of cash on hand to take advantage of market "dips." Once again, we are not suggesting that you try to predict market movements, only that bear markets can produce as much despair as bull markets can produce hope.

KEEPING TRACK OF YOUR INVESTMENTS

There are three items you should keep track of, two qualitative and one quantitative. The qualitative ones concern how you place your orders and the potential for abuse, along with

EXHIBIT 11–1.   DOLLAR-COST AVERAGING

Month	Amount Invested	Price Per Share	Shares Bought
January	$360	$20	18
February	$360	$30	12
March	$360	$40	9
April	$360	$30	12
May	$360	$40	9
June	$360	$60	6
Total	$2,160		
Average Price		$36.67	
Shares Bought			66
Average Cost Per Share	$32.73 (= amount invested divided by shares bought) (= $2160 ÷ 66)		

what you can do to prevent it. The quantitative one deals with tracking your investment performance.

Tracking How You Place Your Investment Orders

As a buyer or seller of securities, you tell your broker how you want your order executed. You could, say, authorize a transaction to be executed "at the market." This is a *market order* and means that your order will be filled, or completed, at the best price available. In this case, you would be buying at the current ask price and selling at the current bid price (the difference is called the *bid-ask spread*). Your order may be filled at the same price as the last trade, or close to it if stock is not available at the last-traded price. But when you authorize your broker to buy "at the market," be aware that you will not know how much you will be paying for the stock.

An alternative is to place a *limit order*, in which case you specify the price you expect to pay. Let's say you offer to buy shares at a price below the most recent trade. Your order might fill at the lower price if a willing seller offers the stock, but if no such seller can be found, your order will not be filled. A limit order may be a day order—one limited to the day you placed it—and will expire at the market's close; or the limit order might be left open until it is canceled, in which case the order is *good 'til canceled*. If you place such an order, remember you did so, as it might not be filled until weeks later.

Two other types of orders can help to protect your investments: the *stop order* and the *limit order to sell*. The stop order is a special form of limit order that tells the broker's representative on the exchange floor to sell your shares if the price drops to a level you specify. Thus, you can avoid a major loss on shares you own by entering a good 'til canceled stop order.

For example, suppose you own shares bought at $35, but they are now trading at $45. You decide to protect at least some of your profit against a possible future drop in price, and you enter a stop order to sell your shares at $40. A stop order set too close to a current price could be tripped off by a temporary blip down, after which the price rises again. (Recall from Chapter 8 on technical analysis that this brief movement down followed quickly by a move up is called a whipsaw.) If the market turns against you, and the price drops to $40, your stop order automatically becomes an active order and is executed. Although you have lost $5 per share from a recent price, you protected $5 per share of your profit above its cost basis.

A limit order to sell functions like a stop order, protecting you in a sale. If you are holding stock at $45 and wish to lock in a profit on a rise, you may place a limit order to sell if your stock reaches, say, $50.

Stop orders can be changed at will, so a *trailing stop order* may protect more of your profit if you monitor prices regularly. A trailing stop order is one that moves up as the price rises. Continuing with our example, suppose that the price of your stock moves up to $50 from $45. With the stop order set at $40, you could lose 20% of your profit in a serious downturn. To protect more of your profit, you could move the stop limit up from $40 to $43. If the stock continues to move up, call your broker and change the limit again.

As you trade, be aware of what are called *wash sales*. A wash sale occurs when you sell and buy back essentially the same security within 30 days. A rule imposed by the IRS voids the practice of taking capital losses to offset gains. Doing this with mutual funds is easier, because switching funds does not violate the wash sale rule.

Tracking Your Investments to Prevent Abuse

You might have heard a broker's license sometimes referred to as a "license to steal." Indeed, the opportunity for abuse in dealings between securities firms and investors is always tempting to the greedy. Newspaper accounts record all too often the abuse of fiduciary responsibility in all of the following:

- Selling and buying junk bonds

- Fraudulent multimillion-dollar real estate deals

- Highly questionable investment advice

- Insider trading scandals involving highly placed company officials, major players at brokerages, and institutions responsible for the savings of small investors

Such large-scale, unsavory activities are widely reported, but abuses that occur between retail brokers and individuals are less often publicized, hence less well known. Your best defense against such abuse is to be aware of the tricks and tactics of the trade and avoid them. This is not to say that all brokers are given to shady practices, but enough engage in them to warrant watchfulness on your part.

Much of the abuse between broker and client results from a conflict of interest; never forget that the broker needs a steady stream of commissions. Common activities that tend to enhance the income of brokers to the possible disadvantage of investors are described in the following sections.

Watch Out for Churning. Churning refers to excessive trading in an account. The broker, with the tacit approval of the client, engages in frequent trading for the express purpose of generating more commissions. Selling one block of stock in order to generate cash to buy a different block of stock yields two commissions.

Churning often peaks near the end of each month, when a broker may feel pressed to meet a goal or a quota. Often the broker will sell a stock that has advanced in price and shows a profit, citing the gain to the client. The pitch may be that the price for that stock has moved up and is now likely to stall— better to get out and move into another stock that the broker believes is about to move up. In a bull market (i.e., one that is moving up), such tactics may appear reasonable to the unsophisticated investor who relies on the broker for advice.

The reverse may occur in a bear market (i.e., one that is moving down), when the broker advises the client to get out of a stock that is declining to avoid a greater loss. The pitch may then be to move the cash generated from the sale into a defensive stock, one likely to retain its value in a down-trending market. A defensive stock may be one of the major food companies or a utility, as both industries tend to hold their value during a recession, simply because people still must eat and turn on the lights. What may not be apparent to the uninformed investor is the price level of defensive stocks. Many will have been bid up in price by others taking positions in those same stocks months earlier when early signals of a declining economy appeared. Ordinarily, according to the usual agreement signed between client and broker, the broker must obtain the client's approval for each transaction. However, some brokers fail to follow procedure and make trades on their own, often to the disadvantage of the client.

Your defense against churning is to pay close attention to the paperwork you receive from the broker. Just be aware that this paperwork is designed to simplify the work of the firm's computer rather than to inform you, the client, so take the time to learn how to read the monthly reviews of account activity. Check that every transaction was made with your approval. If you find transactions that you did not approve prior to execution, inquire promptly. Likewise, if you detect an unproductive volume of trading, advise your broker to stop it.

Find out whether you have a *discretionary agreement* with your broker, which allows the broker to use his or her own discretion in trading for your account without your prior approval. Thus, a broker operating with a discretionary agreement can more easily churn your account and may invest in companies riskier than you might approve. If you now have a discretionary agreement with your broker, revoke it. Requiring a broker to check with you before trading is one way of keeping the broker's feet to the fire. If your broker has to check with you, he or she will most likely engage only in trades in whose outcome he or she has confidence.

Be Savvy about Unsuitable Investments. When you hire a broker, you will be asked to spell out your goals and operating parameters, usually on a standard disclosure form. You may be asked about your interest in capital gains versus income, about whether your attitude is conservative or aggressive, and about acceptable risk levels. This form goes into your record as a statement of your intentions and goals.

A broker may recommend investments far outside the limits on your disclosure. You may have indicated that you are conservative and desire to invest for income with liquidity. A broker who sells you a limited partnership to finance some real estate, oil development, or an apple orchard is not following your expressed goals, as these investments tend to be extremely risky, long-term, and illiquid. Further, limited partnerships require investors to meet suitability limits, such as a minimum net worth outside one's residence and a high salary level. Such suitability requirements are established by the Securities and Exchange Commission and state security departments to limit partnership offerings to sophisticated investors with enough financial resources to withstand a loss if the project goes sour. However, the broker may push such partnerships because they generate higher commissions than stocks and bonds.

Your defense against unsuitable investments is to question your broker about the details of any recommended investment. Learn enough about various alternatives so that you can rate the risks on your own. Before you venture into an unknown field of investing, do your homework. Before committing to a large investment, ask your accountant or a knowledgeable friend to review it. Do not depend entirely on recommendations from your broker.

Know the Risks of Initial Public Offerings (IPOs). Shares in an initial public offering can be a very risky investment with little promise of a big payback to compensate for the added risk. An IPO may be one of two kinds: a public offering by a company seeking funds for expansion or an initial offering on a closed-end mutual fund. Underwriting IPOs enables small companies to grow. A company making a public offering of shares to raise funds for expansion usually has an excellent track record—years of steadily rising sales, rising profits, proven managers in place, and promising business plans for expansion once new funding becomes available. Many IPOs go on to unqualified successes, such as Nordstrom and Microsoft. However, despite the rosy projections featured in the prospectus issued by the IPO underwriters, not all companies prosper after raising new cash.

One way to judge the general opinion of the professionals about an IPO is to ask your broker about shares. If many shares are available and your broker offers you as many as you want, regard the issue as suspect and avoid it. Other investors, possibly more knowledgeable than you, have passed on purchasing the shares, and this accounts for their ready availability.

On the other hand, if a forthcoming IPO generates considerable media attention, the shares may become a hot issue. But unless you are a frequent investor who buys and sells in large-dollar terms, your broker will not offer shares to you. When a hot issue hits the market, many investors enter buy orders even before the share price is announced, and brokers swamp the market with orders. Too few shares are available to satisfy the demand and may be rationed to brokers. The quick summary on IPOs is this: If you can buy IPO shares readily and in any quantity, do not. If IPO shares are likely to be profitable, you probably won't be able to buy them unless you have a close relationship with your broker.

The second type of IPO is the closed-end mutual fund. These IPOs are probably one of the biggest ripoffs in the investment business. You should avoid buying shares in closed-end funds at the initial offering for one simple reason: they are overpriced. Let's say your broker offers you shares in a new closed-end fund without a commission. You buy at the asking price. But your broker earns a concession (i.e., a commission) from the fund manager equal to 6% to 8% of the money invested. If you take 7% as an average, what you bought for each $100 invested is $93 of assets.

For a few weeks, until all of the shares have been sold, the underwriters will probably support the price, mainly by buying any shares being offered at a price lower than the IPO price. After the initial period, shares are left to find their own price level. Many decline to a discount relative to their net asset value (NAV). Discounts of 15% to 25% percent are common. If you are interested in a closed-end fund, wait for several months and buy shares at a discount.

Beware of Boiler-Room Sales. High-pressure salespeople who operate at some remote location often engage in fraudulent sales activities. These salespeople are particularly adept at promoting oil and precious metals, either as stock or as commodities. They may contact you because your name appears on a list of subscribers to some financial publication, or because you asked for information in response to a sales piece you received in the mail, or simply because you live in an area known to be affluent.

Telephone swindlers may sound authentic while offering great deals. Don't forget the adage, "If it sounds too good to be true, it probably is." Refuse to deal with anyone unknown to you who approaches you by telephone. Don't be tempted by promises of huge profits. If special deals were available in platinum or obscure oil stocks, you would be able to access them through your local broker at a lower cost. If a boiler-room solicitor contacts you, simply hang up; it's your best protection.

Resolving Disputes with Your Broker

Not everything unfortunate that happens between a broker and a client is the result of trust abuse. Simply, there are risks inherent in the trading process and not all of your investments are going to have the result you desired. This raises the main question between brokers and clients: Who is responsible for losses?

If your broker recommends a stock and you approve the transaction with a full understanding of the facts, and the price of the stock declines, can you take your broker to arbitration and hope to win? It is doubtful. You cannot expect to earn a profit on every transaction. Brokers may work with some undisclosed ratio of profitable to losing trades, but a 70% ratio of profitable trades represents a high success ratio. This means that out of every ten transactions, three may go sour. If you suffer one of these losses following full disclosure by your broker, you have no actionable recourse.

Overall market declines are not the responsibility of the broker, either. For example, during the wild sell-off on October 16, 1987, some clients were unable to reach their brokers to enter a sell order. Likewise, brokers were sometimes unable to execute a sell order. Problems of this magnitude occur only when the market is in a freefall, when everything and everybody is in an uproar. You may believe you have cause for complaint in these unusual situations, but the status of the environment can be cited as a defense if you take such a case to arbitration.

If you believe you have a legitimate grievance, consider taking a stepped approach as you seek resolution. Every brokerage has a written policy for resolving disputes and grievances. Any defense under this policy requires you to retain all paperwork, confirmations, certificates, and monthly statements. Armed with solid documentation, you can attempt to resolve your problems in two ways: in-house and through arbitration.

Resolving Problems In-house. If you discover a problem in your monthly statement from the broker, call it to his or her attention. You may discover any one of the following:

- A trade you did not authorize

- A trade you authorized but was not made (through the negligence of your broker)

- A violation of your margin agreement

- Misrepresentation of some kind

If you discover a trade you did not authorize, and you have not signed a discretionary agreement, notify your broker within a day or two, if possible. Undoing a trade must be handled quickly. Other problems can be brought to your broker's attention within a couple of weeks. If your complaint is legitimate, the broker's firm should resolve it promptly.

If your broker cannot, or refuses to, resolve your complaint, your best recourse is to try to have your complaint resolved through the broker's grievance resolution process. In this case, set up an appointment with the broker's supervisor or the office manager (sometimes a single person serves both functions). At this meeting, explain your problem and be prepared to back up your complaint with documentation. If the office manager cannot resolve your grievance, contact the firm's compliance department, which may be located at a headquarters office if the firm maintains a number of branch offices. If this proves unsuccessful, your next stop is to contact the regional manager or the firm's president. Exhaust every avenue within the brokerage firm before taking your complaint to outsiders.

If you fail to get satisfaction within the firm, you can file complaints with the following organizations:

• Security Exchange Commission

• National Association of Securities Dealers

• Your state's securities department

• The NYSE (if the security is traded on this exchange).

Be prepared for delays, however, if you take your grievance to a state securities regulatory body, as investigations are often backed up. Once a grievance with these bodies is being investigated, a filing for arbitration or a suit in court, which you may subsequently initiate, will be held pending resolution of the investigation.

Using Arbitration to Settle Disputes. Your final step is to take an unresolved complaint either to arbitration or to court. Taking it to court may not be as easy as it sounds, because agreements presented by many brokers to new clients contain an arbitration clause that effectively precludes the client from taking a case to court. Although arbitration decisions are final and may not be appealed, they offer a number of advantages over litigation:

• Disputes are almost always resolved far more quickly in arbitration than in state or federal courts.

• Costs for arbiters, attorneys, and arbitration hearings are lower than similar costs in court.

• According to the Security Exchange Commission, investors receive a higher percentage of their claim for damages against brokers in arbitration than they do in court cases.

Also, be aware of your right to choose the forum, which can be any of the following:

• National Association of Securities Dealers

• New York Stock Exchange

• American Arbitration Association

Consult an attorney who is knowledgeable about securities arbitration. Securities dealer arbitration hearings are held around the country; the ones concerning the New York Stock Exchange usually take place in New York. You or your attorney should obtain the rules or procedures and all the necessary documents for filing a claim from the forum you select. You will be charged filing fees.

An arbitration case begins by filing a *Statement of Claim* in the form of a detailed letter with supporting documentation. The party bringing the claim is called the claimant. A small claims procedure limits costs and time. Small claims are typically decided by a single arbitrator from submitted written data. At the arbitrator's discretion, he or she may hold a hearing and/or request additional documentation. Claims of $25,000 or more are conducted by a panel of three arbitrators:

• One industry arbitrator, that is, someone who works within the brokerage industry, or has recently done so.

• Two public arbitrators, people who have no current or past ties to the brokerage industry; they may be attorneys or others with a working knowledge of legal procedures and securities trading.

The arbitrator or arbitration team renders a decision either immediately or within a few days. There is no appeal from an arbitration decision. If your claim is considered valid and damages are specified, the brokerage pays and that is it. In some blatant cases of broker misconduct, attorney fees incurred by the claimant are charged to the broker. Otherwise, you are liable for your own legal expenses.

KEEPING TRACK OF YOUR INVESTMENTS' PERFORMANCE

Whether you are a passive or active investor, would you be satisfied with investments that appear to be increasing significantly in value? Among the reasons to consider when answering this question are the returns: Are they high enough to enable you to reach your goal? How would you know?

To help you answer these questions, assume that you need to accumulate $100,000 in 15 years. You plan to save $300 per month out of your income to do so. You plan to put the money in the Vanguard 500 Index fund. Let us further assume the fund is expected to earn 10% per year. With these factors, will you reach your goal? If you invest $300 per month for ten years, this leads to about $61,400, not nearly enough for you to meet your goal. After all, you only have five years left to accumulate another $38,600. Will $300 a month be enough? Is a 10% return high enough? The answer is yes. In fact, you will end up with about $124,300, more than enough to reach your goal. Note the power of compounding: it took you ten years to get to $69,000, but only 5 more years to get over $55,000 more, an additional 80%.

But we still have not determined whether your investments are on track to meet your goals. To find out, you can track the performance of your investments, monthly, quarterly, annually, or all three. Although monthly statements are often the norm, tracking investments on a quarterly basis is reasonable and relatively simple. For example, let us say you invested in the S&P 500 or in a fund that tracked the index very closely. At the end of every quarter (i.e., in March, June, September, and December), you can check how well your investment is doing by reading the financial section of metropolitan and financial newspapers that report the S&P 500, such as the *Wall Street Journal* and the *New York Times*, or by checking the Internet. For example, between September 2002 and March 2003, we found the following closing values for the S&P 500:

September 2002	815.3
December 2002	879.8
March 2003	848.2

You can see that the index was up over the period, from 815.3 to 848.2, but by how much? Yes, 848.2 minus 815.3 equals 32.9, but what is this in percentage terms? In addition, you should account for any income payments that you have received, in this case, dividends. In other words, your gain (or loss) consists of two parts:

• The capital part is the difference between the asset's beginning value and its ending value.

• The income part is just that, whether it is interest from bonds, dividends from stocks, or rents from properties. These points can be succinctly and easily expressed, as follows:

$$[(\text{Ending value} - \text{Beginning value} + \text{Income})/\text{Beginning value}] \times 100$$

For example, between September 2002 and December 2002, the S&P 500's rate of return was:

$$[(879.8 - 815.3 + 4.25) \div 815.3] \times 100$$
$$= 8.43\%$$

Between December and March, its return was:

$$[(848.2 - 879.8 + \$3.90) \div 879.8] \times 100$$
$$= -3.15\%$$

This formula for rate of return, sometimes referred to as total return, is really nothing more than the percentage change. What was the average rate of return between the two periods? To do it right, first divide each return by 100 and add 1:

$$8.43 \div 100 = 0.0843$$

then:

$$0.0843 + 1 = 1.0843;$$
$$-3.15 \div 100 = -0.0315$$

then:

$$-0.0315 + 1 = 0.9685$$
(because the return is negative)

Multiply the two numbers:

$$1.0843 \times 0.9685 = 1.050$$

Finally, take the square root of the result and subtract 1, yielding 0.0248. Multiplying the final result by 100 yields 2.48%.

If you had three returns, you would multiply the three numbers and take the cube root; if you had four returns, you would multiply them and take the fourth root; and so on. For each group, remember to subtract one and multiply by 100.

If you are aiming for 10% per year, is 2.48% good enough? At first glance, it may not seem so. Consider, though, that the return

is *quarterly*, not annually. If your portfolio continues increasing at this pace for the next three quarters, you will be on track to reaching your goal. Indeed, your return for the year would be 10.3%.

How do you get 10.3% from 2.48%? You might be inclined to think that your return, over four quarters, would be:

$$4 \times 2.48\% = 9.92\%$$

Recall, however, the discussion in Chapter 1 on compounding, or "return on return." You would be earning 2.48% on *top* of what you already earned through March, 2.48% on top of what you had earned through June, and 2.48% on top of what you had earned through September, or:

$$(1.0248) \times (1.0248) \times (1.0248)$$
$$\times (1.0248) = 1.103$$

Subtracting 1 and multiplying by 100 gives 10.3%. The first 1.0248 pertains to December 2002 through March 2003. The second one is from the end of March through the end of June. The third one runs from the end of June through the end of September, and the fourth one from September through December.

The point is, by following these simple formulas, you can get a good idea whether you are on track to reaching your goals. The key lies with the *rate of return*. As long as the return averages to 10% per year, you can rest easy.

The percentage change formula works equally well with any investment for any period. For example, Coca-Cola's rate of return for March 2003 was:

$$[(\text{March closing price} - \text{February closing price} + \text{March dividend}) \div \text{February closing price}] \times 100$$

or:

$$[(\$40.48 - \$40.22 + \$0.22) \div \$40.22]$$
$$\times\ 100 = 1.19\%$$

Its (one-day) return for April 1, 2003, was:

[(April 1 closing price − March 31 closing price) ÷ March 31 closing price] × 100

or:

$$[(\$40.39 - \$40.48) \div \$40.48]$$
$$\times\ 100 = -0.22\%$$

No dividend was paid on April 1, so the dividend income is zero. By the way (as mentioned in Chapter 2), if you are interested in the dividend payment, remember two things: the dividend yield and the ex-dividend date.

As a final point, performance includes not only the *return* on your portfolio, but also its *risk*. To keep matters simple, check the beta of the portfolio. If you are choosing your own securities, you need to weight each one based on the proportion invested. For example, let us say you have allocated a $50,000 portfolio among the three stocks shown in Exhibit 11–2.

The weight is the percentage invested in each security. For instance:

$$\$25,000 \div \$50,000 = 0.50$$
$$\$10,000 \div \$50,000 = 0.20$$
$$\$15,000 \div \$50,000 = 0.30$$

The added weights should equal 1 (that is, 0.50 + 0.20 + 0.30) because the entire $50,000 is allocated to the three companies. Each company has its own beta. All you need to do is to multiply the weight by the beta. After doing so for each stock, add the results to get the *portfolio beta* of 0.715. If the portfolio beta is within your risk tolerance, then you have reason to feel comfortable.

SOME THINGS TO AVOID

To conclude, we review what we believe to be the most important action to avoid from each of the previous ten chapters:

- **Avoid being concerned with day-to-day market movements.** If you don't, you are likely to deviate from a buy-and-hold strategy, which is generally superior to frequent trading.

- **Avoid penny stocks.** Their price may be attractive, but their return to risk is not.

- **Avoid investing too much money in Treasury bills and certificates of deposit.** After taxes and inflation, over time, your return will likely be almost nothing.

- **Avoid investing in load funds with big expenses.** These funds are likely to yield performance after adjusting for loads and expenses.

EXHIBIT 11–2. PORTFOLIO BETA ACROSS THREE STOCKS				
Company	Amount	Weight	Beta	Beta × Weight
Coca-Cola	$25,000	0.50	0.35	0.175
Intel	$10,000	0.20	1.80	0.36
3M	$15,000	0.30	0.60	0.18
Totals	$50,000	1.00	—	0.715

- **Avoid naked options.** These are too risky even for risk-tolerant investors.

- **Avoid making big bets on commodities.** In terms of return to risk, you should look elsewhere.

- **Avoid speculating with stock index futures.** Trying to time markets accurately is practically impossible.

- **Avoid investing in companies with no earnings.** These are bad bets for risk-averse investors.

- **Avoid holding losers too long.** Better opportunities lie elsewhere.

- **Avoid investing too much in one area.** Ignoring the benefits of diversification is a mistake.

SUMMARY

Regardless of whether you are an active or passive investor, whether you do your own trading or you have an advisor do it for you, you would be wise to track your portfolio's performance, in terms of both return and risk. As you do so, keep an eye on economic activity, paying special attention to the actions of the Federal Reserve System. And whatever the conditions may be, remember to build a diversified portfolio that properly reflects your risk aversion, and use a buy-and-hold strategy.

SIMPLE WAYS TO MEASURE RISK

This appendix is for readers who have a quantitative orientation. If you are familiar with Excel, Microsoft's spreadsheet program, and know some basic statistics (such as mean and variance), then you will be able to understand the material given here. And even if you are not, by following the step-by-step instructions you will be able to master the techniques in a few hours or less.

To measure and assess risk, we need to know the monthly rates of return on an investment. To get them, we begin with a company's historical stock prices, which are widely available from financial newspapers and the Internet, and we compute historical rates of return from them. For this example, we'll use the rates of return for Coca-Cola from 1998 through 2002. These 60 observations are listed in Exhibit A–1.

EXHIBIT A–1. MONTHLY RATES OF RETURN FOR COCA-COLA: 1998–2002

−2.91	−2.53	−1.40	−4.84	−7.22
5.98	−2.19	−15.34	−8.56	8.32
13.08	−3.68	−3.10	−14.54	10.74
−2.02	10.90	0.67	2.28	6.21
3.30	0.64	12.96	2.63	0.09
9.29	−9.26	7.96	−4.69	1.17
−5.86	−2.33	6.74	−0.89	−10.83
−19.10	−1.23	−14.13	9.13	2.13
−11.30	−19.10	5.04	−3.75	−5.59
17.24	22.29	9.54	2.21	−3.10
3.91	14.36	4.02	−1.56	−1.37
−4.37	−13.46	−2.69	0.41	−3.95

The concept of risk here has to do with the *fluctuation* in Coca-Cola's returns. For example, the return in January of 1998 is −2.91%. In February, it is 5.98%, followed by an increase in March of 13.08%. In April, though, the return declines by −2.02%. Do you think you could have predicted these returns, or at least come fairly close? A more important question is: Do these returns unsettle you? This is what risk is all about: the possibility that your expectations will not be met.

To estimate Coca-Cola's risk, finance measures fluctuations, in this case in the monthly returns. The more they fluctuate month to month, the more risky the security is said to be. The fluctuation is measured by *variance*, which indicates how much a security's return varies from its average return.

To get the variance for Coca-Cola, at any open cell, with all 60 returns listed in exhibit A–1, type:

$$=var(a1:a60)$$

and press the Enter key. This should give you 75. This is total risk: the sum of the systematic and unsystematic risks.

To estimate the correlation between the returns of two securities, or the degree of association between them, we'll begin with rates of return for Coca-Cola, PepsiCo. and Intel, shown in Exhibit A–2.

EXHIBIT A–2. MONTHLY RATES OF RETURN FOR COCA-COLA, PEPSICO., AND INTEL					
Coca-Cola	PepsiCo.	Intel	Coca-Cola	PepsiCo.	Intel
−2.91	−0.34	15.39	6.74	3.08	−0.14
5.98	1.03	10.69	−14.13	−6.92	12.19
13.08	16.96	−12.95	5.04	8.24	−44.48
−2.02	−7.04	3.58	9.54	5.30	8.27
3.30	2.85	−11.61	4.02	−6.31	−15.39
9.29	0.91	3.74	−2.69	9.56	−21.02
−5.86	−5.46	13.92	−4.84	−11.08	23.09
−19.10	−28.41	−15.67	−8.56	4.56	−22.79
−11.30	5.62	20.51	−14.54	−4.34	−7.86
17.24	14.65	4.01	2.28	−0.30	17.49
3.91	14.62	20.72	2.63	2.16	−12.57
−4.37	5.65	10.14	−4.69	−0.94	8.31
−2.53	−4.59	18.89	−0.89	5.51	1.89
−2.19	−3.67	−14.86	9.13	0.79	−6.14
−3.68	4.30	−0.91	−3.75	3.51	−26.87
10.90	−5.74	2.96	2.21	0.44	19.43
0.64	−3.87	−11.62	−1.56	−0.17	33.86
−9.26	8.96	10.09	0.41	0.42	−3.69
−2.33	0.64	15.95	−7.22	2.88	11.41
−1.23	−12.35	19.17	8.32	0.81	−18.47
−19.10	−10.63	−9.58	10.74	2.28	6.51
22.29	13.73	4.21	6.21	0.77	−5.91
14.36	−0.36	−0.94	0.09	0.16	−3.40
−13.46	2.01	7.34	1.17	−7.01	−33.83
−1.40	−3.20	20.20	−10.83	−10.91	2.80
−15.34	−5.86	14.25	2.13	−7.89	−11.16
−3.10	8.55	16.76	−5.59	−6.21	−16.66
0.67	5.20	−3.90	−3.10	19.36	24.53
12.96	10.91	−1.64	−1.37	−3.68	20.80
7.96	9.22	7.21	−3.95	−0.26	−25.42

We would expect Coca-Cola's returns to be more strongly correlated with Pepsi's returns than with those of Intel. To confirm this, we must compute a *correlation coefficient*, which is a number that lies between negative 1 and positive 1. Note that it can also equal either negative or positive 1. For example, if we correlate Coca-Cola's returns with PepsiCo.'s returns, we will get a correlation coefficient of positive 1. Recall that the objective is to find low correlation coefficients. So the farther away the coefficient is from positive 1, the more unsystematic risk (i.e., diversifiable risk) we will be able to eliminate.

To determine the correlation coefficient between Coca-Cola's returns and PepsiCo.'s returns, go to an empty cell in the Excel spreadsheet and type the following:

$$=correl(a1:a60,b1:b60).$$

Now press the Enter key. That should give you a correlation coefficient of 0.49. This is relatively high. We would like to find something closer to 0. Let us try Intel's returns. Go to another empty cell and this time type:

$$=correl(a1:a60,c1:c60)$$

and press the Enter key. The number you should get is about −0.08, much lower than 0.49. If you conclude that Coca-Cola and Intel are a better fit for your portfolio than Coca-Cola and PepsiCo., you are right.

GLOSSARY

12b-1
Fees collected from mutual fund investors for sales and promotions.

401(k)
A tax-deferred savings plan set up by employers to which employees can contribute directly from their salaries. Employers may match the contributions.

403(b)
Similar to a 401(k), the 403(b) applies to employees of tax-exempt organizations, such as schools.

529 account
A college savings plan that grows on a tax-deferred basis.

accounts receivable
Sales on which the company has yet to receive the money.

active investing
An investment strategy that tries to beat a benchmark, such as the overall market.

actively managed
Description of a mutual fund that is not tied to an index.

advance-decline
The difference between the number of securities that show higher prices versus those that show lower prices.

American Depository Receipt (ADR)
A stock representing the shares of a foreign-based company.

American Exchange Index
A measure of stock market performance of the American Stock Exchange (AMEX).

American option
An option that can be exercised at any time.

American Stock Exchange (AMEX)

arbitrage
Profit from the simultaneous sale and purchase of a security, usually across different markets.

arbitrageur
An investor who engages in arbitrage.

ask price
The price that a seller of security is asking for.

at the money
An option in which the strike/exercise price equals the underlying security price.

bear market
A period, usually in months, when stock market measures are generally falling.

beating the market
Earning a risk-adjusted rate of return that consistently outperforms that of a broad market index.

behavioral finance
A field of finance proposing psychology as a foundation for explaining exceptions to efficient markets theory.

beta
An index of systematic risk normalized around 1; securities with betas greater than 1 are considered "aggressive," while those less than 1 are classified as "defensive."

bid price
The price that the buyer of a security is willing to pay.

bid-ask spread
The difference between the ask price and the bid price.

bill
A security with a maturity of less than one year.

Black-Scholes options pricing model
A model used to find the price of an option.

block
10,000 shares.

blue chip
A security from a financially strong company.

board of directors
The governing body of a corporation.

bond
A security with a maturity in excess of ten years.

book value per share
The value at which an asset is listed on the balance sheet divided by the number of shares outstanding.

breakout
The movement of share prices out of a trading range on the upside through the resistance level, or on the downside through a support level.

broker
An individual who charges a fee for executing the purchases and sales of an investor's securities. Classified into two groups: full-service brokers give investment advice; discount brokers do not.

bull market
A period, usually in months, when stock market measures are generally rising.

buy-and-hold strategy
Buying securities and holding them for a long time, regardless of price fluctuations.

call
An option giving the investor the right to buy an asset.

callable
In terms of a bond, one that can be "called in" before maturity (and then reissued at a lower interest rate).

capital gain
The price appreciation in the value of a security.

cash equivalents
Highly liquid, short-term securities considered part of cash on a company's balance sheet.

cash flow
The amount of cash a company brings in and spends for a specified period.

cash flow per share
Cash flow divided by shares outstanding.

certificate of deposit (CD)
A time deposit issued by depository institutions.

churning
Frequent buying and selling of securities within a client's portfolio by a broker to increase his or her commission income.

closed-end funds
A description of a mutual fund that issues a fixed number of shares that are not redeemed.

commercial paper
A short-term IOU issued by corporations in good financial standing.

commodities
Any of many bulk goods traded on exchanges.

common stock
A security representing corporate ownership and carrying voting rights.

compound annual growth rate (CAGR)
The growth rate compounded annually.

compounding
The principle of "interest on interest," or "return on return." As your money grows, the amount you earn in the current period is based on everything you have earned up to the previous period.

confidence index
A measure of investor temperament about financial markets.

contingent redemption charge
A fee imposed by a mutual fund for redeeming shares, usually for a premature redemption.

contrarian
An investor who invests in securities when others are selling them, and vice versa.

convertible bond
One that can be converted to stock.

corporation
A form of business organization whose worth is measured in terms of the worth of its stock.

correlation

A measure of the association between the returns on two securities.

correlation coefficient

A measure of correlation that ranges from negative 1 to positive 1.

cost of goods sold

An expense that reflects the cost of generating revenue.

Coverdell Education Account

An education savings account, similar to a Roth IRA, that grows on a tax-deferred basis.

covered

An options term indicating that the investor holds shares in the written option.

current assets

Balance sheet items that include cash, marketable securities, accounts receivable, and other assets that can be converted to cash fairly easily.

current liabilities

Balance sheet items that include accounts payable, interest owed, and other short-term obligations.

current ratio

A measure of a company's capability to pay its debts, calculated as current assets divided by current liabilities.

current yield

The annual interest payment divided by a bond's current price.

day trading

The process of making many trades in a single day.

debenture

Unsecured debt issued by corporations.

declaration date

The date of the next dividend payment, including the amount, as stated by the board of directors.

default risk

The risk that the bond issuer will not make payment on interest and principal.

defined benefit

A savings plan, through an employer, based on a formula that gives the exact amount an individual will receive on retirement.

defined contribution

A savings plan, through an employer, in which a certain amount is reserved per period for an individual's retirement.

delta

The change in the price of an option relative to the change in the price of the underlying security.

depreciation

An expense that reflects the usage of a long-term physical asset.

derivative

Any asset whose value is derived from another asset.

descending triangle reversal

A pattern of price declines that takes on the appearance of increasingly smaller triangles.

discount rate

The rate of interest the Federal Reserve System charges banks on loans.

discretionary agreement

An agreement that allows a broker the discretion to trade securities without the client's prior approval.

diversification

The act of investing in dissimilar assets for the purpose of reducing investment risk.

dividend

The income payment associated with common and preferred stock.

dividend payout

The amount of dividends paid by the company.

dividend reinvestment plan (DRIP)

A plan in which dividends paid by a company or mutual fund are automatically reinvested in additional shares.

dividend yield

The dividend payment divided by the price of the stock.

dollar-cost averaging
A method of buying securities according to a fixed schedule, regardless of price.

double-bottom reversal
The opposite of the double-top reversal; *see next entry*.

double-top reversal
An increase in the price of a security, followed by a decline in it, followed by another rise, and then another decline, giving the appearance on a graph of the letter M.

Dow Jones Composite
A measure of stock market performance based on 65 stocks.

Dow Jones Industrial Average (DJIA)
A measure of stock market performance based on 30 stocks.

Dow Jones Industrial Average Model New Deposit Shares (DIAMONDS)
An exchange-traded fund that mimics the 30 Dow Jones Industrial stocks.

Dow Theory
With respect to the Dow industrial and transportation averages, the idea that the market is trending upward (or downward) whenever either average breaks through a critical high point (or low point).

downtick
A transaction that has taken place below its previous price.

earnings
A synonym for net income or profit.

earnings per share
Net income (minus dividends on prefered stock) divided by the number of outstanding shares.

earnings surprise
When a company's reported earnings per share are different from what analysts had expected.

efficient diversification
Diversification based on the idea of low correlations across security returns, and in a way that reduces risk while preserving rate of return.

efficient markets theory
The idea that there are no undervalued or overvalued securities.

entry price
The purchase or sales price of a futures or index options contract.

eurodollar
Dollar-denominated deposits in banks outside the United States.

European option
An option that can be exercised only at the end of its term.

exchange-traded fund
A security that trades like a stock but is tied to an index.

ex-dividend date
The date on which the dividend payment belongs to the seller of the stock rather than the buyer.

exercise
The act of executing an option; with stock, trading in the option for shares.

exercise price
See strike price.

expected return
The rate of return that you expect to earn on an investment.

expense ratio
The fraction of the assets expended to run a mutual fund.

face value
The stated principal amount on a bond.

Federal Reserve System
The nation's central bank.

filter rule
A trading rule based on a price change exceeding a predetermined percentage.

finance
The study of the art and science of money and asset management.

financial futures
Indices of stocks, bonds, and currencies.

fixed income
A term referring to a security with a fixed, periodic payment.

fixed-income trust receipt (FITR)
An exchange-traded fund representing fixed income securities.

foreign currency exchange risk
The chance that investors will lose money when exchanging foreign currency for home currency.

forward contract
A cash transaction in which the price of a commodity is agreed on today for delivery in the future.

fully priced
A stock price that is unlikely to rise without gains in earnings.

fundamental analysis
The study of a company's financial numbers and other relevant criteria for the purpose of determining the worth of the security.

futures contract
An agreement to buy or sell a commodity for future delivery.

futures market
A market in which futures contracts are traded for delivery at a specific forthcoming date.

futures overlay
A risk-reduction strategy in which your investments are hedged against an index.

gamma
The change in delta relative to the change in the price of the underlying security.

general obligation bond
A type of municipal bond backed up only by the local government's taxing power.

Ginnie Mae
A bond issued by the Government National Mortgage Association.

going long
Buying a security with the expectation that its price will rise.

going public
The first-time sale of shares of stock to new investors.

good 'til canceled
A term used in placing limit orders.

gross domestic product (GDP)
A measure of a nation's production of goods and services.

hard currency
A currency easily converted to another currency.

head-and-shoulders reversal
A pattern in security movements that takes the shape of the human head and shoulders.

hedge ratio
The percentage of the investment being hedged.

hedging
Reducing risk.

high-yield bond
A synonym for a junk bond.

hindsight bias
A feature of behavioral finance whereby investors believe they could have predicted the correct outcome after the actual outcome has occurred.

holder-of-record date
The date set by the corporation to determine who is entitled to receive a dividend.

holding company depository receipt (HOLDRS)
An exchange-traded fund, consisting of twenty stocks, offered by Merrill Lynch.

individual retirement account (IRA)
An account that provides an opportunity to defer taxes on the investment gains and income.

in the money
For a call option, when the strike/exercise price is less than the underlying security price; for a put option, when the strike/exercise price is greater than the underlying security price.

inflation
A sustained increase in the general price level.

initial margin
The percentage of the price of a security that can be margined.

initial public offering (IPO)
The term for "going public."

intrinsic value
For a call option, the difference between the security's price and the underlying strike/exercise price; for a put option, the difference between the underlying strike/exercise price and the underlying security's price.

inventory
An asset that reflects stored materials and goods not yet sold.

investment-grade bond
A bond with a Baa/BBB rating or higher.

iShares
Worldwide exchange-traded funds offered by Barclay's Global Investors.

January effect
The term given to the observation that January is one of the best months to be in stocks.

junk bond
See noninvestment-grade bond.

lay off
In commodities and futures trading, to transfer risk from the hedger to the speculator.

leverage
To borrow capital in the expectation of increasing your investment returns.

limit order
An order placed with a broker stating a price or other condition that the security must attain before it can be executed.

limit order to sell
An order to sell a security when the price rises to a specified level.

load funds
Mutual funds that charge a commission whenever its shares are sold.

London Inter-Bank Offer Rate (LIBOR)
A short-term interest rate used as an international benchmark.

long-long
A position in currency trading used to hedge foreign exchange risk.

long-term debt ratio
Long-term debt as a percentage of total liabilities.

long-term debt to stockholders' equity ratio
Long-term debt divided by stockholders' equity.

long-term equity anticipation security (LEAP)
A long-term option.

margin account
A brokerage account in which the investor borrows money from a broker to buy or sell securities.

margin call
Also referred to as a *maintenance call*, the requirement that an investor come up with more cash and/or securities to meet the minimum requirement.

marked to market
The daily settlement of the gains and losses on futures contracts.

market order
An order to buy or sell a security at the current market price.

market timing
Buying securities when market prices are perceived to be low and selling when market prices are perceived to be high.

maturity
The number of periods, usually years, before the bond must be repaid.

mean reversion
The tendency in security prices to move to their long-term averages, especially prices that have been either rising or falling for a sustained period.

money market deposit account
A savings account with limited checking features issued by banks.

money market mutual fund
A fund that invests in short-term debt instruments.

mortgage-backed bond
A bond representing money loaned to a homebuyer.

moving average
An indicator, used in technical analysis, that shows a security's average price over time.

muni-bond
A short form of municipal bond.

mutual fund
Portfolio whose shares are sold to investors.

naïve diversification
Diversification based on the idea that investments should be across a wide variety of assets and industries in order to reduce risk.

naked
The opposite of *covered*.

NASDAQ Index
A measure of stock market performance of the NASDAQ; see next.

National Association of Securities Dealers Automated Quotations (NASDAQ)
An electronic stock exchange geared toward new industries and technology companies.

net asset value (NAV)
A mutual fund's assets, minus the value of its liabilities, divided by the number of shares outstanding.

New York Stock Exchange (NYSE)
A stock exchange using floor brokers to trade shares of large, established firms.

New York Stock Exchange Composite Index
A measure of stock market performance of the New York Stock Exchange.

noise
Colloquial term used to refer to random fluctuations in the prices of securities.

no-load funds
A description of a mutual fund that offers its shares without charges.

noninvestment-grade bond
A bond with a Ba/BB rating or lower, carrying higher default risk than an investment grade bond.

note
A security with a maturity of more than one year but no more than ten years.

odd lot
Fewer than 100 shares of stock.

odd-lot index
A measure of stock trading based on fewer than 100 shares, the normal trading unit.

open-end funds
A description of a mutual fund that continuously offers and redeems its shares.

open interest
The number of derivatives contracts that have yet to be closed or delivered on a given day.

open outcry
An auction system in commodities trading and other securities in which traders communicate with a combination of shouts and hand signals.

operating profit
Profit from the company's own business.

optimal portfolio
A group of securities arranged in a way that either minimizes risk for a given rate of return or maximizes return for a given level of risk.

option
A contract giving the investor the right but not the obligation to buy or sell something.

out of the money
The opposite of *in the money*.

panic reversal
A sudden and sharp change in the price of security.

par value
See face value.

partnership
A business owned by one or more partners.

passive investing
An investment strategy tied to a market measure.

passively managed
Description of a mutual fund that is tied to an index.

pass-through
A group of fixed income securities backed by a group of assets, often used in the mortgage market.

payment date
The date on which the dividend is paid.

PEG ratio
A stock's price-earnings ratio divided by its expected growth rate in earnings per share.

penetration
A component of the Dow Theory in which the Dow Jones Industrials' closing price exceeds the previous high closing price.

penny stock
A stock that sells for less than $1.

periodic rate
The rate of interest per payment period, such as per month.

Pink Sheet
Publication printed on pink paper, listing stock quotes, often of penny stocks.

portfolio analysis
The examination of portfolio construction and performance.

portfolio beta
A portfolio's index of systematic risk.

portfolio curve
Also known as the *efficient frontier*, it represents portfolios that are efficiently diversified, earning the highest rates of return possible for given levels of risk, or incurring the lowest level of risk for given rates of return.

preferred stock
A dividend-paying security but (usually) without voting rights.

premium
The price of an option.

price-book ratio
The price per share of stock divided by book value per share of stock.

price-earnings (P/E) ratio
The price per share of stock divided by earning (profits) per share of stock.

price momentum hypothesis
The idea that "hot" stocks stay hot and "cold" stocks stay cold.

price-sales ratio
The price per share of stock divided by sales (revenue) per share of stock.

primary market
The market in which investors have the first chance to buy new stock.

principal
The face value of a bond; often the original amount invested.

program trading
Computer-based trading by institutional investors.

proprietorship
A business owned by one person.

prospectus
(1) A legal document that describes the company in detail; (2) with respect to mutual funds, a description of a fund's objectives and features.

put
An option giving the investor the right to sell an asset.

put-call parity
The relationship between the prices of puts and calls having the same underlying asset, strike price, and expiration date that exists in an efficient market.

QUBES
Shortened pronunciation for QQQ, the symbol for the NASDAQ 100, an exchange traded fund.

rate of return
The percentage change in the price of an asset, including any cash payments, such as interest and dividends.

real estate investment trust (REIT)
A security that invests in real estate but is traded like a stock.

real GDP
Gross domestic product adjusted for inflation.

recession

A sustained decrease in real GDP, usually for at least two consecutive quarters.

red herring

A registration statement normally filed with the Securities and Exchange Commission.

reinvestment rate

A measure of how much of a company's earnings are being reinvested.

resistance level

The level of stock prices that appears to be a limit on upward movement of prices, as in the upper limit of a trading range.

retained earnings

The portion of profits retained by the company, often for reinvestment.

retention rate

The percentage of earnings not paid out in dividends.

return on equity (ROE)

Net income divided by shareholder's equity.

revenue bond

A bond supported by the revenue from the project it finances.

reverse stock split

A decrease in the number of shares outstanding that leads to an increase in the price per share of stock.

risk

The chance that the actual rate of return will be less than the expected rate of return; the chance that you will be disappointed in the outcome.

Roth IRA

Individual Retirement Account with the special provision that earnings grow free of taxes.

round lot

One hundred shares of stock.

round-bottom reversal

A decline in price followed by a rise in price, whose pattern resembles the bottom of a circle.

round-top reversal

The opposite of a round-bottom reversal.

rule of 70s

Also known as the *rule of 72s*, it is a way to figure out how quickly you can double your money. For example, if you were earning 6% per year on $100,000, it would take you about twelve years (72 divided by 6) to get to $200,000, or $100,000 multiplied by 2.

run

A pattern in the prices of securities when at least two consecutive price changes are the same.

Russell 2000

A measure of stock market performance of small-cap companies.

secondary market

The market in which investors trade securities with each other rather than with the issuing company.

sector fund

A nondiversified mutual fund; one tied to an industry or set of closely aligned industries.

Securities and Exchange Commission (SEC)

Government body charged with the regulation of securities markets and the protection of investors.

securities

Any financial instruments on which a rate of return is expected, such as a certificate of deposit, a note, a bond, or a stock.

securitization

Creating a financial instrument from other financial assets.

selling-climax reversal

A significant decline in a security's price, followed by a recovery, with another smaller decline before the price rises again.

selling short

Selling a security with the expectation that its price will fall (so that the investor can buy it back at a lower price); the opposite of *going long*.

semistrong form

The segment of efficient markets theory that states that public information is useless for trying to find superior trading strategies.

sentiment index
A survey of the opinions of a sample of investment newsletter writers.

settlement date
The date by which a sale must be settled.

shareholder
One who owns shares of stock in a company.

short-interest chart
A trading rule based on the number of shares sold short.

Simple IRA
An IRA-based plan designed for employees of small businesses.

simplified employee pension (SEP)
An IRA-based plan for the self-employed and for employees of small businesses.

sinking fund
A fund that a company sets up to pay off debt before it matures.

small-cap
Stocks of small companies.

soft currency
The opposite of a hard currency.

speculate
To take on risk.

speculator
An investor in the commodities and futures market who is willing to assume the risk that others are hedging.

spot market
A market for commodities sold for cash and delivered.

spread trading
A risk reduction strategy in commodities, futures, and options that entails trading in two different, but related, securities.

Standard & Poor's 500
A measure of stock market performance based on 500 stocks.

Standard & Poor's Depository Receipt (SPDR)
An exchange-traded fund linked to the S&P 500.

statement of claim
A supporting letter used in arbitration cases involving an unresolved financial complaint.

stock
Ownership in a company, as represented by the number of shares held.

stock buyback
When a corporation buys back some its outstanding shares.

stock dividend
A dividend payment more in terms of stock than cash.

stock split
The division of a corporation's shares into more shares.

stop order
A term used in limit orders to protect share value from a significant decline.

straddle
Holding a position in a call and a put at the same strike/exercise price.

StreetTRACKS
Exchange-traded funds put out by State Street Global Advisors.

strike price
The price at which an option investor may call or put shares to another investor holding the opposite side of the option; also known as the *striking price* or *exercise price*.

strong form
The segment of efficient markets theory that states that insider information is useless for trying to find superior trading strategies.

subordinated
Debt that ranks below other debt.

support level
The level of trading prices at the lower end of a trading range.

systematic risk
Risk that affects all securities, to one degree or another, and hence is not diversifiable.

technical analysis
The study of a security's historical price and volume data for the purpose of determining future prices.

tender
Acceptance of an offer; a settlement.

theta
A change in the price of an option relative to a reduction in the time to expiration.

time spreading
A part of spread trading involving the prices of contracts with different due dates.

total return asset contracts (TRAKRS)
Futures contracts marketed by Merrill Lynch and linked to a broad-based group of bonds, stocks, and currencies.

trailing stop order
A method of locking in profits as the price of a security rises.

trend
The perceived direction in the price of a security.

trend-following system
A set of rules used for moving in and out of mutual funds.

underwrite
A process by which financial companies (investment bankers) raise funds for organizations, whether in stocks or bonds.

unsystematic risk
Risk that is unpredictable, unique to a stock or bond, and in turn is diversifiable.

uptick
(1) A transaction that clears at a price above the price of the previous transaction; (2) trading at a higher price.

U.S. Department of Treasury
The federal government body in charge of issuing and paying on all U.S. Treasury bills, notes, and bonds.

U.S. savings bond
A small-denomination debt instrument issued at a discount by the U.S. Treasury Department.

Value Line Index
A measure of the performance of stocks tracked by Value Line.

Vanguard Index Participation Equity Receipt (VIPER)
Exchange-traded fund marketed by the Vanguard Group.

variance
A measure of a security's risk, centered on the fluctuation in a security's rate of return.

volatility
The fluctuation in the price of a security.

wash sale
The repurchase of a security within thirty days of a sale of that same security to establish a loss.

weak form
The segment of efficient markets theory that states that past price and volume data are useless for trying to identify superior trading strategies.

whipsaw
A situation in which an investor's transaction is followed by an opposite reaction, such as buying a security just before it significantly falls, or selling one just before it significantly rises.

Wilshire 5000 Index
A measure of stock market performance across the New York, American, and NASDAQ stock exchanges.

write
The act of selling an option.

yield
A bond's coupon yield, or the annual coupon interest, divided by the bond's par value.

yield to maturity
The expected rate of return if the bond is held to maturity.

zero
A security sold at a deep discount from its face value.

REFERENCES

Internet

http://www.forbes.com
http://www.lycos.com
http://www.morningstar.com
http://www.yahoo.com

Periodicals

Barron's, 200 Liberty Street, New York, NY 10281.

Hulbert Financial Digest, 5051B Backlick Road, Annandale, VA 22003.

Investor's Business Daily, 12655 Beatrice Avenue, Los Angeles, CA 90066.

Mutual Funds, Morningstar, 225 West Wacker Drive, Chicago, IL 60606.

The Value Line Investment Survey, 220 E. 42nd Street, New York, NY 10017.

The Value Line No-Load Fund Advisor, 220 E. 42nd Street, New York, NY 10017.

The Wall Street Journal, 200 Liberty Street, New York, NY 10281.

Books

A Random Walk Down Wall Street. 7th ed. Malkiel, Burton G. W.W. Norton. New York, NY: 1999.

Inefficient Markets: An Introduction to Behavioral Finance. Shleifer, Andrei. Oxford University Press. New York, NY: 2000.

International Investments. 4th ed. Bruno Solnik. Addison-Wesley-Longman. Reading, MA: 2000.

Investment Analysis and Management. 7th ed. Reilly, Frank K. and Keith C. Brown. South-Western. Mason, OH: 2003.

Investments: A Global Perspective. Francis, Jack C. and Roger Ibbotson. Prentice Hall. Upper Saddle River, NJ: 2003.

Investments: Portfolio Theory and Asset Pricing. Vol. 1. Elton Edwin J. and Martin J. Gruber. MIT Press. Cambridge, MA: 1999.

Mutual Funds. Haslem, John A. Blackwell. Malden, MA: 2003.

Portfolio Management Construction & Protection. 3rd ed. Strong, Robert A. South-Western. Mason, OH: 2003.

Portfolio Selection: Efficient Diversification of Investments. Markowitz, Harry. Yale University Press. New Haven CT: 1959.

Stocks For The Long Run. 2nd ed. Siegel, Jeremy. McGraw-Hill. New York, NY: 1998.

Stocks, Bonds, Bills, and Inflation. Ibbotson Associates. Chicago, IL: 2003.

Stock Traders Almanac, 2003. Hirsch, Yale and Jeffrey A. Hirsch, Old Tappan, NJ.

The 100 Best Stocks to Own in America. 1st-7th eds. Walden, Gene. Dearborn Financial. Dearborn, MI: 1989–2002.

The 100 Best Stocks You Can Buy. 1st-6th eds. Slatter, John. Adams Media. Avon, MA: 1996–2001.

The Motley Fool Investment Guide. Gardner, David and Tom Gardner. New York. Simon & Schuster: 1996.

The Wall Street Journal Guide To Understanding Money & Markets. Wurman, Richard Saul, Alan Siegel, and Kenneth Morris. ACCESS Press. New York, NY: 1989.

Understanding Financial Statements. 5th ed. Fraser, Lyn M. and Aileen Ormiston. Prentice Hall. Upper Saddle River: 1998.

Articles

Ahmed, Parvez and Sudhir Nanda. "Style Investing: Incorporating Growth Characteristics Into Value Stocks," *Journal of Portfolio Management*, 27 (Spring 2001), 47–59.

Badrinath, S.G. and Omesh Kini. "The Robustness of Abnormal Returns From the Earnings Yield Contrarian Investment Strategy," *Journal of Financial Research*, 24 (Fall 2001), 385–401.

Barber, Brad M. and Terrance Odean. "Trading Is Hazardous to Your Wealth: The Common Stock Investment Performance of Individual Investors," Journal of Finance, 55 (April 2000), 773–806.

Bauman, W. Scott, C. Mitchell Conover, and Don R. Cox. "Are the Best Small Companies the Best Investments?" *Journal of Financial Research*, 25 (Summer 2002), 169–186.

Broad, Manual B., Arthur B. Laffer, and Michael A. Petrino. "Democratic and Republican Administrations; Their Effect on Both Large and Small Cap Stocks; A Seventy-Two Year Study: 1926-1998," Laffer Associates. (November 1998), 1–4.

Fama, Eugene. "Random Walks in Stock Market Prices," *Financial Analysts Journal*, 51 (January-February 1995), 75–80.

Goetzmann, William N. and Roger G. Ibbotson. "Do Winners Repeat? Patterns in Mutual Fund Behavior," *Journal of Portfolio Management*, 20 (Winter 1994), 9–18.

Gold, Stephen C. and Paul Lebowitz. "Computerized Stock Screening Rules For Portfolio Selection," *Financial Services Review*, 8 (no. 2), 61–70.

Johnson, Robert R. and Gerald R. Jensen. "Stocks, Bonds, Bills, and Monetary Policy," *Journal of Investing*, 7 (Fall 1998), 30–36.

Lakonishok, Josef A., Andrei Shleifer, and Robert Vishny. "Contrarian Investment, Extrapolation, and Risk," *Journal of Finance*, 49 (December 1994), 1548–1571.

Metrick, Andrew. "Performance Evaluation With Transactions: The Stock Selection of Investment Newsletters," *Journal of Finance*, 54 (October 1999), 1743–1775.

Pari, Robert. "Wall $treet Week Recommendations: Yes or No?" *Journal of Portfolio Management*, 14 (Fall 1987), 74–76.

Rich, Steven P., and William Reichenstein. "Predicting Long-horizon Stock Returns: Evidence and Implications," *Financial Analysts Journal*, 50 (January–February 1994), 73–76.

Sharpe, William. "Mutual Fund Performance," *Journal of Business*, 39 (January 1966), 119–138.

Siegel, Jeremy J. "The Nifty-Fifty Revisited: Do Growth Stocks Ultimately Justify Their Price?" *Journal of Portfolio Management*, 21 (Summer 1995), 8–20.

Siegel, Laurence B. and David Montgomery. "Stocks, Bonds, and Bills After Taxes and Inflation," *Journal of Portfolio Management*, 21 (Winter 1995), 17–25.

Treynor, Jack. "How To Rate Management of Investment Funds," *Harvard Business Review*, 43 (January–February 1965), 63–75.

INDEX

NOTES